AF560265

LORD WILLIAM BENTINCK AND METCALFE

Encyclopaedic History of Indian Freedom Movement Series

LORD WILLIAM BENTINCK AND METCALFE

Era of Reforms

Edited by

OM PRAKASH

ANMOL PUBLICATIONS PVT. LTD.

NEW DELHI - 110 002 (INDIA)

ANMOL PUBLICATIONS PVT. LTD.
4374/4B, Ansari Road, Daryaganj
New Delhi - 110 002
Ph.: 23261597, 23278000
Visit us at: www.anmolpublications.com

Lord William Bentinck and Metcalfe: Era of Reforms

First Edition, 2004

ISBN 81-261-1514-9

[Responsibility for the facts stated, opinions expressed, conclusions reached and plagiarism, if any, in this book is entirely that of the Editor. The Publisher bears no responsibility for them, whatsoever.]

PRINTED IN INDIA

Published by J.L. Kumar for Anmol Publications Pvt. Ltd., New Delhi - 110 002 and Printed at Mehra Offset Press, Delhi.

Contents

Contents

Preface

'Golden bird' as India was known in yore days, rich in natural resources and well-developed cottage industries it was considered an affluent country. Indian spices, fabrics and other handicrafts were in great demand the world over. In the lure of having these goods and riches, many European powers made adventurous voyages to locate India.

The story of European expansions in Asia forms one of the great epics of modern times. India was the cornerstone of European imperialism in Asia. It was the lure of the lucrative 'Indian trade' which incited European adventurers to seek a new route to India, thus inaugurating a new era of contact between these two distant lands. Among the European empires in Asia, the British empire was the most enduring and prosperous one. And India was the finest jewel of the British dominion. It is worthwhile to remember that European exploration and adventure in the east were encouraged by the great demand in Europe for the products from Malabar like spices and calicoe cloth. Symbolically, the European age in Indian and indeed Asian history began with the landing of Vasco-de-Gama at Calicut on the 27th of May 1498. During this period, there was a continuous struggle between European traders and their native rivals and among the Europeans themselves. By the end of the eighteenth century this struggle for supremacy had been resolved in favour of the English.

The European traders were originally in the position of supplicants before the native rulers in India. For example, when William Hawkins arrived at the court of Jehangir with a letter from King James I asking for trade facilities, he had brought with him, a gift of 25,000 Gold pieces. As Lane Poole observes,

"There was nothing to suggest the most distant dream that in two centuries and a half the slight introduction Hawkins was then effecting between England and India would culminate in the sovereignty of a British Queen over the whole empire."

But unlike their European rivals like the Portuguese and the Dutch, the English made their bid for power in India only when the powerful Mughal empire had begun to decline. In any case the Portuguese and the Dutch had only small coastal settlements in India even at the height of their power and influence in this country.

By the end of the seventh Century, the Portuguese had been displaced by their Dutch rivals in Malabar and in the islands, of the East Indies. As for the Dutch, they were compelled by force of circumstances to regard the factories "which they established on the main land merely as marketing points for the products of an Empire which had its capital at Batavia in the East Indies."

Moreover, the Dutch power in India was largely jeopardised on European battle fields.

The wars with England and France drained the resources of this nation. Thus, it was left to the French to provide real opposition to the English in India.

The same pattern can be detected in the story of European activity in Malabar. Here the intensity of their rivalry was greater because of three main reasons. Malabar with its many fine harbours and backwaters was more accessible from the sea, increasing the scope for European interference.

Thus, European powers who came to India with the intention of trade snatched the political power and sovereignty from the local states, principalities and feudal lords. And established complete control over India. After over hundred years colonial rule, the feeling of national integration and freedom from the clutches of foreign power developed among the Indians. Thus, began the saga of freedom movement.

This encyclopaedic study is phased into two most significant and historic diversions having deep bearing on varied kinds of events which moulded the destiny of millions of people of Indian sub-continent. These events having complete political overtones, became a glaring phenomenon with the downfall of the Mughal Empire almost with the commencement of the 18th century. The ambitious piercing eyes of four European powers — the British, the French, the Portuguese and the Dutch—did cast upon several gainful economic successes in India.

Of these powers, the East India Company's government, with well organised force, bureaucracy and diplomats achieved phenomenal successes against their adversaries. The first phase,—therefore has been marked from Plassey to the Mutiny of 1857 (The First War of Independence) when the Company's role came to an end.

The second phase, naturally, came very much in the hands of the British Government functioning under the Whitehall and ended with the dawn of Swaraj on 15 August 1947.

This multi-volumes study would take up several themes, viz. political, socio-economic, religious, constitutional, educational, press, revolutionaries, local pioneers, legislation, revenues and judicial policy, on-going process of reaction — violent and non-violent, moderates and extremists, local and all India movements, reaction of the British Raj, efforts for conciliation, significant Acts passed by the Central Legislature, the impact of two global wars, 1914-1919 and 1939-1945; Congress, Muslim League, Hindu Mahasabha and the British Policy, a significant change in Britain soon after 1945, the Labour Government of Clement Attlee and Partition of India in August 1947.

In the first lot eleven volumes have appeared while in the present second lot ten volumes are being brought out namely the Marathas and their administration; Lord William Bentinck and Metcalf era of reforms; Raja Rammohun Roy: the reformer; Mutiny and its aftermath; History of Anglo-Sikh wars;

Emergence of Maharaja Ranjit Singh; Lord Hastings and his administrative measures; Ranjit Singh administration and British policy; British policy of intervention and expansion; and Lord Wellesley and policy of expansion.

This prestigious project is arranged, managed and looked after by a team of most dedicated and long experienced scholars of modern Indian history.

In gathering the authentic information, we have taken liberty to draw the material from the learned works of many great scholars in the field. We are deeply beholden to all those whose works are partially cited or substantially made use of in the project. I am indebted to Mr. J.L. Kumar, Managing Director, Anmol Publications Pvt. Ltd., New Delhi for his constant inspiration and moral support and finally to bring out this work. Last but not the least I am thankful to all those who have assisted me one way or other while preparing the manuscript.

—**Om Prakash**

1

Lord Amherst and William Bentinck

John Adam and the Press: Lord Amherst Governor-General: first Burmese War: the Barrackpur mutiny: sack of Bharatpur: Oudh: the Noozeed case: Lord William Bentinck Governor-General: Bird's Land Settlement of the North-West Provinces: Charter renewal, 1833: Bentinck and native States: British travellers in Central Asia: Avitabile: Alexander Burnes.

John Adam's brief sway was remarkable only for his action against the Press. There had been Calcutta English journals since 1780. In Warren Hastings's time they were scurrilously personal, ravelling in the wide range of material afforded by a settlement as non-moral as any cinema-crazed community of today. Checks were supplied by duels, assaults on editors, or vigorous executive action whenever Mrs. Hastings or her friends got too annoyed. In Cornwallis's time the Press was fairly well behaved; no one wanted to libel a Governor-General so respected and so respect worthy. Wellesley and Minto maintained a thorough oversight; and under them.

> 'this dread of the free diffusion of knowledge became a chronic disease....continually afflicting the members of Government with all sorts of hypochondriacal day-fears and nightmares, in which visions of the Printing Press and the Bible were ever making their flesh to creep, and their hair to stand erect with horror. It was our policy in those days to keep the natives of India in the profoundest possible state of barbarism and darkness, and every

attempt to diffuse the light of knowledge among the people, either of our own or the independent states, was vehemently opposed and resented.

Lord Hastings followed, holding opinions liberal in the extreme and completely contemptuous of misrepresentation; he thought that India should be educated, and the Press left free to say what it liked. Munro for once was on the illiberal side, considering a free Press incompatible with despotic government.

It must be remembered that the British community in India was below the level of responsibility of even the eighteenth-century public in England. It was not a question of whether seditious lawyers and 'babus' should be allowed to write at large, but of whether every attempt of Government to cut down perquisites or economies on administration—and every personal grievance against executive action or merely against some individual—should be open to the imaginative letters of disgruntled anonymity. "Brutus" was, not improbably, a rising member of the Civil Service"[1]—some junior civilian who found the pagoda-tree a little higher than his friends had led him to suspect; and "Cleophas" a liberal-minded major on the general staff', who remembered better times before these jacobins came to ruin everything. These gentlemen, in Mrs. Winston Churchill's admirable phrase, 'stood no nonsense from facts', and lived in a society which saw no reason why anyone should stand any nonsense from them.

Adam's action, however was stupidly taken on narrowly bureau critic grounds. The editor of the *Calcutta Journal,* James Silk Buckingham, had brought out with him a sense of absurdity; and India had increased his natural light-heartedness. Madras had been unfortunate in its Governors, with the fine exception of Munro; a gentleman who occupied this position, 'to the regret of the public',[2] was given an extension of his term. Buckingham announced the news inside a black border, to Adam's exceeding wrath. Government had a fervent partisan, one Bryce, a Church of

Scotland minister; Bryce started a rival journal, trouncing Buckingham in a manner which the Supreme Court, appealed to by the trounce, decided was libelous. When Bryce was consoled with the lucrative post of Clerk to the Stationery Department, Buckingham was amused, and said so; he pictured the revered gentleman entangled in tape and envelopes when he should be pondering sermons. Thereupon Adam, 'one of the odd oligarchy of Calcutta—an honest, uncorrupted, good-hearted and very able man, with a mind warped by the chronic condition of bureaucracy, to which he had been so many years condemned',[3] rose from his desk, and 'smote heavily,' in regulations which took all the pith and manhood out of the journals of the day'. Bucking man's licence to reside in India was cancelled; he was 'deported, ruined, and became for years a continual running sore in the flesh of the East India Company and British Parliament'. He got into the House of Commons, 1832, and the Company found it wise to allow him a pension of £200 a year.

Metcalfe disapproved of Adam's action. But this was the one period when Metcalfe did not matter.

Between the Company and Burma unsatisfactory relations had persisted for over thirty years. When Burma conquered Arakan, 1784, there was an influx of refugees into the Bengal delta, which already swarmed with pirates, mostly Portuguese and Mugs (mixed Bengalis and Arakanese). Burmese troops made no scruples about following them up, and Sir Shore for the sake of peace surrendered their prey on condition that they retired with it. In Wellesley's time there were armed clashes, but he was too occupied with bigger wars to attend to the business. Fugitives continued to pour in, begging piteously not to be sent back; the Burmese continued to chase them in British territory. The Court of Ava informed the Company, in 1817, that if they did not return to their doom 'the vagabond Mugs...the Lord of the Seas and Earth would be obliged to reassert his authority over such places as Dacca and Murshidabad—undoubted apanages of the crown of Arakan[4] Lord Hastings was the wrong person to address such a menace to. However, war did not come until Lord Amhersts' time.[5] It broke out in 1824.

To-day it seems strange to read, in the *Life of Henry Lawrence*.[6] that there was 'a panic that the Burnas had taken Chittagong, and were pushing up to Calcutta in their war boats.' But after years of over-running their neighbours the Burmese were filled with conceit, and had conveyed their good opinion of themselves to others. The encounters between them and the Company's troops, though trivial, had been numerous, and the latter had generally got the worst of them. The Burmese were now checked in Kachar (February, 1824), but their most famous general, Maha Bandula, annihilated a detachment at Ramu in May.[7] The eastern frontier seemed threatened, and Bandula carried a set of golden fetters for the Governor-General. But the British struck from the sea, —occupied Rangoon May, 1825 and proceeded to win victories. It was an absurd war, against an enemy who did much tom-toming, and tattooed his body with ferocious beats to make himself invulnerable, but also dealt skilfully in underground pits behind stockades. It was a cruel war also. The Burmese refused to grant or accept quarter. When they took prisoners–and there were some British reverses, whose repercussions in India were important they executed them, the British frequently coming upon the sight of the hung-up bodies. Maha Bandula, recalled from the Bengal frontier to meet the invaders, was struck by their care of wounded prisoners. Savagery was seen to be not a law of nature; the campaign grew tolerable in consequence. Sickness wrought great mortality, so that both sides were glad when peace was made (Treaty of Yandabo, February, 1826); the British were then getting uncomfortably near the Burmese capital. Maha Bandula, a genuinely remarkable man, though with barbarous methods of instilling courage into his men, had been killed by a rocket a year previously. No one will grudge the Burmese Court its official version of events:[8]

'White strangers of the west fastened a quarrel upon the Lord of the Golden Palace. They landed at Rangoon, took that place and Prome, and were permitted to advance as far as Yandabo; for the King, from motives of piety and regard to life, made no preparation whatever to oppose them. The strangers had spent vast sums of money in their enterprise, so that by the time they reached Yandabo their resources were exhausted, and they were in great distress. They then petitioned the King, who in his clemency and generosity sent them large sums of money to pay their expenses back, and ordered them out of the country'.

The large sums of money were an indemnity of one million sterling. Assam, Arakan, and the Tenasserim coast were annexed.

'Exaggerated reports of the strength and ferocity of the Burmese troops'.[9] had swept through India:

"The peasants on the frontier fled in dismay from their villages; and every idle rumour was magnified so industriously by timid or designing people, that the native merchants of Calcutta were with difficulty persuaded to refrain form removing their families and property from under the very guns of fort William'.

It was just such a disquiet as some of us remember on a smaller scale, when the *Emden* was working havoc among Indian shipping and shelling Madras. It brought about at Barrackpur, the Governor-General's place of residence near Calcutta, another rehearsal of the Great Mutiny. We are told that the sepoys had got above themselves, by reason of 'their pride in the successes that had been achieved in the campaigns against Pindaris and Marathas',[10] which 'bred a spirit of insubordination', such as perhaps their more observant members noticed from time to time in their European comrades, particularly the officers. Moreover, an attempted invasion of Burma through Arakan was accompanied with pestilence and appalling mortality. The sepoys, high caste men, were furnished with precisely the same grievance that had repeatedly been held to justify mutinous behaviour of company's officers, a heavy financial loss. Coolies, carriers, drivers, were offered higher pay than the infantry, to induce them to enlist for service which was dreaded; sepoys were told they must continue on the lower rates for which they had contracted. They 'also had a real material grievance owing to the impossibility of obtaining land transport, which had to be provided by the men themselves under the rules then in force', while the requirements of Government had gathered up most of the available beasts.

Vincent Smith remarks: 'As usual, the genuine grievance was made the occasion for raising the cry of religion in danger'.[11] The grievance, at any rate, was seen and admitted by many regimental officers, who tried to help the men from their own pockets. But 'strait-laced officialdom at headquarters was inflexible. The men were under engagement to provide their own carriage, and government declined to relieve them of the responsibility'.[12] The 47th Native infantry refused to move or to ground arms, and remained on the Barrackpur parade-ground,

> 'as described by some who witnessed the scene...dazed by excitement...men so much bent on mischief as possessed by some fatal infatuation...."with ordered arms in a state of stupid desperation, resolved not to yield, but making no preparation to resist".[13]

After warning, guns were opened on them, making the parade-ground a shambles. The survivors

> 'fled in all directions, and were instantaneously dispersed. Above 800 muskets and uniforms were found in the adjacent fields and roads. The Court-martial sat immediately. The ringleaders (six) were hanged the next morning. Many hundreds since have been found guilty and sentenced to death but this was commuted to hard labour for fourteen years on the public roads. Five other ring leaders were executed afterwards, and one man whom the mutineers regarded as their Commander-in-Chief was hung in chains in front of the lines.... All the officers (native) were dismissed the service and their

guilt proclaimed at the head of every regiment in their native language....

'....our situation was awfully alarming. Lord Amherst resolved not to leave the house, and I determined not to quit him. Sarah behaved heroically, and, though ill, declared she would remain, and kept up her spirits, as we all did as well as we could.[14]

It is generally considered that the episode should be judged retrospectively, through the lens of what happened thirty years later:

'It did not appear that the Sepoys had contemplated active resistance, for though in possession of ball-cartridge, hardly any had loaded their muskets. Sir E. Paget was much blamed for resorting at once to the extremist measure; but the events of 1857, which began at the same station of Barrackpore, throw a truer light on the graity of the crime of military mutiny'.[15]

'The punishment was just, but the fate of the regiment was unspeakably pathetic.... The name of the regiment was effaced from the list of the army. Those who blame the rigour shown in 1824 may, perhaps, ask themselves whether lenity might not have been misconstrued. No one felt more keenly than the Governor-General the pain of the spectacle'.[16]

though he did not obtrude himself too closely upon it. However, 'nothing cheered and pleased him more than the proof he was hereafter to receive of the return of a better feeling among the soldiers...the 39th Native Infantry and the 60th Native Infantry volunteered services to go anywhere that Government ordered them'.

In 1826 took place the one considerable military action of Lord Amherst's administration inside India. The Bharatpur Raja died, 1825, perhaps without assistance; his nephew murdered the regent and took prisoner the new prince, who was six years old and, but for the swift interposition of Sir David Ochterlony, Commissioner at Delhi would probably have joined 'the long list of Indian prices born to near a throne to escape each by a poisoned opiate, or the dexterous hand of an athlete'.[17] He was not deliver up when Ochterlony demanded; the long-desired casus *belli*, aggravated by much vaunting defiance, was furnished against the grim fortress which India believed impregnable. This time the British commander, Lord Combermere's, before storming blasted a tremendous breach: his men rushed in through the smoke and terror. The enemy suffered a loss of 8,000, cut off by the cavalry almost to a man; the British casualties were 600. Lord Combermere's enthusiasm for financial gain attracted some comment; Metcalfe observed that while he was ostensibly acting as the young Raja's protector, that child was plundered of even his brass pots. The General awarded himself 6 of the 48 lakhs of treasure found, which has been censured by even recent historians as overstepping proper bounds.[18] But to a Government generally moving from one triumphant campaign to another, the army had long been all-powerful; experience had proved repeatedly the danger of coming between it and its captures. And we who live on the wrong side of the World War can surely be happy in the spectacle of bygone jollity, of men happy and victorious, women gay and unbothered:

> 'It may cheer the present generation to hear of past illuminations and rejoicings which are almost like those in a fairy tale, in which everyone is victorious and comes home unharmed. On the king's birthday, April 24, there is a grand entertainment at Government House; Combermere and Bhartpur in lamps on the right, Campbell and Ava in coloured lamps on the left, wreaths round the pillars, George IV in the centre also in lamps, with the appropriate accompaniments of star and crown. In the great ballroom were transparencies representing Lord Combermere leading the young Raja into Bharatpur, followed by his staff while a figure of Civtory waved a laurel wreath. Also Sir Archibald Campbell on horseback with his steamer in the background, the Dagon Pagoda, and a nymph-like figure scattering olive

branches-India, Peace, Victory and other appropriate inscriptions were liberally scattered about, and the company danced till 3 o'clock morning.

'Rejoicings, alas, do not last for ever....[19]

We must turn to finance. ' "Adapt your revenue to your ruling requirements" was the contention of Sir Charles Metcalfe. "Adapt your military requirements to the exigencies of economical finance" was the unceasing burden'[20] of those mean-spirited men, the Directors. 'And in a sense the Directors were right. The disaffection created by excessive or inappropriate imposts in no whit less dangerous than weak battalions, and the problem of finance pressed very heavily on the minds of those responsible. Luckily the King of Oudh again proved a very present help, in 1825 and 1826 providing a million and a half sterling, thereby 'soothing the anxiety of the conscientious but impecunious John Company'.[21] Another helper was the Maharaja of Gwalior. Daulat Rao Sindhia died, 1827; and his wishes as regard an adopted child and his favourite wife's regency were respected, in consideration of a loan of eighty lakhs, whose interest was to be spent on a British subsidiary force.

His Majesty of Oudh had monetary anxieties of his own, Oudh having continued for forty years the prey of European harpies. As far back as 1798 Sir John Shore had refused to include in a treaty a clause making the Company the guarantor of alleged loans, which in the usual manner-dishonesty and 36 per cent usury—had 'swelled to an amount calculated to excite a feeling of astonishment at the vast amount of rank vegetation springing from so inconsiderable a seed'[22] as the alleged original assistance. Successive Nawabs, harassed by pimps, pandars, dancing girls, and 'conscientious but impecunious John Company' very busy with new wars, had accepted the aid of generous-minded European; and in return had dispensed bonds 'with truly oriental magnificence. Had these securities been satisfied in due course, the vizier would have set an example altogether new in India'. But, as Thornton observes, finding a theme adequate to his vivacity of ironical meiosis, the Wazir 'did not thus violate the principles upon which Eastern rulers ordinarily administer their pecuniary affairs'. Each Wazir (later, king) knew that he was dealing with venomous crooks, and he himself was usually a crook in his own fashion. Oudh for close on a century resembles a still living carcase on which thousands of bloated insects were battening.

The 'creditors' decade after decade, pressed for settlement of their steadily mounting claims, which no amount of such piecemeal composition as was progressively obtained could wipe out. The nature of these claims was by now pretty generally understood, and a committee of the East India Company recorded (May 31,1822) that 'loans at such an exorbitant rate of interest cannot justly be considered in any other light than as gambling transactions. But better times were coming for the creditors. As one by one the men who remembered when there were sill native States not without qualities that called out respect—when a Gurkha war was a frightening campaign, and Bharatpur a still unconquered fastness, when Englishmen and Indians met as foes but as foes who still had hours of friendly equality—as Munro, Scotland's noblest gift to India, died, as an Elphinstone and then a Malcolm went, as Webbe and Graeme Mercer died, and Metcalfe was withdrawn into the Calcutta Secretariat already a man torched with mortal disease and lingering on only until his place could be filled, as certainty of immeasurable superiority settled on British minds. It was felt that Indians had no particular rights beyond that of accepting the government provided for them, without demurs as to cost or kind. That this cost was immensely swollen by the voracity of unofficial Europeans troubled the best officials, and made the (Metcalfe was here an exception, for entirely liberal reasons) steadfast against lifting the licence on non-Company personnel or allowing 'colonization' on any scale. But most took it in the light-hearted spirit of the old saying, the 'Nizzy pays for all: 'this was a period when the good fortune of those who were desirous of preying upon the people of India was in the ascendant'.[23] Nevertheless, the

Oudh creditors received a series of checks in 1834, when Lord Ellenborough, supported by the Duke of Wellington (who was exceedingly will informed as to what lengths adventurers habitually went to, and held strong views about what he called 'these gentry'), asked a numbers of questions which were resented but not satisfactorily answered. Ultimately, 'after much tedious argument', during twenty years—and with this we may dismiss an unsavoury topic—'political influence procured a decision more favourable to the claims of the European money-lenders, against various native debtors in Oudh than was consistent with the honour of the British government'.[24]

The partial check which rapacity experienced in 1834 was due to some extent to its victory in 1832, a triumph so astounding that it set men thining. During the worst times of the Madras corruption, various officials tramped up claims against the Zemindar or Noozeed, some based on bonds given by him, when in prison, to his jailor, Mr. James Hodges. The claims were so obviously worthless, even in those days, that they were left alone, after the *zemindari's* affairs had been finally settled in 1803, for thirty years. Nevertheless, the House of Lords in 1832 accepted them, though opposed at every stage by the whole power of the East India Company. The connoisseur of malversation should look into this once-notorious case; it would teach him something of the possibilities if really skilful dishonesty.

Opposition to acceptance of whole claim (million and a half sterling) against Oudh was due also to slowly growing perception of the value of Oudh as an unofficial treasury whenever the Company needed special subventions. Its annexation was always an event hovering more or less close to materialization; and, referring to this possibility, Sir Robert Peel in 1834.

> 'solemnly deprecated....the commencement of the exercise of sovereignty, by appropriating eleven hundred thousand pounds sterling of the property of the territory to the liquidation of a claim, for which it did not appear

that the British State had ever made itself in the slightest degree responsible'.[25]

The Nepal War had acquainted British officers with the pleasure and health of Himalayas sojourning. Lord Amherst in 1827 started the custom of summering at Simla, which perhaps is his strongest title to remembrance. The three Governors-General who followed Lord Hastings were less powerful than the brood of vigorous soldiers with 'the knacks of executive success', whose velour and spirit of conquest were within a quarter of a century to make the Company's dominion into an empire as superb as any the world has seen. There might be discontent beneath the surface, but it was discontent absurdly helpless. Courage, enterprise, physical and moral strength, were all on the rulers' side.

Lord William Cavendish-Bentinck arrived, July 4, 1828, and began with unpopularity having to enforce stringent economies. These were of course accompanied with threats of mutiny by the military personnel, but had far-reaching administrative results, and after a considerable interval were saving half a million sterling in civil affairs and (rather more quickly) a million in the army. He abolished the Provincial Court of Appeal and Circuit, which had become proverbial for their dilatoriness and uncertainty of decision',[26] a gain financially and judicially. He licensed the direct passage of opium from Central India (where then, as now, certain States grew it largely) to Bombay, diverting it from Karachi; the British government secured the profits which the Amirs of Sind lost. The action 'practically ensured a valuable contribution, paid for by the Chinese drug-taker, to take the peace of the alleged payment to the Company by the English teadrinker'[27] R.M. Bird put through the Land Revenue settlement of the North-West (the modern Uttar Pradesh), Allahabad being given a separate Board of Revenue. Most impotent of all, the urgency of economy led to the extension of 'the uncovenanted services', already begun by Lord Amherst, a wide devolution of important administrative and judicial duties to an Indian personnel, as far less costly than a solely European one.

The company had lost its monopoly of the Indian trade in 1813. Another twenty-year period closed in 1833, and opinion in England was setting steadily and increasingly against renewing the charter. Probably the charter would have gone if it had not been that by 1833 Lord William Bentinck's immense reforms in moral and social practices has made a very different and far better impression aboard than the surfeit of victories which in the dawning of modern thought and modern ethics were wearying and even disgusting people. The Company's activities put up 'a better show', and what would probably have been denied to a Wellesley or Hastings was granted to Bentinck. The China trade monopoly, however, went the way of the old Indian one. It had been grudgingly continued, and as the Burmese operations opened up the Far Eastern trade increasingly, and its profits were seen to be 'far in excess of its dimensions',[28] the demand that it be thrown open proved too strong to be resisted. China has disappointed the West in recent years, but in 1830 its people were satisfactory beyond their neighbouring; 'the capacity of the Chinese for consuming opium and paying silver then seemed to be unlimited. Moreover, the East India Company was accused of profiteering in tea, a commodity which bulked largely in their annual profit of over a million sterling from the Chinese trade.

It is interesting to note that practically all the items which make up the present-day controversy (or, rather, the controversy of a yesterday that is only just finished) were established by 1830. The home remittances amounted to three millions sterling, which the Company covered by the profits of Chinese and Indian goods sold in London. Five years of Lord Amherst's administration had seen average annual deficits in the Indian revenues of close on the same sum; and the rule of Lord Hastings and Amherst together had resulted in a total deficit of nearly nineteen and a half millions. Bentinck turned the deficits into what was a two millions surplus when he left; showing what was possible if wars were avoided and revenues used for the ordinary administrative routine.

The Company had done England service, immensely augmenting commerce, adding to national pride, weakening and humiliating France and Holland. It drew dividends from its possession of India, and would have to be bought out if deprived of India. The Act of 1833, passed after discussion before 'empty benches and an uninterested audience' of the House of Commons and a less languid treatment by the House of Lords reprieved the Company for twenty more years. The Proprietors' dividends became definitely chargeable on Indian territorial revenues, but were backed by collateral British Government stock.

The *Calcutta Gazette* (October, 1833) hailed the charter's renewal by calling for 'a general illumination and a display of fireworks', which were granted, and brought much satisfaction to a populace always agreeably avid for *tamashas*. The new regime came into force in the spring of 1834.

Bentinck's orders, arising naturally out of the need and demand for economy, were to leave native States alone. This he could not altogether do. In suppressing *thagi* he obtained the help of Oudh, Hyderabad, and Gwalior, the Marathas daubers behaving much more amicably than during lord Hastings's drive against the Pindaris. He failed in his attempts to apply pressure on the Central States over the opium trade, however, and had to fall back on the arrangement whereby the Malwa opium was sent through British Indian ports. Mysore since Purnaya's retirement in 1811 had been robbed and terrorised till a peasants' revolt came in 1831; the Company suppressed this, and took the country over in trust,[29] almost certainly the only possible course. An Oudh minister who tried to reform administration was unsupported by the Power whose citizens were largely responsible for that kingdom's drawn-out wretchedness, and he was driven out. The Raja of Coorg, a murderous ruffian who refused to hold any relations with the British, was deposed after considerable fighting, in which the Governor-General acted as Commander-in-chief, and Coorg was annexed. The Political Commissioner in Delhi was murdered, and the culprit, a chieftain, hanged, to the menace of a rising.

Jaipur, after disturbances amounting to civil war, the murder of a British officer and the wounding of the Resident, and the child-raja's death, possible by poison, was given a Council of Regency for a new child-king. Gwalior broke into internecine quarrels, Indore sank into disorder, Baroda became truculent and hostile, Udaipur drifted towards the condition which was presently to stir Henry Lawrence's contempt and his skepticism of Tod's rose-coloured pictures of the Rajputs.

All this completed the working out of the modern relationship of princes and paramount power in its main technique except for Hydrabad, which (as befitted its long and practically unbroken alliance) was treated as a case apart. Hydrabad sank now into chaos of the worst kind, left to its ruler's devices, which tended only towards show and luxury.

The peninsula and all Hindustan conquered, the Company looked earnestly to their western borders. Ranjit Singh, 'the Lion of the Punjab', was sinking fast to decrepitude. In October, 1831, Bentinck drew him into a camp of several days' duration, at Rupar, on his marches; 'those sons of glory those two lights of men', displayed themselves on an Oriental counterpart of 'the Field of the Cloth of Gold',[30] and concluded a treaty of perpetual amity, which, as a matter of fact, was to last for another seventeen years—a long period for such treaties.

It was in Bentinck's time that the major bugbear of the century entered Indian politics. Russia, steadily encroaching on Persia and Turkestan, made the Indian Government cast roving eyes abroad, seeking fresh alliances with buffer States, pondering annexations which would provide a batter frontier. Cutch was theirs already; and in 1825 Sind had been awed by the presence of 'a hostile demonstration'[31] on its frontiers. In journeys, sometimes open, sometimes in disguise, the Company's agents assiduously collected geographical and military information concerning their neighbours. There had been Elphinstone's mission to Kabul, Malcolm's two missions to Persia. Central Asia was not as bigotedly closed to British infiltration as it afterwards became (thanks, mainly, to the two Afghan Wars). From 1819 to 1825, Moorcroft and Trebeck, two men not in any covenanted service, but spared by adventurous courage and curiosity, explored (as horse-dealers and merchants, predecessors of Kipling's Afghan in *Kim*) Ladakh, Kashmir, Afghanistan, Balkh, Bokhara. Moorcroft died in the vast snowy loneliness behind the Hindu-Kush, disappointed that he had not stirred the Indian Government to overcome their apathy and fear of annoying the Sikh Power. He wrote to Metcalfe, who as Resident in Delhi had helped him and sympathized:

> It is somewhat humiliating that we should know so little of countries which touch upon our frontier; and this in a great measure out of respect for a nation that is as despicable as insolent, whose origin was founded upon rapine, and which exists by acquiring conquests it only retains by depopulating the territory.'

His view of the Sikh was largely coloured by the prejudice he found in Afghanistan. Ranjit Singh, after rising to supreme power among his people, had steadily pushed back the border tribes and their suzerain in Kabul, in 1834 wresting from them Peshawar. He was aided by soldiers broken in the downfall of Napoleon, most prominent being Avitabile, 'the ferocious Neapolitan', whose methods revolted Henry Lawrence, his guest during some of the Afghan War:

> 'All that can be said in his favour is, that he has savages to deal with—but why should he deal with them as a savage? He might be as energetic and as summary as he pleased, and no one would object to his dealing with a lawless people in such manner as would restrain them in their practices; but he might spare us the scenes that so frequently occur in the streets of Peshawar, equally revolting to humanity and decency.[32]

Avitabile blew from guns, impaled, flayed have alive, left men naked and honey-smeared in the sun to die. Yet Lawrence thought him, though just the picture of one of Rubens' Satyrs, one of the world's masterminds; and to his wife he added, 'Remember....that I have eaten of his salt, and that he has been civil to me. We must therefore, in telling the truth, do so in mercy. But the Sikhs added, to cruelty ruthless as their foes', fighting qualities which make Moorcroft's adjective 'despicable' ring queerly in our modern knowledge of them.

Moorcroft was before his time, but only a few years before it. The time came suddenly, bringing with it the man. Alexander Burnes at the age of sixteen arrived in Bombay, 1821; and 'at a period of his career when the majority of young men are mastering the details of company drill, and wasting their time in the strenuous idleness of cantonment life.',[33] was a noted linguist, and while yet in his teens the official Persian translator to the Sudder Court. In 1831 he was sent up the Indus, from 'the enlightened desire' of Lord Ellenborough, President of the Board of Control, ' to ascertain' that river's 'commercial possibilities.' The Sind Amirs were told that they were to throw open their river. Burnes's ostensible mission was to take a present of fine English horses to Ranjit Singh.

Metcalfe, in a Minute of Council (October, 1830), contemptuously called the camouflaged expedition 'a trick unworthy of our government, which cannot fail when detected, as most probably it well be, to excite the jealousy and indignation of the power on whom we play it.' The Amirs watched with dismay; one spectator at the riverside lifting his hands and crying 'Sind is gone, since the English have seen the river, which is the road to its conquest. But Burnes went on, and was received honourably by Ranjit Singh, who was delighted with the horse. Returning, at Ludhiana he met a former Amir of Afghanistan, Shah Suja, whom his own people had driven out in 1809 and repulsed twice in attempts since; Shah Suja spode warmly and longingly of the joy it would be to him to be back in Kabul, with an English Resident and the English using his country as a high-road between Europe and India. Full of enthusiasm, Burnes obtained passports from the Indian Government for an overland journey 'to England', a journey which took him over Afghanistan, the Central Asia khanates, Persia, and by sea back to Bombay. In justice to the man who was destined to play so prominent a part in the silliest and most unjust war ever waged by the Indian Government, it is fair to say that the stated emphatically that Shah Suja lacked both energy to recover his throne and tact to keep it, while he found the ruling Kabul chief, Dost Mohammed, a far superior man, and his people 'simple-minded, sober', 'of frank, open manners, impulsive and variable almost to childishness'.

Burnes's travels made a tremendous impression. In India, and then in London, he was lionised excessively; fashionable ladies besought him to honour their gatherings, statesmen and scholars listened eagerly to him. Special missions to Sind (1835) and Kabul (1837) followed. All this he enjoyed immensely. The rest of his career will emerge in the course of narrative. Kaye observes pityingly:

> 'It was the hard fate of Alexander Burnes to be over-rated at the outset and under-rated at the close of his careers'.

REFERENCES

1. *Life of Metcalfe*, ii. 249-50.
2. Higginbotham, *Men Whom India Has Known*, 42.
3. *Life of Metcalf*, ii. 249-50.
4. Anne Thackeray Ritchie and Richardson Evans, *Lord Amherst* ('Rulers of India') 73.
5. 1823-28.
6. Edwardes and Merivale, 35
7. H. H. Wilson, *Documents illustrative of the Brumese War, 41*.
8. Crawfurd, *Embassy to Ava*, i. 304.
9. Snodgrass, *Narrative of the Burmese War*, 74.
10. *Lord Amherst*, 149.
11. *Oxford History of India*, 649, But religion (that is to say religious ritual) *was* in danger; 'the usage of caste compelled each man to take his own set' (*Lord Amherst*, 148) of cooking utensils, for which no transport could be obtained. As for Vincent Smith's 'as usual', the extreme rarity with which disaffected elements raised the cry of 'religion in danger'—the effective cry possible, for which

plausible excuse always existed—is admiringly commented on by distinguished soldiers all through the troubled times which continued with scant intermission ever since Lord Wellesley's governor-generalship.

12. *Lord Amherst*, 150
13. *Op. cit.* 15.
14. Lady Amherst's *Journal.*
15. Sir Herbert Edwardes and Herman Merivale, *Life of Sir Lawrence*, i. 59.
16. *Lord Amherst*, 153-4.
17. M. Martin, *The Indian Empire*, iii. 426.
18. 'The glory of the achievement was dimmed by the excessive rapacity for prize-money displayed by Lord Combermere' (*Oxford History of India*, 653). Cf. Marshman (*History of India*, 356): 'The laurels of Bhurtpore were tarnished by the rapacity of the military authorities; he considers rapacity' open to criticism before it becomes 'excessive'.
19. *Lord Amberst*, 158.
20. *Op. cit.* 33.
21. *Op. cit.* 182.
22. Thornton, *History of the British Empire in India*, vi. 2-3.
23. *Op. cit.* vi 9.
24. Montgomery Martin, iii. 422.
25. Thornton, vi. 20.
26. Demetrius C. Boulger *Lord William Bentinck*, 16.
27. *Op. cit.* 121.
28. *Op. cit.* 10.
29. It was restored in 1868.
30. See Emily Eden, *Up the Country* (Oxford University Press, 1930), 186.
31. Kaye, *History of the War in Afghanistan*, 175.
32. Henry Lawrence, Adventures in the Punjab, chapter ii.
33. Kaye i. 175.

2

Changing of Hindu Thought and Ambitions

The widening gap: fears of old-time officials: Metcafe and intelligent and influential native gentlemen of Calcutta: William Carey: Rammohan Roy: Henry Vivian Derozio: Dr. Richardson: the Brahmo Samaj: the Bengal Renaissance: Michael Dutt: the education controversy: introduction of travel by steam: Malcolm and the Bombay Supreme Court: Metcalfe as acting Governor General.

Bentinck's entertainments were magnificent; and 'he achieved fame by permitting Indians to drive to the Governor-General's house in carriages',[1] at a time when superiority on one side, and timidity on the other, had grown to such lengths that

> 'on going to a station no Englishman thought of calling on the notables of the district, as was once done as a matter of course; instead, certificates of respectability were required of the notables before they could be guaranteed a chair when they visited the officer.... In Calcutta many writers expected every Indian to salute them.'

Lord William did some thing, by precept and example, to mend matters. But it was a passing improvement only; and racial relations in Bengal continued what they are still—the amazement of the society of India's saner regions. Elphinstone was scornfully aristocratic even among his own people. But he knew well that India had its own aristocracy, whose friendship was worth regarding. He told Malcolm (May 24, 1819):

> 'The picture you draw of he state of India, as-it is likely to be for the next four or five years, makes me regret that you are likely so soon to leave it. It has sometimes struck me that the fault of our younger politicians—who have never seen the Indian states in the days of their power—is a contempt for the natives, and an inclination to carry everything with a high hand'.

Towards the end of Lord Hasting's time, he wrote what many felt about conditions in Bengal;

> 'Sir, Henry Strachey, in his report laid before Parliament, attributes many of the defects in our administration in Bengal to the immeasurable distance between us and the natives, and afterwards adds that there is scarcely a native in his district who would think of sitting down in the presence of an English gentleman. Here every man above the rank of a hircarra sits down before us, and did before the Peshwa; even a common ryot, if he had to stay any time, would sit down on the ground. This contributes, as far as the mechanical parts of the society can, to keep up the intercourse that ought to subsist between the governors and the governed; there is, however, a great chance that it will be allowed to die away. The great means of keeping it up is for gentlemen to receive the natives often, when not on business'.[2]

Admitting the degradation, and in many things depravity, which had overtaken the native populations, there was, nevertheless, in Bengal a stratum of Indian life where liberal sentiments were cultivated, and modern enlightenment was beginning to marry with ancient culture and courtesy. There is pathos in the Address given to Metcalfe in 1835, when he was preparing to close his superbly beneficent career, 'signed by more than five hundred of the most intelligent and influential native gentlemen resident at the capital'; and in the understanding and sympathy of his reply:

> 'Our opportunities of estimating the private qualities that have earned you the love of your countrymen have necessarily been few. But it would be a reproach to our hearts and understanding, if we did not come forward to proclaim our sense of the inflexible regard for equal justice, and utter contempt for abuse, corruption, and chicanery, which have uniformly marked your official career'.

> 'I greatly lament that a difference in religion and customs should operate, as it does, in great degree, to prevent the benefits of social intercourse between the native and European communities in India; and consequently to preclude that personal intimacy, and that knowledge of private character, which are the chief cements of mutual attachment. You can neither share in our convivial enjoyments nor take an interest in our amusements; and it is much to be regretted that nothing has yet been devised, which being suited to the habits and tastes of both parties, might lead naturally to that frequency of intercourse, which is so much to be desired, as tending to unite all in the bonds of affection. I trust that time will effect this desirable result, and remove the obstacles which retard it'.

The process Metcalfe preyed for had already achieved notable (though by Government unsuspected) progress. William Carey, excobbler and Baptist missionary, settled at Serampur in 1799, finding in Danish territory the toleration refused in lands under Company control. For over forty years he laboured with a practical wisdom and a catholic enthusiasm for every kind of enlightenment, which both recall John Wesley. He and his colleagues introduced printing; and Bengali prose saw its birth in the translations and treatises of pandits working under their direction. Bengal itself also produced a great man. Rammohan Roy (1774-1833), while yet a boy, saw the unwilling death of his brother's widow on her husband's pyre; emotional and intellectual revolt stirred together, and he found himself driven out on a path as lonely as any ever trodden by a valiant spirit. To his knowledge of Sanskrit, Persian, Arabic, he added English, Greek, Hebrew, that he might read the Bible; and he sought out such European acquaintance as was possible to a native of Bengal. In 1820, he published *The Precepts of Jesus the Guide to Peace and Happiness*, and was soon involved in a controversy with the Serampur missionary Dr. Marshman, to whom his rejection of Christ's deity was a heresy outweighing his close approach to Christianity in other matter. But he found allies in the Unitarians of England, and gathered a band of Bengalis atheistically minded like himself, who formed the nucleus of the Brahmo Samaj; he ravaged orthodox Hinduism with his attacks on suttee, idolatry, and the manifold mischiefs and errors of contemporary religion. There are noble strains in Hindu thought, and India has never lacked saints and mystics; but Hinduism was passing through a most unhappy phase, and countenanced a multitude of revolting practices. Rammohan Roy's courage by 1820, or even earlier, 'raised such a feeling against me that I was at last deserted by every person except two or three Scotch friends, to whom and to the nation to which they belong I will always feel grateful'. He thought Bentinck's prohibition of suttee premature and inexpedient. But his support of the action in England (which he visited in 1830, and where he died, 1833), in private and before the Select Committee of the House of Commons examining Indian affairs, was invaluable in procuring the rejection of the appeal of over five hundred leading Bengalis to the Privy Council, against the prohibition.

Elphistone in 1822 noted

> 'the wonderful improvement of the natives that begins to be discernible, in Bengal especially. There is a Bengalee newspaper, which discusses all subjects and is interesting even to English readers, though of course often puerile and often mistaken.
>
> 'Ram Mohun Roy, wisely retaining the name and observances of a Hindoo, is writing books in favour of Deism and many natives begin to discover curiosity and

interest about the form of their government as well as its proceedings, together with a strong spirit of reform as applied to the science, religion, and morals of their nation. Amidst all this there is a great deal of cant, affectation, and imposture, Bengaless talking about liberty and philanthropy, and declaiming against the efforts of the Tories to crush the infant liberty of the Press....but even to use this sort of language without understanding it is wonderful advance and from admiring the sound, people must come to relish the sense.'

No more finely gifted a man than Elphinstone ever went to India. But he could not guess how great a thing was beginning.

Bengal had other spirits swift and brave, and filled with intellectual fire. A half-caste Portuguese, Henry Louis Vivian Derozio, in 1826, at the age of seventeen, joined the staff of the Hindu College, Calcutta (now the Presidency College). Derozio's life flamed out quickly. To him truth and beauty were a passion and their attainment worth infinitely more than the keeping of life. His own verse, a flood romantic, flushed, luxuriant, was valueless; but his enthusiasm and selflessness swayed his students wildly. Such an emancipation seemed to be coming to intellectual Young Bengal that the orthodox compelled his dismissal. His defence, though unavailing, was noble:

'Entrusted as I was for some time with the education of youths peculiarly circumstanced, was it for me to have made them pert and ignorant dogmatists by permitting them to know what could be said upon only one side of grave question?....I never teach such absurdity.'

He started a daily paper, *The East Indian* but before he could make a new career, cholera killed him, December 23, 1831.

The Hindu College had found another remarkable teacher, Dr. Richardson. Thanks to such men as these, Bengal not only gained the intellectual primacy of India, but-possessed it so firmly established the even to-day the largest half of current literature in such a language as Gujarati is translation from Bengali; there is no Indian vernacular which does not still exist in a state of considerable dependence on this the most vigorous of them all. The Derozio school cared nothing for nationalism, despising everything Indian, awake to one fact only, that at last intellectual freedom had come, and that nothing else mattered. Movements long spent in Europe found renewal here; the French Revolution long its ideas, the late eighteenth-century philosophers, such poets as Shelley and Byron. More than vigorous, they were often reckless, against superstition; students would fling beef-bones into the houses of the orthodox, would go round shouting, 'We have eaten Mussulman bread', would stage ceremonies of mock-conversion to Islam. They showed great earnestness for social reform; and when Dr. Alexander Duff founded in 1845 what is now the Scottish Churches College, he won swiftly from the highest Hindu families a group of converts whose after-career proved them of outstanding ability and character. Among them were Lalbihari De, whose *Folk Tales of Bengal and Bengal Peasant Life* enjoyed long spell of use in schools; and Kalicharan Banerji, Registrar of Calcutta University, one of the founders of the National Congress (*circa* 1885), a man influential in Bengali literature. Krishnamohan Banerji, another man destined to matter greatly in his country's life, in 1833 left the Derozio group, with their scorn for all religion as superstition, and was baptised. For a while it looked as if Bengal, led by it bound intelligentsia, was at the start of a mass movement into Christianity recalling the early centuries of Christian missions in Europe. Macaulay's belief that enlightenment would kill Hinduism and bring in Christianity, so derided now, in its context was a reasonable guess. But as with the Oxford Movement, that contemporary drift of Anglicanism towards Rome—one stirring similar hope, alarm, and rage—a Dr. Pusey was found in Hinduism, in Debendranath Tagore, father of the poet, and the consolidator, practically the real founder, of the Brahmo Samaj. 'Wait to bit! I will stop all this', he said, when he heard of Duff's success. In his *Autobiography* he tells us how he went from house to house cementing opposition. The Brahmo Samaj did what orthodox Hinduism was powerless to do; providing a half-way house where men could worship without idolatry and the cruelties which passed for religion, it stayed the exodus. The Brahmo Samaj today is a dying institution. But for seventy years its influence was all-pervading in every higher walk of Bengali life, and it produced a secession of men for whom the only adequate adjective is 'noble'. Without them, Bengali intellectual life would have been almost negligible, whereas with them it was a beacon to the rest of India, which Bengal saved by her example, as she was saying herself by her exertions. The great house of the Tagores, in their more influential members, were Brahmos, a galaxy of genius and accomplished talent; they were supported by a society intensely individual, highly and variously cultured, energetic in effort, upright in conduct. Christian missions continued to win an occasional convert who mattered, notably Madhusudhan Datta, better known by his baptismal name of Michael—the greatest poet of nineteenth century Bengal, author of the epic, *The Death of Meghnad,* introducer of blank verse and the sonnet. But the Brahmo Samaj provided what awakened consciences asked, without compelling an absolute break with Hindu society.

With these spiritual movements secular reforms were also working. The early' thirties, the period of the working of renewed revolutionary activity in Europe and of the beginning of electoral democracy in England, saw the passing from the Indian scene of the great figures, alternately soldiers and statesmen, moving at ease amid the frightened (yet with them trustful) princes of the land, self-confident, happy, athletic, preferring the saddle to the Councillor's seat, when on campaign hunting in the intervals between battles. A very different man was about to appear. The 1833 Act provided for an additional member of the Governor-General's Council, to codify the laws. As this, Mr. Thomas Babington Macaulay came, in 1834. He had thoughts on other than legal matters, and is perhaps best remembered in connection with India by his famous Minute on Education.

We must retrace our steps a little. The idea of State-controlled, State-organised machinery for universal education was as foreign to the English civil servants of his day as it would have been to the group of Indians like Rammohan Roy, Dwarkanath Tagore, and others who led the reformist movement. It is true that a system of that kind had been instituted in Prussia after 1806, but in almost every other country the primary responsibility for bringing up a child lay with the parent and the Churches. Government participation in England was confined to grants-in-aid, and these, which were on a small scale, did not involve any State, control until 1856, when the vice-President of the Council of Education was made responsible to Parliament. Forster's Education Act was to follow fourteen years later, but this did not destroy the dual system. A considerable part of English elementary education is still in Church schools. State interference is small both in the Public Schools and Universities. The English certainly did not bring to India any predilection for a unified secular educational system, yet this was what was actually developed during the twenty years preceding the mutiny and was defined in the Directors' despatch of 1854, which determined the organisation of education throughout British India. Looking back over early a century of educational effort, the evils of State system are sufficiently obvious, the failure of a secular Westernised education is writ large over India, but it is difficult to see what alternative lay before Bentinck and those who worked with him and after him. The Government entered unwillingly into the field of elementary education because the existing facilities were inadequate and there was no other body with the necessary driving force to undertake this work. It decided to support a modern Western type of higher education, but only after a long controversy, in which many English opposed and many Indians supported the view which Bentinck finally adopted. Both decisions followed inevitably from the decay of Hinduism and the disordered state of the country.

The state of education in India before the British occupation is, unfortunately, a favourite subject for political dissertations. This has led to a certain confusion of thought about the various types of indigenous teaching, of which three were of importance in the eighteenth century. The ideal training for the Brahmin youth is of great antiquity, and represents an extremely high standard of education. After assuming the sacred thread at the age of eight, the boy would spend fourteen years away from his home under the personal supervision of his *guru,* or in the forest *asram*. Such an upbringing was always confined to a very small and highly privileged class, and was probably common in the hey-day of Brahminism, before the spread of Muhammadanism. This was not a type of education in between *guru* and *chela* might be an inspiration to University teachers, as it has been to Rabindranath Tagore in his *asram* at Santiniketan. Two other institutions catered for a wider but still limited range of boys. These were the Muslim and Hindu schools which were common in the towns and large villages. Both suffered during the eighteenth century from the continual disorders which disturbed most parts of the peninsula, but they were found in many districts when they came under British rule, and their work and scope are described in early reports. Most of them were of a very primitive nature, being usually attached to a temple or mosque. This meant the exclusion of the lower castes and the primitive tribes, and it is typical of the early attitude of the Government towards elementary education that almost the first elementary State schools were for the children of Bhils, Khonds, and of criminals whose parents could not send them to religious schools. The Muslim schools taught the Quran and some Persian to a few elder boys, but there is little evidence about the standard of teaching. In the Punjab, which was annexed later, indigenous education was surveyed with a move modern eye.

> 'The Hindu schools were rare being either colleges in which Brahmin boys learnt Sanskrit and received a half-professional training, or elementary school where sons of Hindu shopkeepers were taught to keep accounts and read and write the traders' scripts. The few Gurmukhi schools that existed were of a purely religious character.

> The best feature of the indigenous schools was that they were not confined to the religious and mercantile classes but were open to the few agriculturists who cared to attend them'.[3]

These schools continued to function, and some of them have survived till today. They had the usual weaknesses of isolated religious schools, and they only reached a very small proportion of the population. In 1835 Bentinck instituted an enquiry into the state of indigenous education in Bengal and Bihar, and found that under five per cent of the male population attended these schools, but that 'certain classes of the native population, hitherto excluded by usage from vernacular instruction, have begun to aspire to its advantages'.[4] The more accurate survey of the North-West Provinces some ten years later showed that 'of a population which numbered in 1843 23,200,000 souls, and in which were consequently included more than 1,900,000 males of a school-going age, we can trace but 68,200 as in the receipt of any education whatever'. In all the recently acquired territory adult literacy was proportionately far lower than amongst the young.

The evidence does not suggest any widespread system of what would now be called popular education, but a fair amount of local effort by Hindu pandit or Muslim maulvi, and this would be supported, here and there, by grants from local princes. The training of elder Hindu boys, confined to a small section of the population, was obscurantist and ineffective.

> 'The ancient scriptures of the country, the famous records of numerous Hindu sects, had long since been discredited. The Vedas and Upanishads were sealed books. All that we know of the immortal Mahabharata. Ramayana, or the Bhagavad Gita was from the execrable translation into popular Bengali, which no respectable young man was supposed to read.'[5]

Persian, Sanskrit, and Arabic were taught, all of which were, from the Indian standpoint, 'dead' languages, though Persian remained the language of the courts until the time of Lord William Bentinck. Vernacular learning and vernacular literature were at a very low ebb, and were not considered a suitable medium for instruction.

> 'Though the past had produced very much that was noble and popular in vernacular literature, such as the Hindi work of Tulsidas or the Marathi of Tukaram, the existence of which the opponents of vernacular ignored, it was certainly true as they urged that very little was begin produced at the time'.[6]

Such, roughly, was the position which confronted the Committee of Public Instruction which had been set up in 1823, and to which Bentinck looked for advice on education, and it was in this body that the struggle took place between the 'Orientalists' and the 'Anglicists' which culminated in Macaulay's famous minute, and the initiation of a policy which was to have such a profound effect on the future of India. Two points were in dispute—the type of education to be given in such colleges as received public assistance, and the best method for encouraging popular elementary education. The dispute which took place over the first question has rather obscured the importance of the policy adopted for the second.

The battle between 'Anglicists' and 'Orientalists' was fought out over the allocation of the Government grant to a few colleges in Bengal. Some of these had been founded under European initiative—such as the Muslim Madrassa at Calcutta, which was founded by Warren Hastings, and the Sanskrit College at Benares, which owed much to Jonathan Duncan. All of them however, except the *Vidyalaya*, the Hindu College, were definitely Oriental in character. The *Vidyalaya*, which finally became the Presidency College, was founded in 1817 by a group of reformist Hindus, led by the English secularist watchmaker, David Hare. These Hindus, of whom Rammohan Roy was the most prominent, were anxious for a new type of education. They believed that the teaching of science would help to abolich certain social evils in the Hindu system, that it would make it easier for Indians to take their part in Government service, and that practical and engineering training would help to make their country prosperous. The Committee of Public Instruction was divided, but not along racial lines. Several Europeans were keen Orientalists, including Wilson, the principal of the Hindu College; others took the line, which was ultimately adopted by Bentinck, that if the government contributed money it should be invested in some form of 'useful' training. The discussion was closely connected with the 'suttee' controversy, and the Orientalists suffered a severe blow because Wilson had doubted the wisdom and practicability of abolishing the practice. Bentinck finally gave his decision that the 'object of the British Government should be the promotion of English literature and science'.[7] The 'Anglicists' had won the day. As a foretaste of the expected revolution in Hindu mentality, the Medical College was opened to Indian students in 1837, and the orthodox Hindus heard to their dismay of Brahmins dissecting human bodies 'with even more than the indifference of European professional men.'[8]

Once it had been decided to encourage a modern type of education in the colleges, the use of English as a medium of instruction followed inevitablity. The choice lay between English and either Sanskrit or Arabic. There was at the time a strong prejudice amongst educated Hindus against the use of the vernaculars for higher education, an attitude which had an exact parallel in medieval Europe. William Arnold, writing in 1840, notes the Punjabi scholar's strong objection to the use of Urdu.[9] Bentinck was guided solely by practical considerations. He believed that science would be the subject must taught, and, as between English and a 'dead' language, he preferred the former. He certainly had no feeling against the vernacular languages, and he gave a great impetus to their study when he abolished Persian in the law courts and substituted the vernacular as the official language in all except the highest courts. He was, however, anxious to foster the growth of a small educated class, who would know

English and through that knowledge bring Western ideas to India. There was much talk at that time of what has been called the 'filtration' theory. Macaulay emphasises this idea in his minute of February, 1835. 'It is impossible for us, with our limited means, to attempt to educate the body of the people. We must do our best to form a class who may be interpreters between us and the millions whom we govern; a class of persons, Indian in blood and colour, but English in taste, in opinions, in morals, and in intellect. To that class we may leave it to refine the vernacular dialects of the country, to enrich those dialects with terms of science borrowed from the Western nomenclature, and to render them by degrees fit vehicles for conveying knowledge to the great mass of the population'. These ideas held the field for some twenty years, and led, especially in Bengal, to an excessive concentration on a modernised higher education. Looking back after a century of it, it is easy to see why Bentinck and his officials were too optimistic. The Hindu system divides the population into water-tight compartments, most unsuitable for filtration. The educated *Zeminder* did not return to his village and educate his tenants, or even undertake scientific farming. Science has not taken the place in education which was expected in 1830, and the higher castes have shown an overwhelming preference for literary and legal studies, which they are not likely to impart to others. The reformist movement amongst the educated classes was based on the Brahmo Samaj, and almost disappeared in the revival of Hindu orthodoxy, of nationalist sentiment, which followed the mutiny. Yet Macaulay's forecast[10] has come partly true. We have formed a definite English-speaking 'class of persons', though they have no desire to act as interpreters for the Government. The vernaculars have become of greater relative importance, but is the vernacular Press rather than the text-book which has penetrated into the villages. The dialects may not have been 'refined', but they have certainly been 'enriched by the assimilation of foreign words and foreign idiom.

Steam was an event almost more revolutionising than eduction itself. In August, 1830, Bentinck decided in favour of the Red Sea route over the slow Cape one, for letters and tidings. After his governor-generalship, giving evidence in 1837 before a Select Committee of the House of Commons, he brought forward an argument for steam communication by the shortest route, which reads now like a prophecy which has been ironically fulfilled:

> 'It is through the means of a quite safe and frequent communication between all India and England that the natives of India in person will be enabled to bring their complaints and grievances before the authorities and the country; that large numbers of disinterested travellers will have it in their power to report to their country at home the nature and circumstances of this distant portion of the empire. This result I hope will be to rouse the shameful apathy and indifference of Great Britain to the concerns of India; and by thus bringing the eye of the British public to bear upon India it may be hoped that the desired amelioration may be accomplished'.

'In every way the West made it clear that it had come to remain. From 1830 onwards the Government possessed a summer capital in Simla, which had been in part annexed after the Gurkha War and in part purchased from the Maharaja of Patiala. Darjeeling was bought from the Raja of Sikkim in 1835. Bentinck also established the hill station of Ootacamund, in the Nilgiris of South India.

The mood and methods of the old brigandage were changing into those of modern industrialism and capitalism. The process of readjustment proved painful, as every such process must in intensely conservative circles. When in 1835 the five chief mercantile firms of Calcutta failed, the financial dislocation, following on the Palmers' failure in Lord Amherst's time, hit the Company's servants specially hard. It was difficult to know how money could be safely kept, in a country where commercial morality had been so low during so many decades.

ADMINISTRATION UNDER LORD WILLIAM BENTINCK

Bentinck and the new spirit in England: reaction against Hinduism: Bentinck's reforms: judicial changes: police: suppression of thagi and suttee: effect of these campaigns on administration: Sir Charles Metcalfe.

The arrival of Lord William Bentinck marked the beginning of a new era in numerous ways. His seven years' rule proved a peaceful interlude between two periods of severe and costly campaigning, and thus made it possible to achieve reforms which were long overdue. Helped by his previous experience in Madras and a more efficient staff of officials, he consolidated and reorganised the administration which since the time of Cornwallis had been hastily adapted to the newly conquered countries. His own instincts were those of a Liberal reformer. He believed in peace, retrenchment, and reform, in free competition, free trade, and a strictly limited sphere of State action. In Sir Charles Metcalfe he had an admirable chief of staff who supplied the local knowledge and some of the driving force behind the reforms. These touched nearly every side of Indian life and formed the basis of the paternal Government of the Victorian era. Bentinck initiated new policies in the spheres of finance, justice, and education. Freedom from war gave him a larger European staff and greater confidence in taking unpopular measures. He was able to turn his attention to the civilisation of savage tribes and the abolition of certain religious and social customs, such as suttee and female infanticide.

This epoch is important from another point of view. Bentinck and the younger officials who came out in the twenties brought with them some of the new spirit which was causing a religious and social revival in England. For some years Wilberforce and Fowell Buxton had been exposing the horrors of slavery, and Sir James Mackintosh had been inveighing against the barbarities of the criminal code. They were beginning to have their effect. By 1830 over a hundred felonies had been removed from the category of capital offences, and English law became little more bloodthirsty than Muslim. In 1834 slavery was abolished throughout the British colonies. The Poor Law of 1834 helped to restore the working mans' self-respect. In 1833 also, Keble preached his sermon on National Apostasy and Newman published the first of the *Tracts for the Times*. They started a movement which was to have considerable influence upon many of the pre-Mutiny officials. A new leaven was working within the small English community, in India, a new school of officials and officers began to make its influence felt. It was to show itself in a revolt against the lax morality common amongst Europeans in the East, against the patronage of idolatry by the Government, and against certain Hindu customs.[11] The English began to believe that they had a moral mission in India, that they represented a higher civilisation, a better religion. The younger men came out to India and received an impression of a country where crime flourished, and the mass of the people were steeped in a form of savagery which they connected with the Hindu religion.

Trevelyan, writing in the middle' thirties on Indian education, talks of 'suttee, Thuggee, human sacrifices, Ghaut murders, and other excrescences of Hinduism and expressly enjoined by it'.[12] This was the view of many contemporaries, and the moral was only emphasised by the horrid example of the older generation of Englishmen, with 'their black wives running about picking up a little race, while their husbands please them by worshipping the favourite idol.[13] Evangelical activities in England were beginning to have their repercussions in India. Phrases like 'churchwarden to Juggernaut' and 'wet-nurse to Vishnu' embarrassed a Government which held that the policy of complete impartiality required the attendance of the Company's officers at Hindu and Muslim religious festivals. Government offices were still closed on such days, but open on Sunday, and a cocoanut was officially broken at the beginning of the monsoon. The question was to become still more acute under Lord Auckland, when Sir Peregrine Maitland, the Commander-in-Chief at Madras, resigned his post rather than punish a British soldier who refused to take part in a ceremonial parade in salutation of a Hindu deity. These ideas were beginning to affect the expatriated Englishman when Bentinck came to India. They had their counterpart in that reformist movement amongst certain sections of educated Hindus of which Rammohan Roy was the leader. Hinduism at that moment was at a low ebb, and the more enlightened Indians turned Westward for inspiration. Many Englishmen of that period would have subscribed to Macaulay's view, written in 1836, that 'if our plans of education are followed up, there will not be a single idolater among the respectable classes in Bengal thirty years hence'. The revival of orthodox Hinduism did not become vigorous or widespread[14] till after the Mutiny. When Bentinck arrived, nearly thirty years were still to pass before that catastrophe. His reforms started an era of great administrative activity, somewhat marred by the secularist complacency of the early Liberalism.

One of Bentinck's first tasks was both dangerous and unpopular. Since the Charter Act of 1813, which separated the Company's political and trading activities, there had been a rapid increase in the expenditure under the former head. By 1827 this had risen from about sixteen million yearly to over twenty-five million, and the difference was only partially covered by receipts from the newly added territories. There was a deficit of a million in the last year of Lord Amherst's term of office, and Bentinck sailed for India with definite instructions to cut down civil and military salaries and allowances, and reduce expenditure generally. The army was mulched of half its *batta,* the extra allowance which the officers had come to regard as a permanent addition to their pay. Special committees examined and reduced the expenditure of each Presidency, cutting down the irregular military forces and part of the civil establishments. The work required great tact and firmness. These Bentinck possessed, but he recovered from the odium engendered by those early years and to most Englishmen he remained 'the clipping Dutchman' until he retired.

The judicial system had been little altered since the time of Cornwallis, and the Provincial Courts of Appeal were showing signs of deterioration. The administrative side of the civil service has usually attracted the ablest men, and this tendency was especially marked when new areas were being brought under control. The Courts had become, in Lord William Bentinck's words, 'resting-places for those members of the service who were deemed unfit for higher responsibilities'. The general standards of administration had improved, but the Courts remained hopelessly in arrears, both with the civil appeals and also their gaol-deliveries. The Courts were now abolished, and their criminal jurisdiction transferred to the Commissioners of Revenue. This experiment was a failure, and the Sessions duties were then allotted to the civil judges, who were instructed to hold a monthly gaol-delivery, and thus became the forerunners of the present District Judges. Their magisterial powers had, of course, to be transferred, and were given to the District Collectors, a 'blending of Somerset House and the Old Bailey' which survives in spite of obvious theoretical objections. The main collector of revenue and head of the police, the Sessions Judge with criminal and civil jurisdiction—were thus established. The concentration of power in the hands of the European District Magistrate was originally justified by the difficulty of initiating cases against gangrobbers, many of whom were protected by *Zemindars,* and by the need of a single authority in times of disorder. The system received a new lease of life in the Mutiny, and has continued since, though the revenue work is more stereotyped, and the District Magistrate has become more like a French *Prefet*, co-ordinating in each locality the many activities of a modern government.

Bombay, after Elphinstone's departure, saw a temporary revival of that struggle between a High Court, created in 1823, and the Executive, which had so disturbed Bengal forty years earlier. The Court claimed jurisdiction over every person in Bombay territory, then extended far beyond the port and adjacent islands. On October 6, 1828, the Presiding Judge told the world where, in his opinion, the Governor stood:

'Within these walls we own no equal, and no superior but God and the King. The East India Company, therefore, all those who govern their possessions, however absolute over those whom they consider their subjects, must be told, as they have been told ten thousand times before, that in this court they are entitled to no more precedency and favour than the lowest suitor in it'.

Malcolm, the Governor, was properly determined not to be beaten down, 'not by honest fellows with glittering sabres, but quibbling, quill-driving lawyers,' and won support from the Governor-General and Lord Ellenborough, President of the Board of Control. The latter wrote from London, in February 1829, that 'their law is considered bad law; but then their errors in matters of law are nothing in comparison with those they have committed in the tenor of their speeches from the bench.' The dispute was temporarily settled by the appointment of Malcolm's own Advocate-General as Chief Justice, a timely reminder that patronage still went to those who supported the Company, and the Privy Council rejected the claims of the Supreme Court. The controversy aroused much talk, because Malcolm's indiscretion allowed a private letter of the Board of Control's President to get into the Press, with the result that 'Lord Ellenborough, of whom little before had been known in India, suddenly became famous'[15] But the Privy Council's action settled the trouble for the time being; and Malcolm, whose qualities were better fitted for a solely Oriental stage than for one systematised and in process of modernisation, was able to leave the cares of his governorship, and pass to activities in which he was perfectly at home, riding through Kathiawar to Cutch, where he harangued Rajput chefs and dewans on the horrid custom of infanticide. He was respectfully listened to; and returned, hunting and slaying by the way,[16] in the manner of the old joyous times when even a campaign had been for its leaders more than half play, with battle and the chase alternating and easily passing into one another. Meanwhile, the establishment of the 'rule of law' had suffered a temporary setback, from which there was a quick recovery. Malcolm was typical of a vanishing age, even he knew that his beliefs and principles were doomed to defeat:

> I have tried to deal some heavy blows at these costly and dangerous fabrics yclept Supreme Courts; but they are too essential for the objects of power and patronage, and to feed the rising spirit of the age, for me are any man to prevail against them.' (October 19, 1828.)

A weakness of the Cornwallis Regulations had been the very cautious and limited use of Indian judges for civil cases. From time to time their jurisdiction had been slightly increased, but the first real extension was made in 1827, when more subordinate judges were appointed and *Sadar Amins* were empowered to try suits involving double the former amount. In 1831 Lord William Bentinck established a superior type of Indian civil judge authorised to try cases involving property to any amount, and with salaries rising to £ 720 a year. The principle of appointing more Indians to positions of importance was discussed before the Parliamentary Committee of 1832-3, many witnesses arguing that this was the only method of keeping down areas of work, and avoiding a more expensive administration. The next ten years saw the appointment of Indian deputy-collectors in 1837, and deputy-magistrates in 1843. In the latter capacity they were able to pass sentences of imprisonment up to three years. In this way some real recognition was made of the principle contained in 87th clause of the Charter Act of 1833. 'Be it enacted that no native of the said territories...shall by reason only of his religion, place of birth, descent, colour, or any of them, be disabled from holding any place, office, or employment in the said Company.' Up to the time of the Mutiny the employment of Indians was being extended at a moderate rate. In 1857 there were some 256 Indian officials drawing over £360 a year, and 2590 held various appointments of a lower grade. Nearly every civil case was by this time being tried originally before an Indian judge.

The tracking and apprehension of criminals has always proved a more difficult task than the organisation of criminal justice. Cornwallis had taken the management of the 'police' into Government's hands, and introduced the *thanadari* system, with Indian *darogas* in charge of each police district, but the rank and file of the police force were the village watchmen, 'an enormous ragged army who eat up the industry of this province.'[17] The idea of an organised disciplined body of men had hardly been conceived in any part of the world. It was considered a great innovation when Sir Robert Peel reorganised the London Metropolitan Police in 1829, the year after Lord William Bentinck had become Governor-General, and England had her first 'Peelers.' In 1830 few governments thought it their duty to provide a 'patrolling' police force with recognised stations any more than they would have thought it incumbent upon them to provide universal juvenile education. Regular policemen were first found necessary in the large cities, but in other countries, as in India, the expenses were entirely defrayed by the residents. The extension of this system into country districts, and the co-ordination of the various forces, has proved a very slow process which is far from complete even in countries like the United States, where a sheriff may still have to summon a posse of fellow-citizens to pursue a criminal. Bentinck did not alter the *thanadari* system, but he organised, what might be described as a 'flying squad' to deal with the specific crimes of *thagi* and dacoity. His successor, Lord Auckland, improved the pay and standing of the *darogas*, but the village watchmen remained dependent upon the other villagers for their support, and shortly before the Mutiny it was recognised that, while the special department was doing excellent work, the *thanadari* system was functioning very badly. The matter was under discussion in 1856, when a minute by the Governor of Bengal sketched out a policy which would have turned the watchmen into regular Government servants.

The suppression of *thagi* was a notable achievement of the pre-Mutiny era. The *Thag,* or more accurately *phansidar,* was a member of one of those hereditary criminal castes which have always been a feature of Indian life. Some of these, like the *Chapperbunds,* and the *haranshikaris,* still survive to worry the police officer by their cunning thefts. The *phansidar,* or 'noose-holder,' was unusual because his invariable method of procedure was to murder before robbing. Working in gangs, which were bound together by strict religious vows to the goddess Kali, the *phansidars* would ingratiate themselves with travellers, and then strangle them and bury them. They formed a powerful confederacy operating over the whole of the north of India, and supported by many landowners, through whom they disposed of their booty. For some years after the British occupation their activities were screened by the Maratha and Pindari Wars, but the existence of the professed *Thag* had been established by Lord Hastings's administration and in 1829 a special department under Colonel Sleeman was appointed to deal with them. The methods by which these gangs were finally dispersed, and a description of their habits and curious mentality, have been recounted in two classic works.[18] Some idea of their depredations can be gathered from Sleeman's report of 1840, when the number of 'ascertained well known and bloody Bhils' in Oudh alone was given as 274, and of the twenty approves one confessed to 931 murders in 40 years, and another to 508 in 20 years. Over 1500 *Thags* were apprehended in the first six years.

In 1837 Colonel Sleeman was also entrusted with the suppression of dacoity, but here the task was much more difficult. Many Indians of all classes must have known about the operations of the *Thags,* and in some cases assisted them and profited by them, but a far larger and more influential section of the population were accessory to the dacoities. There were parts of India where dacoity was as much a national pastime as bull-fighting in Spain. It was considered by its participants as an honourable profession.

> 'Whilst talking over their excursions...their eyes gleamed with pleasure, and beating their hands on their foreheads and breasts, and muttering some ejaculations, they bewailed the hardness of their lot, which now ensured their never being able again to participate in such a joyous occupation.[19]

They could not be hunted down with the ruthlessness employed against the *Thags*, and for some years they were protected by the insistence of the law courts upon proof of specific offences, when all that could normally be proved was that a prisoner belonged to a gang of dacoits. This was partially corrected by an Act of 1843, but the difficulty of obtaining evidence still proved a great hindrance, and the professional dacoits learnt to operate near the borders of Indian States, where their pursuit was made harder by questions of jurisdiction. In Western India the most persistent robbers were the Bhills, whose settlement and reclamation by Outram was a wholly admirable work.

The Government's duty was clear in the case of *thagi*, and also of dacoity. It was impossible to justify murder for the sake of robbery, even though the perpetrators might claim to be religious devotees. Other savage customs presented greater difficulties. The religious element was stronger, the element of gain was less. As our officials spread over the country, they were brought into touch with new side of Indian life, about which their predecessors had been ignorant or indifferent. Some of these offended strongly against all European ideas of civilisation. The three most important, not only in themselves but in the way they affected the Englishman's idea of India, were the *meriah* human sacrifices in Orissa, the prevalence of female infanticide, and the custom of 'suttee' or widow-burning, which was common throughout Bengal and Northern India. The first was confined to certain backward sects, but the other two were practised by the highest castes, and the last was enthusiastically approved by all classes.

The *meriah* sacrifices of Orissa were first noticed in the report of an official (Russell), May 11, 1837. There suppression was a slow business, not completed until the end of Lord Dalhousie's time, if then. The main work was done by General Campbell. The sacrifices were to the spirit of natural fertility, a sanguinary form of the *Iti* or *Itu* worship still existing in rural North India. At Chinna Kimedy she took the form of an elephant, at Gumsur and Boad of a bird. The Khonds who practised the rite sometimes allowed *meriah* girls to live until they had children by Khond fathers. These children were reared for sacrifice, and were well treated. Before being put to death they were exchanged for similar children in another village, apparently because their own village had ties of affection with them. The sacrifices were always in public. They took varying forms, all inexpressible cruel, consisting of the cutting of the flesh off the living victim.

Campbell was away on the Chinese War, 1842-7, and had to take up the work of suppression afterwards with renewed vigour. His task was pursued with immense patience and kindness. In Chinna Kimedy the people were suspicious, since it was rumoured that he himself was collecting materials to sacrifice to the water-spirit, because a tank he had made had dried up; also, that his elephants needed periodical meals of human beings. He began by giving cotton cloth and strings of bright beads to those who had female children (he was simultaneously trying to extirpate infanticide), and threw open his tent to full examination. ('It is the house of a god!' His astonished visitors exclaimed.) He tried also, with scant success, to introduce vaccination. In 1853, towards the end of his long campaign, he discovered that this formula was being used in the now *meriah*-less worship:

> Do not be wrathful with us, O Goffess, for giving you blood of beasts instead of human blood! Vent your anger

on this gentleman, who is well able to bear it. We are guiltless'.[20]

Between 1837 and 1854, 1506 merihas were rescued.

The killing of girl babies was commonest amongst the warlike castes in Central and Western India, and is a natural development of a primitive civilisation in which an unmarried woman is considered as unchaste, and a fair proportion of the men are killed in war. Some castes carried the habit to extreme lengths. The Rajkumars kept very few of their female children, and the custom was prevalent throughout Rajputana. It was extremely difficult for the early administrators to deal with this problem. The systematic murder of children was an affair of the zenana. The mother was usually the executioner. She either did not feed the child, or 'rubbed a little opium on the nipples of her breasts'. Considering the extreme privacy of the zenana, it was impossible to deal with specific cases, and the only practical method was to bring Government pressure to bear upon the leaders in areas where the very small proportion of female babies showed that the custom was in force. One economic reason for female infanticide was the high dowries demanded amongst certain castes, such as the Mairs. In Kathiawar the Political Agent, Willoughby, instituted an 'infanticide fund' from which presents were made to members of the Jharijah tribe who preserved their daughters, while maximum sums were fixed for dowries. As the country became more settled it was possible to keep better registers of births, and infanticide became more localised and even before the Mutiny had tanded to disappear amongst all except a few castes.

'Suttee' presented a more difficult problem, and the subject has had far more publicity outside India. *Sahamrana*, the 'dying in company with' one's husband, is very ancient Indian rite. The Anglo-Indian word 'suttee' is from *sati*, the woman who performs the rite, usually by immolating herself on the funeral pyre. It seems to have been confined to the higher castes of the Hindus, though the weavers of Tippera practised a still more objectionable variant in burying their widows alive. The Moguls attempted to discourage the custom whenever it came under their notice. Tavernier says that 'the Governors, who are Mussalmans, hold this dreadful custom of self-destruction in horror, and do not readily give permission'.[21] Manucci describes a case at Agra, in which the woman was rescued, and the Brahmins complained, whereupon Aurangzeb 'issued an order that in all lands under Mogul control, never again should the officials allow a woman to be burnt'.[22] It was discouraged in the neighbourhood of Delhi, where Metcalfe when Resident was able to prohibit it, but was common amongst the Brahmins of Bengal and throughout the Hindu States. When a prince died there was something approaching a holocaust. In 1780 sixty-four women burned at the death of Raja Ajit Singh of Marwar. As late as the middle of the nineteenth century, during the anarchy of the last days of Sikh rule in the Punjab, such wholesale 'suttees' were frequent. Wives and concubines were burnt in numbers after the deaths of Kishari Singh and Basanta Singh. Suchet Singh's death was reputed to have been followed by the burning of ten wives and three hundred concubines. For some years the various Europeans who came to India noticed and disapproved of the practice, but could not prevent it except in small compact areas. The French prohibited it at Chandernagore, the Danes at Serampur, the Portugueses at Goa.

From the Hindu point of view *sahamarana* was an extremely popular semi-religious spectacle. It was attended by large crowds, and redounded to the credit of the deceased husband and his family. There was no opposition to the practice from Indians until about 1820, when a few educated and Westernised Hindus, led by Rammohan Roy, started a reformist movement. The higher Muslim officials disapproved of 'suttee', but, like the earlier. British servants of the Company, they had a no police force at their disposal and no means of preventing such occurrences. Occasionally English officials would interfere when a case came to their notice. Mr. Brooks, Collector of Shahabad, feasibly prevented a suttee in 1789. The Collector of Gaya, in 1805, stopped the burning of a girl of twelve. It was only when the administration became better organised, and more Englishmen began to move about the country, that the extent of these and other practices was fully understood. William Carey, the missionary, brought the subject of widow-burning before the Bengal Government by carrying out an unofficial census of 'suttee' occurring within thirty miles of Calcutta. He placed the figures-there were 438 in 1803—before Lord Wellesley, who had already forbidden one religious practice, that of exposing children at Saugor Point, and was disposed to take the same action about widow-burning. Unfortunately he referred the matter to the Nizamat Adalat, the court of appeal in criminal law.

The Nizamat Adalat displayed its accustomed pedantry, and advised the Government to be guided by 'the religious opinions and prejudices of the natives', and for the next twenty-five years a vacillating policy was followed. The Government took the advice of leading Hindu pandits, who replied that the practice was 'recognised and encouraged by the doctrines of the Hindu religion', and for some years attempts were made to regulate the 'suttee', and 'to allow the practice in those cases in which it is countenanced by their religion, and to prevent it in others in which it is, by the same authority, prohibited'.[23] The effect of this action was to legalise the purely voluntary immolation of a widow who was over sixteen and not pregnant, and in pursuance of this policy the police were ordered to get early information of an intended 'suttee', and to see that the widow was neither drugged nor forcibly burned. It was a lamentable procedure, for the police officer would almost invariable be a Hindu or Muslim of the poorer classes, and in either case would not be too critical, while his presence would give an impression that the Government's approval had been obtained. This official sanction had one good effect. As more European officers came out to undertake magisterial and police work in the districts they began to investigate these cases, and to discover the sordid economic reasons as well as the sheer love of cruelty which formed the background to so many cases of *sahamarana*.

By the twenties there was a strong move for prohibition amongst the officials in the more settled areas. The evidence of Mr. Ewer, the Superintendent of Police in Lower Bengal, had great weight. It may be quoted at length as a fair description of most 'suttees'.

> 'There are many reasons for thinking that such an event as a voluntary Suttee very rarely occurs; few widows would think of sacrificing themselves unless overpowered by force or persuasion, very little of either being sufficient to overcome the physical or mental powers of the majority of Hindoo females. A widow, who would turn with natural instinctive horror from the first hint of sharing her husband's pile, will be at length gradually brought to pronounce a reluctant consent because, distracted with grief at the event, without once friend to advice or protect her, she is little prepared to oppose the surrounding crowd of hungry Brahmins and interested relations... In this state of confusion a few hours quickly pass, and the widow is burnt before she has had time to think of the subject. Should utter indifference for her husband, and superior sense, enable her to preserve her judgment, and to resist the arguments of those about her, it will avail her little--the people will not be disappointed of their show; and the entire population of a village will turn out to assist in dragging her to the bank of the river, and in keeping her on the pile.[24]

Bentinck's Regulation prohibiting widow-burning was not issued until 1829. Both Lord Hastings and Lord Amherst had considered this step, but had deferred action partly from fear that such an order could not be made operative, but chiefly because they thought it might lead to disaffection in the sepoy army then on active service, and to disturbances in the recently ceded districts. Nothing of the kind actually occurred, but men like Sir Charles Metcalfe, while concurring in the prohibition, believed that it might 'produce a religious excitement, the consequences of which, if once set in action, cannot be foreseen'.[25] Rammohan Roy himself considered that the order was premature.[26]

In Bengal and Bihar there was opposition to the Regulation, but it took only a legal form. An appeal was made to the Privy Council, and after many delays heard and dismissed. The enforcement of the Regulation was made effective throughout the provinces within a year or two. It took another generation before the practice was abolished in all the Indian States. In Southern India *sahamarana* would seem to have been dying out before the Regulation was made, but over Bengal, Bihar, and parts of what are now the Uttar Pradesh the prohibition was directly contrary to public sentiment, and the tradition in favour of the rite has survived even until modern times. The not infrequent cases when widows commit suicide in their own homes are commented upon with approbation in the Indian Press, and the occasional cases of widow-burning which have occurred in the last thirty years have always aroused great popular enthusiasm. In the last recorded case, in August, 1932, events seem to have followed very much the course described by Mr. Ewer, over a century before.[26]

This long campaign to suppress certain types of indigenous crime had a notable effect on British administration. The English officials of the early Victorian period were convinced that they had to deal with a degenerate race, and this impression was only intensified when, passing beyond the old Mogul Empire, they came into contact with the savage hill chieftains of the Himalayan foothills. There is no more need to pass final judgements on early Hindu morality than upon, say, the mercantilist theory. Able apologists have from time to time defended the *saharmarana* rite,[28] and future generations may hold that female infanticide is a lesser evil than the unchecked growth of population which has characterised these later years. The point which must be emphasised is that from about 1830 onwards English officials were imbued with the idea that they were, in Macaulay's phrase, undertaking the 'stupendous process' of reconstructing 'a decomposed society'. They expressed their contempt for the older type of Company's servant by saying they were 'Hinduised', and this attitude developed into a kind of racial aloofness which became more marked as English women began to settle in India with their husbands. There is a definite change of outlook between the earlier administrators, like Munro, Elphinstone, and Malcolm, and their successors who in 1849 set to work in the newly annexed Punjab. The latter were more ruthless, more spiritually arrogant, and less disposed to delegate any real responsibility to Indians. The tendency to isolate themselves from the Indian was to become still more marked after the mutiny. This attitude was visible in every department of our administration. The annexationist policy of Lord Dalhousie was largely inspired by the difficulties which he encountered when urging the abolition of 'suttee' and female infanticide in the Indian States. Part of the opposition to using Indians in an executive capacity was due to a fear of weakening the administration in its struggle against such barbarities. Men like Elphinstone and Munro had envisaged an India in which the British did little more than keep the peace. Leaving the administration in Indian hands, they would have trusted to education to cure such evils as they believed to exist. The next generation of officials was conscious of the clash between two civilisations, one of which they believed to be improving, and the other to be in the stages of degeneration.

On Lord William Bentinck's going, in March, 1835, Sir Charles Metcalfe acted as Governor-General for a year. He abolished the Inland Transit Duties, a great assistance to commerce, and removed the restrictions on the Press. The latter action aroused the Directors to boundless indignation, and settled all question of his confirmation as Governor-General, which had long been canvassed with much vacillation. He stuck to his opinions with characteristic courage and though the objection to officials being appointed to the supreme place was upheld (when for once it might wisely have been waived), he was considered good enough for two colonial governorship, of Jamaica and Canada.

REFERENCES

1. T.G.P. Spear, *The Nabobs,* 140. See the whole chapter, 'Racial Relations'.
2. *Life.* ii. 82-3.
3. See Trevaskis *The Land of the Five Rivers,* 179. The quotation is from a Punjab Administration Report.
4. *Third Report on the State of Education in Bengal.*
5. For an account of the decay of Hindu learning prior to the revival which took place after the Mutiny, see P.C. Mazumdar's *Life and Teachings of Keshab Chandra Sen,* from which this quotation is taken.
6. Arthur, Mayhew, *The Education of India,* 84.
7. The decision was given in a resolution dated March 7, 1835. Macaulay's well-known minute recommending this course was dated February 2 of that year.
8. C.E. Trevelyan, *On the Education of the People of India,* 1838, p. 33.
9. Director of Education in the Punjab. See p. 318.
10. See Appendix C for Macaulay's Minute.
11. The reaction of a younger civil servant to his older fellow-countrymen are shown in that curious novel *Okfield* written by Matthew Arnold's brother, W.D. Arnold, who died (1859) after a few years in India. See Matthew Arnolds commemorative poem, *A Southern Night.*
12. C.E. Trevelyan. *The Education of the People of India,* 1838, p. 83. Trevelyan later Sir Charles Trevelyan, was a prominent official of the Mutiny period. He was a brother-in-law of Macaulay.
13. A. Mayhew, *Christianity and the Government of India,* 48.
14. The 'counter-reformation', led by Debendranath Tagore (the poet's father) against Dr. Duff's success in Christian propaganda in the forties, was local.
15. Kaye, *Life of Malcolm,* ii. 532.
16. 'Thirty-one hogs slain in the last two days by the spears of our party; and I have had an opportunity of showing the boys that

his honour's dart is as sure and as deadly as the best of them'. (March 7, 1830.)

'I am just returned from Cutch in high health, having besides the inspection of our western frontier and the revision of establishment, had glorious hunting and shooting—wild hogs, elks, deer, foxes, hares, black partridges, and quails, almost to a surfeit. It has been a great treat.'

17. Hunter, *The Annals of Rural Bengal,* 335. He was writing in 1860, before the new force was organised.
18. *Confessions of a Thug,* by Colonel Meadows Taylor (first published, 1839); *Rambles and Recollections,* by W.H. Sleeman.
19. Colonel Sleeman's Bhudduck Report, 1849, quoted by Kaye, *Administration of the East India Company.*
20. *Narrative by Major-General John Campbell, C.B., of his Operations in the Hill Tracts of Orissa for the Suppression of Human Sacrifice and Female Infanticide,* Printed for Private Circulation, 1861.
21. *Travels in India* (Oxford University Press), ii. 162 *et seq.*
22. Manucci, *A Pepys of Mogul India* (Murray), 124.
23. Government resolution of December 5, 1812. Reply to an enquiry from an official in Bandalkhand.
24. Ewer's evidence is given in Peggs *India's Cries to British Humanity* (Second Edition, 1830), 14. See also Edward Thompson, *Suttee,* passim.
25. *Life of Lord Metcalfe,* J.W. Kaye, 1858, ii. 78.
26. Miss Collet, *Life and Letters of Raja Rammohan Roy,* 146.
27. See The *Times,* September 2, 1932. 'A Brahmin of Fatehpur Sikri died on Monday. His widow was determined to commit suttee, but was dissuaded. A mob collected at her house and demanded that she should burn herself. The police locked the woman in the house, but the mob broke in and dragged the woman to the burning ghat. The mob was erecting a pyre when the police fired, killing three persons and wounding five, and rescued the woman.'
28. See, for example, Ananda Coomaraswamy, *The Dance of Siva,* Modern writers, however, adopt a very different line of argument from that of the orthodox Hindus who opposed Bentinck in such papers as the *Chandrika.*

3

The Afghan War

Miss Emily Eden: a popular potentate: and an attentive creature, his Majesty of Oudh: Low suppresses a revolution: Shah Suja: Eldred Pottinger and Herat: the Tripartite Treaty: the Sind Amirs: the Khan of Khelat: occupation of Kandahar: death of Meharab Khan: growing perplexities: surrender of Dost Muhammad: murder of Burnes and Macnaghten: retreat from Kabul: our Sikh allies: Sale and Pollock: Lord Ellenborough Governor-General: Roman proclamations.

Lord Auckland, the new Governor-General, a bachelor, was accompanied by his sisters Fanny and Emily. The latter was to write a commentary, witty, vivacious, skilled in perception of all that lay on the surface, the best book ever written by any foreigner merely visiting India, perhaps the best journal of any kind in our language. It shows us a great Whig noble–a languid, gracious, punning gentleman—completely unaware of anything that passed beneath the ludicrous aspect of absurd rajas, queer peoples outlandishly dressed and quaintly mannered, little pushing officials and their scheming flirting womenfolk. He and his sister are revealed in their intimacy of amusement at the bourgeoisie and bureaucracy surrounding them. Miss Eden's political views are all 'snap judgments', based on what those nearest to the Governor-General (and, necessarily, often farthest from the scene involved) told him. When in the second phase of the Afghan

War disasters come thick and fast, ignorant jauntiness gives way to reckless fierceness eager for vengeance.

Auckland, however, began well enough, with usual long leisured tour upcountry. He was away from Calcutta from October, 1837, to March, 1840, a stretch of time which brings home the slowness and difficulty of travel even after steam had come in, and the reality (and on occasion, the value) of 'the time-lag' which has so completely disappeared from modern politics. He was enabled to mix freely with English society and selected natives; his sister reports that he came away

> 'in a great state of popularity in the Upper Provinces; all these people talked of him with such regard and admiration'[1].

Less satisfying was the fact that the huge entourage passed through ghastly famine. Auckland gave freely from his private purse, and instituted an enquiry into preventive measures; the Indian Government's beginnings of famine policy, which were to grow slowly into effectiveness, date from this time. It is significant of the way Governor-General and sister moved throughout in rose-hued mist, that Miss Eden tells us they rejected experienced officials' advice to stop the tour, lest their horde of followers deepen the land's distress. Her characteristically Whig reply was that these followers were a blessing, since good for trade! Neither of them ever came to suspect the extent to which those courses of India, officialdom's dependants, pillage countries through which their masters pass.

The Governor-General was much beset by the King of Oudh, an 'attentive creature'[2] as he had reason to be. Three months before the tour began, close on midnight of July 7, 1837, the Lucknow Resident, Colonel Low, was waked and told that the King was dying. He wrote to the Brigadier commanding the Oudh subsidiary force, to hold a thousand men in readiness to march at a moment's notice; and went to the palace. He found the King's body still warm, blood flowing freely when the Residency surgeon opened a vein; but there was no other sign of life. Part of Low's force was already present, and he placed seals on the treasures, and guards everywhere. The night, a very dark one, was studded with torch-bearers. For the new King, an uncle of the just-deceased monarch, a statement was drawn up, 'that he was prepared to sign any new treaty for the better government of the country that the British Government might think proper to propose'[3].

The late King had assured Bentinck that his putative son was not his. 'The Padshah Begum', mother of the putative son, now installed him, and made a furious assault on the palace. Low, an intrepid man, demanded to see her, and pushed through a dense crowd-witnessing the installation of 'the pretender'. Dancing-girls were swaying and chanting; swords, spears, matchlocks, muskets were being flourished in a forest of torches. The excited mob, ' more like demons than human beings'[4] a menacing 'dance of the imps', closed round Low and two companions, shouting angry and obscene abuse, threatening them with swords and guns thrust in their faces firing muskets. The Begum haughtily refused to withdraw her candidate. Low was seized by the neckcloth, dragged forward, and commanded to congratulate the new king on pain of instant death. He remained steadfast through insult and imminence of murder; and the Begum's vakil, who had the sense to look ahead to what would follow if the Resident were killed, shouted loudly that the Begum's order was that Colonel Low should be allowed to withdraw; and himself led him out. Low, going out, was passed by Colonel Roberts, a brigade in the Oudh service, who presented his offering to the boy and 'then went off and hid himself, to wait the result of the contest'. For contest there clearly must be; and there was as much reason for pusillanimity as there ever is, seeing that Oudh furnished so large a proportion of the Company's sepoys.

The subsidiary force arrived, and Low told its commander the work was 'now in his hands'. The palace gates were blown in, and sepoys stormed the halls. The late King's favourite wife, 'a modest, beautiful, and amiable young woman, who had been forced to join the Begum, in order to give some countenance to the daring enterprise', was let down from a height of twenty-four feet, on a rope of clothes made by a female attendant whose arm was shattered by grapeshot as she followed. By nine o'clock the palace was cleared of insurgents, the King officially sanction brought out of hiding, 'and the Resident exerted himself to soothe and prepare him for the long and tedious ceremonies of the coronation, while the killed and wounded', in all over a hundred, were removed, and the place cleaned for the ceremonial.

After forcing Oudh to accept a new and harder treaty, Lord Auckland betrayed his gravest fault. He was incompetent and casual, and his administration has been more generally condemned than that of any other Governor-General. But all this is trivial beside his habit of suppressing and garbling documents. The treaty was rejected by the Directors, but Auckland told the King merely that *one* clause, that adding Oudh weighs 16 lacks for an additional subsidiary force, had been disallowed. By what Mr. Roberts generously calls 'an inexcusable piece of carelessness',

> 'the treaty was actually included in a subsequent government publication and was referred to as still in force by succeeding Governor-Generals. Upon Lord Dalhousie was thrust the invidious task of explaining to the King that the treaty, which he and former Governor-Generals had believed to be in force since 1837, had really been abrogated two years after that date, and of expressing a tardy regret that the communication of this fact had been inadvertently neglected. Such miserable and unpardonable mismanagement obviously gave too much ground to those who held that the annexation of Oudh was "a gross breach of national faith".[5]

'Neither Lord Hardinge in 1847 nor Colonel Sleeman in 1854 knew that the whole treaty had been annulled. It was left for Lord Dalhousie to discover the truth, as confirmed by Low himself, then a member of his Council, and to acquaint the India House with the extent to which Lord Auckland had evaded their commands'.[6]

When Auckland visited Oudh, the King, a rheumatically, almost bedridden creature, hovered round him, seeking release from the more onerous clauses of the treaty. The Governor-General regarded his attendance as a boring jest, and played with him languidly. There was for example, a magnificent breakfast at Lucknow, on Christmas Day, 1837, when 'G' (George Eden, Baron Auckland).

'sugared and creamed the Nawab's tea, and the Nawab gave him some pilau. Then he put a slice of buttered toast (rather cold and greasy) in one plate for me, and another for F., and B. Said in an imposing tone, "His Royal Highness sends the Burra lady this, and the Choota lady that", and we looked with immeasurable gratitude. At the end of breakfast, two hookahs were brought in, that the chiefs might smoke together, and a third for Colonel L., the British resident, that his consequence might be kept up in the eyes of the Lucknowites, by showing that he is allowed to smoke at the Governor-General's table. The old khansamah wisely took care to put no tobacco in G's hookah, though it looked very grand and imposing with its snake and rose-water. G. says he was quite distressed; he could not persuade it to make the right kind of bubbling noise'.[7]

Superb presents (which by law now went into the Company's resources, when they could not be declined) and the usual round of fights between elephants, rhinoceroses, tigers, followed.

Kaye puts it down to Simla, 'where our Governors-General surrounded by irresponsible advisers, settle the destinies of empire without the aid of their legitimate fellow-counsellors, and which has been the cradle of more political insanity than any place within the limits of Hindostan',[2] that Auckland, who is credited with being a pacific man, ever launched the first Afghan War.

The Durani Amir of Kabul, Shah Suja, lost his throne, 1809, and after many adventures, which included two attempts to reconquer it, had settled down as a Company's pensioner at Ludhiana. Lord William Bentinck would have been glad enough to see him re-established, but explained that it was not the British habit to interfere in other States' affairs. His supplanter, Dost Muhammad, when Lord Auckland reached India, sent his congratulations:

> 'The field of my hopes, which had before been chilled by the cold blast of wintry times, has by the happy tidings of your Lordships arrival become the envy of the garden of paradise..... I hope that your Lordship will consider me and my country as your own'.

On this Kaye allows himself the comment: 'He little thought how in effect this Oriental compliment would be accepted as a solemn invitation, and the hope be literally fulfilled. Three years afterwards Auckland, considering Dost Mahomed's country his own, had given it away to Shah Soojah'.[9]

We have seen that a sprinkling of officers brilliant and daring, with a disinterested love of enterprise that of itself would have sent them forward, were moving, sometimes openly, more often disguised as Muslim devotees, horse-copers, and the like, beyond the Punjab. One of the most gallant, Lieutenant Eldren Pottinger, in 1838 encouraged the Afghan of Herat, when in despair of holding out against a Persian army, and saved the city. British prestige stood high in Afghan regions. Dost Muhammad himself was eager for a British alliance, and for a great while refused to make terms with Russian envoys. But Burnes, who was sent to Kabul, could effect nothing because his hands were empty, both literally and metaphorically. His presents were of slight value.

Nor could he offer anything of political worth. Dost Muhammad was sore over Ranjit Singh's capture of Peshawar (1833), and wished the British to press for its return. This Auckland rightly refused to do. But there was nothing else that the Company would or could offer, beyond the distinction of fighting their battles against the Russian Empire as well as his own. Inevitably, after long reluctance, Dost Muhammad had to begin to compose his differences with Russia and Persia, now acting together on his borders.

This natural course of self-preservation served as sufficient excuse for hostility. Macnaghten, secretary to the Indian Government, was sent to Lahore, and on June, 26, 1838, the Tripartite Treaty between the Sikhs, Shah Suja, and the Company was signed. The British intention was that they should hover as a veast menace, at Shikarpur on the Indus, while Shah Suja, supported by the Sikhs, entered Afghanistan amid the welcome of a delighted nation, Ranjit Singh, further sunk in physical than in mental decrepitude, in the end managed to reverse the method entirely; it was the Sikhs who contemptuously held the passes for a remnant of the shattered British forces to straggle back. For the present he visualised (without enthusiasm) the only kind of attack on the Khyber he thought possible—a thrusting forward of Sikhs, and yet more Sikhs, over the bodies of those first slain, until sheer weight of casualties and numbers bought the passage.

Miss Eden's exultant pages tell how in the autumn 'G' himself, with a huge attendance, came to Ferozpur, close to the Sikh borders, where tremendous junketing took place. Amid a wild tumult of clanging weapons under the fiercer crash of massed artillery and the skirl and blare of military music, the elephants of Maharaja and Governor-General were brought alongside;

> 'and Lord Auckland, in his uniform of diplomatic blue, was seen to take a bundle of crimson cloth out of the

> Sikh howdah, and it was known that the lion of the Punjab was then seated on the elephant of the English ruler. In a minute the little tottering, one-eyed man, who had founded a vast empire on the banks of the fabulous rivers of the Macedonian conquests, was leaning over the side of the howdah, shaking hands with the principal officers of the British camp, as their elephants were wheeled up beside him. Then the huge phalanx of elephants was set in motion again'.[10]

towards the Durbar tent, where presently 'the imbecile little old man' (imbecile only in the physical sense) was tottering between the support of the Governor-General and the Commander-in-Chief. Sir Henry Fane, a superb giant of a man, an undesigned cruel, contrast.

As yet the British had no intention of fighting themselves. 'England was to remain in the background jingling the money-bag'. But the money-bag had to be filled first with something to jingle; and it was not reasonable to expect England to find this metal. The Sind Amirs were cast for the part of providers, Oudh being penniless and Bengal fully occupied with financial performances. Their country had once been in (exceedingly loose) dependence on Afghanistan. It was decided that they should pay' Shah Suja twenty lakhs, which he was to divide with Ranjit Singh. When Ranjit Singh demanded more than ten lakhs, this was arranged by the easy expedient of raising the Amirs' contribution to twenty-five lakhs, of which he was to have fifteen.

The Amirs at this juncture did what in some phases of British rule might have been awkward. They objected to the revival of financial claims by a man exiled from his throne thirty years previously, and produced his formal renouncement of these claims. Colonel Henry Pottinger, the Company's political agent in Sind, submitted that the 'question' of the Amirs being fleeced for the Afghan pretender's benefit was 'rendered very puzzling by two releases written in Korans, and sealed and signed by his Majesty, which they have produced. Their argument now is, that they are sure the Governor-General does not intend to make them pay again for what they have already bought and obtained, in the most binding way, a receipt in full'.

The Governor-General and his advisers, however, had got beyond such pedantry. Pottinger was told to warn the Amirs that

'the interests at stake are too great to admit of hesitation in our proceedings; and not only they who have shown a disposition to favour our adversaries, but they who display an unwillingness to aid us in the just and necessary undertaking in which we are engaged, must be displaced, and give way to others on whose friendship and co-operation we may be able implicitly to rely'.

The treaty by which they had been cajoled into opening the Indus to navigation, in consideration of the Company's solemn promise to convey no military stores along it, was to be set aside 'while the present exigency lasts'. As the Amirs began to betray a sullen reluctance. Pottinger was ordered to assure them that 'neither the ready power to crush and annihilate them nor the will to call it into action, were wanting, if it appeared requisite, however remotely, for the safety of the Anglo-Indian Empire or frontier'.

Macnaghten afterwards complained

'that no civilised begins had ever been treated so badly as were the British by the Princes of Sind. If it were so, it was only because no civilised beings had ever before committed themselves to acts of such gross provocation.... The Amirs viewed all our proceedings....with mingled terror and indignation. Our conduct was calculated to alarm and incense them to the extremist point of fear and irritation; and yet we talked of their childish distrust and their unprovoked hostility'.[11]

As the huge British armies moved through Sind, devastating and eating up, the wealthiest group of the Amirs, in particular those of Hyderabad, became openly disgruntled, almost hostile. Their recalcitrance was eagerly seized upon, and part of the army was detached to bring them to a better sense of their privileges and duties:

> 'Down the left bank of the Indus went Cotton with his troops, glorying in the prospect before them. The treasures of Hyderabad seemed to lie at their feet. Never was there a more popular movement. The troops pushed on in the highest spirits, eager for the affray—confident of success. An unanticipated harvest of honour—an unexpected promise of abundant prize-money—was within their reach'.[12]

But Macnaghten, appalled to see a tremendous military invasion about to degenerate into a freebooting expedition against puny folk, wrote frantic letter to Burnes, to Colvin, to Sir Willoughby Cotton, to Auckland himself. Just in time the Hyderabad Amirs, terrified at the majestic vengeance marching their way, accepted a fresh treaty, by which they were to pay annually three lakhs for the subsidiary force which it was at last to be their privilege, as it had long been that of other Indian States, to support. Cotton, 'to the extreme disappointment of his troops',[13] abandoned 'a pretty piece of practice for the army' and returned to the main business.

The Amirs, to whom it was pointed out that 'friendship, alliance, and unity of interest' with the Company were far better than the independence to which they were so foolishly attached, and that their mulcting, though grievous, was trivial when it was considered what 'vast advantages' they would obtain (arrival of trade and traders, employment for thousands of their meaner subjects, increased demand for grain, etc.), were told further 'that henceforth they must consider Scinde to be, as it was in reality, a portion of Hindostan, in which the British were paramount and entitled to act as they considered best and fittest for the general good of the whole Empire'[14].

These arguments, coming from a Power which was daily giving proof (as it pointed out) of 'moderation and disinterestedness's, carried conviction; the Amirs answered that

> their eyes were opened. They had found it difficult to overcome the prejudice and apprehension of their tribes, who had always been led to think the only object of the British was to extend their dominion. Now they had been taught by experience English strength and good faith.'

It is not to be supposed that there had been no misgivings, no protests. On the contrary, every reputable authority outside India was aghast at what was afoot. Wellesley and his brother, the Duke of Wellington, Elphinstone, Bentinck, all condemned it. Alexander Burnes, whose life was to go in the enterprise, and whose share in the business has been considerably misjudged, had urged that

> 'it remains to be considered why we cannot act with Dost Mahomed. He is a man of undoubted ability, and has at heart a high opinion of the British nation; and if half you must do for others were done for him ......he would abandon Russia and Persia tomorrow .... I think there is much to be said for him. Government have admitted that he had at best a choice of difficulties; and it should not be forgotten that we promised nothing, and Persia and Russia held out a great deal'.

Moreover, London had persuaded the Russian Government to withdraw their envoy, who returned to St. Petersburg and blew his brains out; and Persia raised the siege of Herat (September 9, 1838). There remained, therefore, no shadow of an excuse, ethical or political, for persisting in the enterprise. But Lord Auckland in October issued a minute, in which 'the views and conduct of Dost Muhammad Khan were misrepresented with a hardihood which a Russian statesman might have envied'[15]. Burnes was told that his job was merely to go ahead through the Amirs' country, making requisitions for the army that was following and aweing the people by threats of their destruction if they were backward in assistance[16].

Diverted from passage through the Punjab, by Ranjit Singh's objection, the British moved through Sind and entered Baluchistan by the Bolan Pass, March, 1839. The Khan of Khelat, who had formerly been generous fool enough to protect Shah Suja, was made another unwilling accomplice. 'An able and sagacious man',[17] Mehrab Khan talked reasonably to Burnes (who was now merely a subordinate tool), and told him what others kept on telling the invaders, that Shah Suja was detested and despised and that, though Dost Muhammad could no doubt be conquered, 'we could never win over the Afghan nation by it'.[18] Burnes told Macnaghten that the Khan's country had been swept, as by a razor, clean of grain and greenstuff some of its inhabitants being reduced to 'feeding on herbs and grasses gathered in the jungle ... the small quantities we have procured have been got by stealth'.[19]

Kandahar was occupied in April, the Afghans with deepening resentment watching this restoration of their oft-rejected monarch by a host of *Kafirs*. A clash came at Ghazni, which was stormed in July. Dost Muhammad fled from Kabul, which was occupied in August. The Ghazni carnage was dreadful; and Shah Suja butchered fifty *Ghazi* prisoners. From this incident dates the abhorrence of him which soon became intense, and was understood, if not shared, by many of his British supporters. "The day of reckoning came at last; and when our unholy policy sunk unburied in blood and ashes, the shrill cry of the *Ghazee* sounded as its funeral wail.'[20]

When Shah Suja entered Kabul, 'it was more like a funeral procession than the entry of a King into the capital of his restored dominations'.[21] His public acknowledgment in Kandahar had been a similar failure. Macnaghten had set apart a large space 'for "the populace restrained by the Shah's troops". But the space remained almost empty, and 'no Afghan of repute came forward to pay his reverence to the popular idol of Macnaghten's fancy'.[22]

In Simla, however, things were seen in a far more encouraging light. In May 'G' got the official accounts of the taking of Kandahar, or rather how Kandahar took Shah Soojah, and *would have* him for its King. There never was anything of satisfactory'.[23] Presently 'G'. became an earl, Sir John Keane, the Commander-in Chief of the Indus army, a baron, Macnaghten a baronet, and a 'a shower of honours fell upon the civil and military services'.

Meanwhile the punishment of the wicked had continued steadily. Raging because the march of such a host had not been a picnic, and unable to see 'that the army of the Indus was at least as much the cause, as it was the victim, of the scarcity in Beloochistan',[24] British Indian opinion had fallen into 'the fashion' of attributing 'to the wickedness of Mehrab Khan all the sufferings' which accompanied the campaign. His friendly offices had made possible the passage of the Bolan Pass; and, while he pointed out that no one wished the return of Shah Suja, nevertheless he himself had sheltered the latter, five years previously, when he fled from his rout at the battle of Kandahar. On the morning of November 13, a British-Indian force appeared before Khelat, and stormed it—news which was received with delight. Macnaghten heard it when dining with General Avitable, Commandant of Peshawar. All rose and gave 'the "three times three" of a good English cheer'.[25] On December 3 Miss Eden saw an aide-de-camp 'fidgetting about behind G'.s chair with a note in his hand':

> 'it turned out to be an express with another little battle, and a most successful one. The Khan of Khelat was by way of being our ally and assistant, and professing friendship; did himself the pleasure of cutting off the supplies of the army when it was on its way to Cabul; set his followers on to rob the camp; corresponded with Dost Mahomed, &c.

'There was no time to fight with him then, and I suppose he was beginning to think himself secure; but G. directed the Bombay army, on is way home, to settle this little Khelat trouble.... It was all done in the Ghuznee manner—the gates blown in and the fort stormed—but the fighting was very severe. The Khan and his principal chiefs died sword in hand which was rather too fine a death for such a double traitor; and one in six of our troops were either killed or wounded which is an unusual proportion... Also there will be a great deal of prize money'.[26]

A better authority than Miss Eden sums up the humiliating story:

'For former hospitality, and for protection from sanguinary pursuers, the gratitude of Shah Shooja, under British influence, awarded to Mehrab Khan the loss of his poor capital and a soldier's death. After his honourable fall documents were found which proved the manner in which the Khan had been betrayed and his endeavours to negotiate frustrated; nevertheless it was thought advisable to consummate the threat formerly made, and to place Shah Nawaz Khan, to the exclusion of the son of the fallen chief, upon the masnad of Khelat'.[27]

The day after the battle a British officer (Lieutenant Loveday) looked on pityingly as

'a few of Mehrab Khan's servants brought the body of their master for burial—a fine-looking man. There was one little hole in his breast, which told of a musket-ball having passed through. He had no clothes on, except his silk *pyjammahs*. One of his slaves whispered me for a shawl. Alas! I had nothing of the kind, but luckily remembered a brocade bed-cover, which I had bought in my days of folly and extravagance at Delhi. I called for it immediately, and gave it to the Khan's servants, who were delighted with this last mark of respect, and wrapping up the body in it, placed their deceased master on a *charpoy,* and carried him to the grave'.

The army had reached Kabul, only because Macnaghten lavishly corrupted those Afghan he could reach. The campaign ravaged Indian finances. Withdrawal, however, was impossible; for repression, for punitive measures, for all the abundant dirty work, British officers were indispensable. So the troops were brought in to the capital, and contained for winter on an open plain. Meanwhile, Burnes wrote: 'Bad ministers are in every government solid grounds for unpopularity; and I doubt if ever a King had a worse set than Shah Soojah'. At their head was the Wazir, a man 'old and enfeebled by age. His memory was gone; so were his ears. For some offence against his Majesty in former days, he had forfeited those useful appendances'.[28] Such vigour as remained to him was concentrated into two channels, oppression of the people and loathing of the British. With this valuable assistant the latter had wrought what was almost a miracle, an immense revolution in Afghan feeling, hitherto divided but now become one flaming patriotism. British officers sent for their wives from India.

The Tripartite Alliance was about to lose all but nominal adherence of its Sikh component. Ranjit Singh's body, which had been so long rotting for death, ceased to breathe, June 27, 1839; and a handful of enthralled Europeans watched his barbaric obsequies. Miss Eden, appalled, exclaims:[29]

> 'Those poor dear ranees, whom we visited and thought so beautiful and so merry, have actually burnt themselves... they were such gay young creatures, and they died with the most obstinate courage'.

Her brother instructed his representative at Lahore to express horrow. Horror could be notified only 'unofficially', and was rebutted with polite hint that it was an impertinence.

We descend fast into the shadows of the most sombre and terrible years India has ever known; the terrors of the Afghan slaughters and the Sikh anarchy begin the tale which the violation of Sind, the clash of British-Sikh arms, and the Mutiny are to continue and conclude. Miss Eden's delightful vivacious commentary is soon to be as irrelevant as the piping of linnets in a bombardment. If, contemplating the straightforward wickedness of Lord Auckland's Afghan policy and its dreadful close, we marvel that so inept and recklessly unscrupulous a Power should yet have survived, we may keep faith in an ethical governance of the world (should we desire to keep such faith), by turning our eyes upon the cruelty and cowardice of native Indian.

But our immediate interest is that Ranjit Singh 'was the only man in the Sikh empire who was true at heart to his allies, and all genuine cooperation died out with the fires of his funeral pile'. From now on, the British were in the position of a man who has a wolf by the ears and dare not relax hold. What troops could be withdrawn were withdrawn; it became increasingly plain that no others could be withdrawn. Afghanistan was in for a military occupation whose finish no one could see. British money-bags were emptying; the Commander-in-Chief, Sir Jasper Nicolls, experienced old soldier of another successful war, that against the Gurkhas, at the Governor-General's board kept on stressing the impossibility of endlessly spending at the rate of a million and a quarter sterling a year, on such an enterprise and such a ruler. The rest of the Council seconded him. Lord Auckland, gentle but disinclined for descent into serious controversy with common mortals, shirked and evaded the issue. Sir Alexander Burnes, growing daily wise with a mournful knowledge, a male Cassandra, and like Cassandra doomed to share the ruin he foresaw, remained in Kabul, as he complained 'in the most nondescript of situations'.[30]

> 'It appears to have been his mission in Afghanistan to draw a large salary every month, and to give advice that was never taken. This might have satisfied many men. It did not satisfy Burnes. He said that he wanted responsibility; and under Macnaghten he had none.... He probed, deeply and searchingly, the great wound of

national discontent—a mighty sore that was ever running—and the felt in his inmost soul that the death-throes of such a system could not be very remote'.[31]

Macnaghten, meanwhile, was becoming lost to all ethical consideration, and moral blindness was bringing its inevitable companion, intellectual obsession. Exasperated because he saw questioning in the faces of all but himself, as the hazards and follies of the excursion grew appealingly apparent, he blamed Government's attention to reports of people afflicted with 'the imposthume of too much leisure', who cursed the enterprise, as keeping them away from delectable India 'in a land not overflowing with beer and cheroots'. He plotted wilder adventures yet, and urged that 'we have a beautiful game on our hands if we have the means and inclination to play it properly'. That game was to attack Herat and bring it under Shah Suja's immediate sway; and to annex the Punjab, an action of whose necessity and righteousness men were freely talking, for the Punjab was the only considerable source of revenue still outside British control. Lord Auckland was to 'insist'.

> 'upon the concession of our rights from the ruler of the Punjab.... In addition to the demands already made upon the Sikhs, they should be required, I think, to admit unequivocally our right of way across the Punjab, and in the event of their denying this right, they should be convinced that we can take it'.

Dost Muhammad remained at large, a figure intangible and almost immaterial, flitting through the wild scattered borders of his land. His supporters ('rebels' Macnaghten called them) inflicted petty galling defeats on the invaders; the invaders sometimes routed some trivial detachment of his troops. But while the defeats of the British grew ever more menacing, and each time their prestige shrank visibly, their enemy's defeats were unimportant'. 'I am like a wooden spoon', he said; 'you may throw me hither and thither, but I shall not be hurt'. On September 18, 1840, Macnaghten despondently wrote: 'At no period of my life do I remember having been so much harassed in body and mind as during the past month. The Afghans are gunpowder, and the Dost is a lighted match. On his whereabouts we are wonderfully ignorant'. He talked of aweing Dost Muhammad 'as high as Human', of 'showing no mercy to the man who was the author of all the evil now distracting the country'. Shah Suja, long checked from hewing his subjects in complete Afghan fashion, was delighted, yet surmised, 'I suppose you would, even now, if I were to catch the dog, prevent me from hanging him'.

The dog, however, was not yet caught, and his teeth were presently fastened in his pursuers' flesh. On November 2, on a clear crisp morning of autumn, Dost Muhammad turned at bay. He and his men were poorly mounted, but they were desperate. From his blue standard the native levies fled; and the Afghans charged home the British cavalry. It was a precursor, in pitiful and useless gallantry, of the Khyber and Maiwand. But the ex-Amir, left victor on the battlefield, knew himself no match for these powerful interlopers, Victories such as this could only stir the Feringhis to such an effort as would crush him and his people beyond rising again. He rode through night and the following day twenty-four hours in the saddle; and, the day after the battle of Parwandara, Macnaghten on his evening ride outside Kabul was hailed by a horseman, who told him Dost Muhammad was behind, to surrender. Dost Muhammad himself then rode up; dismounted, cool and debonair as if from his bed; saluted the British envoy and gave him his sword. Macnaghten, who had desired to hang him, was moved and deeply respectful. He returned the sword, and they rode side by side, the ex-Amir asking eagerly about his family. He remained about ten days in Kabul, conversing freely with Macnaghten, who was stirred to chivalrous esteem and admiration by the Afghan's story of his life as a fugitive and his undaunted bearing. His own people, who had remained aloof from His Majesty Shah Suja, crowded to the prisoner's tent burning to show their affection and respect. Shah Suja refused to see him, since he was not allowed to hang him; he 'would not be able to bring himself to show common civility to such a villain'. But Macnaghten delighted to honour 'the dog'; and when the Dost was sent to India wrote, in almost the only words of candour that emerge from the self-deception with which he had enmeshed his mind:

> 'I trust that the Dost will be treated with liberality. His case has been compared to that of Shah Soojah; and I have seen it argued that he should not be treated more handsomely than his Majesty was; but surely the cases are not parallel. The Shah had no claim upon us. We had no hand in depriving him of his kingdom, whereas we ejected the Dost, who never offended us, in support of our policy, of which he was the victim'.[32]

Lord Auckland received the captive generously and respectfully, 'and burdened the revenues of India with a pension in his favour of two lakhs of rupees'.[33]

The British increasingly established themselves. Bungalows were built, gardens were laid out. The Afghan climate suited Feringhi energy. There were race-meetings, jackal and fox hunting, shooting parties, fishing, amateur theatricals. We are told of the 'infinite astonishment' of the people when they saw British officers skating on their lakes. With resentment they noted all the signs of a permanent occupation. This energy was wonderful, and boded no good, conjoined with such ambition; 'the manliness of the Feringhee strangers quite put them to shame'. It put them to shame also in perilous fashion, shame which 'for two long years' burned 'itself into the hearts of the Caubulees'.[34] Afghans of highest family had their harems raided and their women dishonoured.

Then the country cause was given a martyr. Akram Khan, a chieftain who refused to come in, was betrayed for a price, and by Macnaghten's instructions, exercised through nominal Afghan authority, blown from a gun as a rebel.

All through 1841 the storm gathered. Khelat had been recovered from the puppet khan; Duranis, Ghilzyes, and other formidable tribes were rising in revolt. Macnaghten for his services and success was appointed Governor of Bombay, and prepared to leave, rejoicing that everything was 'quiet'. The British, who had occupied a line on the Bala Hissar, the famous fortress overlooking Kabul, gave up their barracks to the aged King's harem and established themselves in an indefensible 'sheep-pen' on flat plain, by a refinement of stupidity putting their arsenal elsewhere. Lord Auckland, having in General Nott an adequate soldier to his hand, preferred to make commander-in-chief in Afghanistan, on Sir Willough by Cotton's retirement, General Elphistone, of whom Miss Eden reports (February 6, 1840): 'He is in a shocking state of gout, poor man! One arm in a sling and very lame, but otherwise is a young-looking general for India.'[35]

Macnaghten, happy in promotion and preparing to go, made light of the warning from every output. At the very time when a formidable conspiracy was meeting constantly in Kabul, he wrote (of a grim little fight which came close to disaster) that he 'hoped the business... was the expiring effort of the rebels', and accepted Burnes's congratulations on 'my approaching departure at a season of such profound tranquillity'. The congratulations must have been ironic; to a native agent's disclosures of peril about to break, Burnes 'stood up from his chair, sighed, and said he knows nothing but the time has arrived that we should level the country'. That very evening (November 1, 1841), we at the house of a chief whom Burnes had called a dog and threatened which the loss of his ears, the conspirators made their plans. Next day Kabul was in commotion, and among the first whom the mob murdered was Burnes.

A massacre followed, of British officers and their families, caught in their pleasant homes. The insurgents were in terror that retribution would come at any moment, and slew and plundered with their eyes watchful for a way of escape. But a British-Indian army remained unmoving, half an hours' march away. Towards evening General Elphinstone wrote to Macnaghten: 'We must see what the morning brings, and then think what can be done'.

Hereafter hardly one act of the British fell below an almost incredible level of imbecility. No disgrace, no humiliation, was wanting, Elphinstone and his troops looked on while the Afghans stormed the fort where the commissariat was stored. The rank and file and junior officers—who hitherto had kept their morale—when they saw their supplies being looted by enemies not four hundred yards away, carrying off their prize 'as busily as a swarm of ants', begged to be allowed to prevent their own starvation. General Elphinstone considered the effort too dangerous, and to Macnaghten (who at least pressed for energetic action) pointed out that his men 'have been all night in the works, are tired, and ill-fed'. On November 13 came a solitary gleam, when Macnaghten took the responsibility on himself and overcame the General's reluctance so far that a detachment attacked a force which was cannonading their cantonment, and rendering it almost untenable. A desperate fight came close to over whelming disaster; for the first time the British soldiery showed that panic terror which was to make this campaign unique in our annals. Called on to advance, as one of their own officers witnesses,[36] with a few gallant exceptions, they remained immovable, nor could the Sepoys be induced to lead the way where their European brethren so obstinately hung back'. At the action's outset, their bayonets had been charged down by the impetuous Afghan cavalry, and ruin had shaken them by the throat. Lady Sale, watching, felt 'her very heart' 'as if it leapt to my teeth when I saw the Afhgan ride clean through them. The onset was fearful. They looked like a great cluster of bees, but we beat them and drove them up again'.[37] One enemy gun was spiked and another smaller one brought back; and the day closed with the keening of Afghan women, and the hillsides dotted with the flitting torches of the burial-parties. The 'was the last success even of a doubtful and equivocal character, which the unhappy force was destined to achieve'.[38]

On December 11 Macnaghten concluded a treaty' whose preamble with humiliating blandness observes:

> 'Whereas it has become apparent from recent events that the continuance of the British army in Afghanistan for the support of Shah Soojah-ool-Moolkh is displeasing to the great majority of the Afhgan nation; and whereas the British Government had no other object in sending troops to this country than the integrity, happiness, and welfare of the Afghans, and, therefore, it can have no wish to remain when that object is defeated by its presence...

Shah Suja was to be given his choice of accompanying the British or remaining on a pension; Dost Muhammad was to be released, the Army of Occupation was to become immediately an Army of Evacuation.

Macnaghten began trying to set one group of chieftains against another, using the weapon of corruption which had formerly served so well. Akbar Khan, Dos Muhammad's son, enticed him to a conference, and shot him with a pistol given by Macnaghten the previous day and accepted with profuse gratitude; 'the Envoy has deeply paid for his attempt to out diplomatic the Afghans.'[39] As the price of safe-conduct to Peshawar, the British were compelled to accept a new and even worse treaty; surrendered hostages: paid individual chiefs large sums: and promised to order the evacuation of Jalalabad and all forts held inside the Afghan border.

The Afghans, however, kept no treaty. Demand upon demand was added, as each was yielded. In the end, all coin in the treasury, all surplus muskets, all the guns except six ammunition, waggons, stores, all were given up. Afghan insolence rose, British depression deepened. Pottinger, who had succeeded Macnaghten as 'Political', was overruled in Council when he 'would have snapped asunder the treaty before the faces of the chiefs, and appealed to the God of Battles'.[40] A rejoicing and fiendish rabble pillaged and insulted and hunted 'a herd of broken-spirited slaves', who on January 6, 1842, set out through the snow.

Sale, who at Gandamak controlled the eastern passes, under Elphinstone's peremptory instructions withdrew to Jalalabad, where presently he was conducting a second 'Defence of Arcot'. Sale, in his own words later, having to choose 'between the alternatives of being bound or not by the convention, which was forced from our Envoy and military commander with the knives at their throats', chose rightly. He and his force had been no party to the compact, and they saw no signs of the Afghans keeping any scrap of the faith they pledged. For the sake of his wretched brethren in Kabul, he deemed it his duty to stay at this advanced post, to succour them as early as possible.

Meanwhile 4000 fighting men and 12,000 camp-followers were enduring the miseries of frost-bite, starvation, and constant attack. The retreat was a mere movement of deer into whose midst wolves kept rushing, picking off a weakling here, striking down another there. Akbar Khan from time to time appeared on the flanks, and demanded (and obtained) more hostages for Sale's evacuation of Jalalabad. The entry of the Kabul Pass was marked by a massacre. Here Elphinstone ordered a halt, and would not stir from his decision. Eldred Pottinger, a prisoner spending the night under a roof, thought of the wretches camped without cover, fire, or food, and persuaded Akbar Khan to promise to take over the British women and children who still survived, and convoy them safe to Peshawar. Akbar Khan, whose own family were in British India, agreed, for he wanted the ladies as hostages. Accordingly, eleven women passed into his keeping their husbands and children accompanying them. The retreat continued (January 10); at the close of that day, one prolonged butchery, only 450 Europeans remained alive. All baggage was lost, every sepoy was dead, of the 12,000 camp-followers a raving, clogging mass of over 300 lived.

From these, under cover of night, the fighting men plotted to escape. But the wretches heard them move on, and 'in the wildness of their fear' surged after them, drawing a massed Afghan fire. Next day the remnant almost reached the Pass of Jagdalak, where they cowered behind ruined walls. The last three bullocks were taken from the camp followers and killed, the European soldiers devouring the flesh raw, slaking it down with handfuls of snow. Two days of desperate fighting, with intervals of negotiation, followed. Generals Elphinstone and Shelton, with a third officer acting as interpreter, were received by Akbar Khan round a blazing fire, and given hot tea, being afterwards kept as hostages.

Akbar Khan probably wished to save the few survivors. But the hillmen, beasts of prey then as now, were determined none should escape. The retreat continued into the Jagdalak Pass, where nearly all of the 150 fighting men who lived were killed. Next day, 25 officers and 45 men reached Gandamak, and were all but about twenty massacred while entering upon invited negotiations. Sixteen miles from Jalalabad, six, all officers, were alive. On January 13 the Jalalabad garrison, straining their eyes from the ramparts, saw one reeling pony in the distance, stumbling forward, with a rider bowed on its neck. It was Dr. Brydon. So closed in 'awful completeness', 'sublime unity', the most terrible disaster that ever overtook a British force.

When the truth, after preliminary rumour, came home in all its century, Auckland knew one spasm of courage, in his Proclamation of January 31, 1842:

> '...A faithless enemy, stained by the foul crime of assassination, has, through a failure of supplies, followed by consummate treachery, been able to overcome a body of British troops, in a country removed, by distance and difficulties of season from the possibility of succour. But the Governor-General in Council, while he most deeply laments the loss of the brave officers and men, regards this partial reverse only as a new occasion for displaying

the stability and vigour of the British power, and the admirable spirit and valour of the British-Indian army'.

The flash went out, and he sank into such dependency that many who received his letters at this period out of pity destroyed such a revelation of a spirit crushed and despairing. One good thing, at any rate, was done. The crisis called for the best soldier, not the most senior; and General Pollock, though a Company's officer, was preferred to the Kings' officers, and placed in command of the troops at Peshawar. In their distress the British called on the Sikhs to implement their part in the Tripartite Treaty, by which their allies were entitled to call on them for help in case of need. They hung back. And on January 10 a sepoy battalion mutinied, demanding increased allowances and coats and gloves before advancing through the cold to Kabul. The other troops fell in, and everything was set for another Barrackpur massacre. Fortunately there was in Peshawar a man as humane as he was intelligent:

> 'It was so dark we could hardly distinguish one another. There was a general hum and whisper. We stood there in a great suspense. An order came for the portfires to be lighted. We could just see Lawrence on horseback, dark and prominent against the sky, vehemently urging and riding here and there. At length we were ordered back. Lawrence had shown the madness of firing on the regiment at such an hour, when we could not discern the different corps, and of exposing to the Sikh army our internal discards...
>
> 'The following day the matter was arranged under Lawrence's counsel, and the Sepoys accepted their pay. I have heard Sir Henry dwell on the dangers of that night, and the difficulty he had to prevent Wild from the suicidal measure of ordering the other Sepoy regiments to compel the 64th. There may have been a deeper danger than we knew: for there is little doubt that all the Sepoys were equally averse to the advance'.[41]

Pollock arrived in Peshawar, February 5; and quietly settled down for two months, while he infused his own confidence and serenity into men who had been handled with imbecility for so long. On April 5 and 6 he forced the Khyber by flanking methods, seizing commanding points instead of merely thrusting through its terrible jaws. On the 16th he relieved Jalalabad. On the 20th he moved forward again, and on September 8 he crowned lesser victories by a resounding one in the Jagadalak Pass; five days later, at Tezin, sepoy and Briton, at last reknit into terrible comradeship, so defeated Akbar Khan that he knew his cause was doomed. Meanwhile, Nott also was fighting his way towards Kabul. Ghazni was recaptured, September 6. Pollock reoccupied Kabul, September 16, Nott joining him next day. On October 9 and 10 the great bazaar was destroyed, 'an inexcusable act of vandalism;[42] perhaps it was, but the consideration which decided its blowing up was the fact that Macnaghten's mutilated body had been exultingly exposed there. Far worse was the deliberate sacking of Kabul, not in the heat of entry, but as a last-minute policy:

> 'Guilty and innocent alike fell under the heavy hand of the lawless retribution.... Many unoffending Hindus, who, lulled into a sense of delusive security by the outward re-establishment of a government, had returned to the city and reopened their shops, were now disastrously ruined. In the mad excitement of the hour, friend and foe were stricken down by the same unsparing hand.[43]

Having covered their name with detestation everywhere, on October 12 the British evacuated the shattered capital. Lord Ellenborough, an exuberant orator and a writer of the high Roman kind, who had succeeded Lord Auckland, February 28, 1842, on October 1 issued his paean:

> '...Disasters unparalleled in their extent, unless by he errors in which they originated, and by the treachery by

which they were completed, have, in one short campaign, been avenged upon every scene of past misfortune; and repeated victories in the field, and the capture of the cities and citadels of Ghuznee and Caubul, have again attached the opinion of invincibility to the British arms.

'The British arms in possession of Afghanistan will now be withdrawn to the Sutlej.

'The Governor-General will leave it to the Afghans themselves to create a government amidst the anarchy which is the consequence of their crimes'.

In England Lord Ellenborough had been opposed to the policy of this War. It is strange that he was capable of the impudence and mixed reasoning of this outburst. Both qualities persist to the end:

'To force a sovereign upon a reluctant people would be as inconsistent with the policy as it is with the principles of the British Government, tending to place the arms and resources of that people at the disposal of the first invader, and to impose the burden of supporting a sovereign, without the prospect of benefit from his alliance'—

truths as self-evident as those with which the American Declaration of Independence opens. Now that they are recognised, late though it be and after unexampled punishment for blindness:

'Content with the limits nature appears to have assigned to its empire, the Government of India will devote all its efforts to be establishment and maintenance of general peace, to the protection of the sovereigns and chiefs its allies, and to the prosperity and happiness of its own faithful subjects.

The rivers of the Punjab and Indus, and the mountainous passes and the barbarous tribes of Afghanistan, will be placed between the British army and an enemy approaching from the West, if indeed such as enemy there can be, and no longer between the army and its sullies.

'The enormous expenditure required for the support of a large force, in a false military position, at a distance from its own frontier and its resources, will no longer arrest every measure for the improvement of the country and of the people.'

In those last words the brazen countenance at last shows some signs of almost shame. The long-delayed internal improvement of much-pillaged India was postponed further by this iniquitous campaign. Hardly anything, and certainly nothing adequate, could be done until after the Mutiny; and then that outbreak crippled Indian finances for many a year longer:

'It is upon record, that this calamitous war cost the natives of India, whose stewards we are, some fifteen millions of money. All this enormous burden fell upon the revenues of India, and the country for long years afterwards groaned under the weight. The bitter injustice of this need hardly be insisted upon.'[44]

The war, moreover, had been waged for solely British purposes, a wild parrying an imagined stroke by Russia, that dread of statesmen in London and Calcutta.

This was all silly and humiliating enough. But on November 16 the Governor-General issued what the Duke of Wellington styled a 'Song of Triumph', his notorious Address to 'All the Princes and Chiefs', 'My Brothers and My Friends', congratulating them because General Nott had torn away from the tomb of 'Sultan Mahmud, that victorious Lord',[45] the gates which in his lifetime (if was alleged) the victorious Lord had brought from Somnath, in Gujarat. The tomb's guardians wept and protested; but no one else was destined to care:

> 'Our victorious army bears the gates of the temple of Somnath in triumph from Afghanistan, and the deposited tomb of Sultan Mahomed looks upon the ruins of Ghuznee.
>
> 'The insult of eight hundred years is at last avenged. The gates of the temple of Somnath, so long the memorial of your humiliation, are become the proudest record of your national glory, the proof of your superiority in arms over the nations beyond the Indus.
>
> 'To you, Princes and Chiefs of Sirhind, of Rajwarra, of Malwa, and of Guzerat, I shall commit this glorious trophy of successful war.
>
> 'You will yourselves, with all honour, transmit the gates of sandal-wood through your respective territories to the restored temple of Somnath.
>
> 'The chiefs of Sirhind shall be informed at what time our victorious army will first deliver the gates of the temple into their guardianship, at the foot of the bridge of the Sutlej.'

The 'people of India', also 'My Brothers and Friends', received their own separate Address.

These Proclamations at first were thought to be a hoax, but were discovered to be genuine. As for the 'gates', they were found to be modern, and not those of Somnath at all; and were finally left to repose in the armoury at Agra.

Lord Ellenborough in December staged a colossal military show at Ferozpur. This was meant partly as a warning to the Sikhs, whose help was 'crabbed' and whose reluctance were angrily discussed, that their turn would come next if they were not careful. All was noise, excitement, flutter fine dresses, fine warriors, fine horses—elephants decorated, caparisoned and painted—triumphal arches gigantic marquees, tinsel, bright-hued cloths, festoons and awnings, 'polyglot emblazonments' of the victorious army's battles, field-days, banquets, speeches and applause. Forty thousand troops and a hundred guns were manoeuvred under the eyes of the Governor-General, the Commander-in-Chief, Sir Jasper Nicolls, Partab Singh the Sikh heir-apparent, Dhyan Singh the Sikh Prime Minister, and a host of happy ladies. The year which began in disaster 'opportunely closed in gaiety and glitter—in prosperity and parade'.[46]

The Governor-General had intended that Dost Muhammad should witness this display of power. But when it was represented to him that this would seem like Roman insolence to a captive, he abandoned the idea. Dost Muhammad was allowed to pass quietly out of India, and reached Lahore, January 20, 1843, where the Sikh durbar received him with genuine honour. He rejoined a people in whom he found 'scarcely a family...which had not the blood of kindred to revenge upon the accursed Feringhees. The door of reconciliation seemed to be closed against us; and if the hostility of the Afghans be an element of weakness, it seemed certain that we must have contrived to secure it.[47] He was enthusiastically welcomed back, and proceeded to give his country again a government wise by contemporary standards, and less ruthless by far than that of its neighbours of the Punjab and the Central Asian khanates.

So ended an episode whose

> 'one consolation—if indeed it can now be called a consolation—was that we had learned a lesson which we could never need to be taught again'.[48]

REFERENCES

1. Emily Eden, *Up the Country*, 391.
2. *Op. cit.* 51.
3. Major-General Sir W.H. Sleeman, K.C.E., *1 Journey through the kingdom of Oude in* 1849-50, ii. 154.
4. *Op. cit* ii. 161.

5. *History of British India*, 355-6.
6. L.J. Trotter, *Lord Auckland* ('Rulers of India'), 29.
7. *Up the Country*, 55.
8. *History of the War in Afghanistan*, i. 312.
9. *Op. cit.* i. 170.
10. *Op. cit.*, i. 389 ff.
11. *Op. cit.* i. 403.
12. *Op. cit.* i. 412.
13. *Op. cit.* 417.
14. See Major-General Sir F. J. Goldsmid, *Jamess Outram*, 170 ff.
15. Sir Herbert Edwardes.
16. For maps see below, Book VI.
17. Kaye, i. 424.
18. Burnes to Macnaghten: Khelat, March 30, 1839. MS Records.
19. Burnes to Macnaghten, April 2, 1839.
20. Kaye, i. 462.
21. *Op. cit.* i. 497.
22. L. J. Trotter, *Lord Auckland*, 86.
23. Emily Eden, *Up the Country*, 290.
24. Kaye, ii. 29.
25. *Op. cit.* ii. 25.
26. *Up the Country*, 348-9.
27. Sir Henry M. Durand, *The First Afghan War and its Causes*, 227-8.
28. Kaye, ii. 18.
29. *Up the Country*, 310.
30. Kaye, ii. 137.
31. *Op. cit.* ii. 64 ff.
32. The reference is to Shah Suja's sojourn as a pensioner in British India, before his restoration.
33. Kaye, ii. 98.
34. *Op. cit.* ii. 143. ff.
35. *Up the Country*, 389.
36. Vincent Eyre. See his *Journal*, passim.

37. *A Journal of the Disasters in Afghanistan,* 1841-2, p. 98.
38. Kaye, i' 223.
39. Lady Saie, *A Journal,* etc., 3.
40. Kaye, ii. 326.
41. Colonel J.R. Becher, quoted in *Life of Henry Lawrence,* i. 300.
42. P. E. Roberts, *History of British India,* 324.
43. Kaye, ii. 369.
44. *Op. cit.* iii. 398.
45. Fitzgenrald's *Rubaiyat of Omar Khayyam.*
46. Kaye, iii. 396.
47. *Op. cit.* iii. 399.
48. R. Bosworth Smith, *Life of Lord Lawrence,* 156.

4

Conquest of Sind and Gwalior Army

The Amirs' candle burns at both end: Napier and Outram: battles of Miani and Dada: various comments on the war: Napier settles new the province: the last Maratha War: battles of Maharajpur and Panniar: dismissal of Lord Ellenborough: Lord Ellenborough on future relations with native States.

'The conquest of Sind followed in the wake of the Afghan War and was morally and politically its sequel'[1] in Sir Charles Napier' expression, 'the tail of the Afghan storm'. Part of the story has already come in the narrative of that campaign. The rest can fitly come mainly in the conqueror's own words.

Lord Ellenborough had reprobated in advance the mischievous activities of any one who should rob India of peace, and warned such that the full majesty of British strength would move against them. In 1841 the Company, having 'acquired by degrees that secondary moral force which belongs to utility irrespective of abstract justice',[2] by virtue of that secondary moral force decided that it should annex Shikarpur, on Sind's northern border and its largest city. The Amirs reluctantly assented. As the British had already seized and kept Karachi, Sind's only port, in the extreme south, 'the Amirs' candle was burning at both ends's. The Amirs were suspected of still harbouring ungrateful feelings, so Sir Charles Napier, recalled from Europe, 'a small dark-visaged old man. . . . with a falcon's glance',[3] 'always more under the influence of excitement than of reason',[4] in September, 1842, was sent to Sind, with the widest possible powers of war and peace. He was a veteran trained under the Duke of Wellington, and imbued with all the master's love of discipline and promptitude; and Lord Ellenborough, when sending him, warned the Amirs, in these 'explicit and honourable' terms, 'stimulated by the lofty ambition of saving India from ruin:'[5]

> 'On the day on which you shall be faithless to the British Government sovereignty will have passed from you; your dominions will be given to others, and in your destitution all India will see that the British Government will not pardon an injury received from one it believed to be its friend'.

The dark-visaged old man with a falcon's glance carried these instructions:

> 'If the Amirs, or any one of them, should act hostilely, or evince hostile designs against the British forces, it was the Governor-General's fixed resolution ever to forgive the breach of faith, and exact a penalty which should be a warning to every chief in India'.

Major Outram 'the Bayard of India', who acted as his 'Political', after cherishing natural enough resentment and suspicion from his memories of a certain lack of enthusiasm in the Amirs's co-operation during the Afghan War had come to feel that their offences were trivial in face of their provocation and the wolf's obvious intention first to charge them with muddying his springs and then to devour them. In February, 1843, he wrote to Napier that he was

> 'unable entirely to coincide in your views, either as respects the policy or justice of, at least so suddenly, overturning the patriarchal government to which alone Sind has been accustomed. . . I say *patriarchal,* for, however we may despise the 'Amirs as inferior to do ourselves, either in morality or expansion of intellect, each chief certainly lives *with, and for,* his portion of the

> people; and I question whether any class of the people of Sind, expected the Hindu traders. . . . would prefer a change to the best government we could give them. . . .
>
> 'It grieves me to say that my heart, and the judgment God has given me, unite in condemning the measures we are carrying out for his Lordship as most tyrannical—positive robbery. I consider, therefore, that every life which may hereafter be lost in consequence will be a murder.'[6]

However, Outram was instructed to force on the Amirs a new treaty. They argued that, 'having never broken the old agreements into which they had entered with the British Government, their was no necessity to impose upon them new and objectionable terms as punishment for an offence they had no committed'. Napier held otherwise, and so did Ellenborough. 'Certain vague charges of disaffection. . . based on evidence now generally recognised to have been unsatisfactory',[7] had been brought against them, the only serious item being a letter which some good scholars considered was probably a forgery but which Napier, who had the advantage of total ignorance of any Indian language, decided was genuine.[8] The main proof, of course, was in the Governor-General's declared conviction that the Amirs could not possibly be genuinely devoted to the Company—a conviction which must be admitted as based on sound reasoning. Napier's own standpoint was disarmingly honest. He wrote in his Diary: 'We have no right to seize Sind, yet we shall do so, and a very advantageous, useful, humans piece of rascality it will be'.[9] Outram's testimony, to which he stood throughout, despite his first prejudice which made him support considerable tightening of the treaty as long as the Amirs were left sovereigns, was:[10]

> 'The information I obtained during my voyage up the Indus, and my previous knowledge of the chiefs of Sind, satisfied me that the reports of their warlike preparations were unfounded, probably promulgated by themselves,

> in hope that our demands would be less stringent, if we supposed them in any way prepared for resistance. . . . I well knew that they themselves were quite conscious of their inability of oppose our power; that they had no serious intention of the sort; and that nothing but the most extreme proceedings and forcing them to desperation would drive them to it'.

Napier destroyed the Amirs's magazines and grain stores, and their fortress of Imamghar. All these actions he considered peaceful arguments. The Amirs, terrified, gave way to Outram's persuasions, and signed a treaty promising to abandon the right of coining money (which was to be issued by the Company henceforth and to bear on one side the effigy of the British sovereign), and to fuel Company steamers on the Indus. But they implored him to leave Hyderabad, before their people got out of hand. The outbreak came, three days later (February 15, 1843), when Outram escaped to a steamer. On February 17, at Miani, Napier routed a horde of Baluchis:

> 'Thick as standing corn, and gorgeous as a field of flowers. . . they filled the broad deep bed of the Fillaillee, they clustered on both banks, and covered the plain beyond. Guarding their heads with their large dark shields, they shook their sharp swords, beaming in the sun, their shouts rolled like a peal of thunder, as with frantic gestures they rushed forwards. . . . with demoniac strength and ferocity. But with shouts as loud, and shrieks as wild and fierce as theirs, and hearts as big and arms as strong, the Irish soldiers met them with that queen of weapons the musket and sent their foremost masses rolling back in blood'[11]

while the guns swept the river-course diagonally, tearing the dense crowd with an appalling carnage. Napier's courage and generalship were both admirable. A desperate fight ended in complete victory, at the cost of 275 casualties; the enemy lost 6000.

> 'The ferocity on both sides was unbounded, the carnage horrible. The General, seeing a 22nd soldier going to kill and exhausted Belooch chief, called to him to spare: the man drove his bayonet deep, and then turning, justified the act with homely expression, terrible in its truthfulness accompanying such a deed; "This day, General, the shambles have it all to themselves".'

Napier next summoned Hyderabad to surrender. Vakils sent to ask his terms were told: 'Life, and nothing more. And I want your decision before twelve o'clock, as I shall by that time have buried my dead, and given my soldiers their breakfasts'.[12] Hyderabad was yielded in haste; its booty, a star drawing envy ever since Alexander Burnes brought British India the report that the Amirs had twenty million sterling hoarded, proved disappointing. The Khairput Amir was routed at Daba (March 24), a repetition of the previous battle, the losses of both sides almost exactly as before. The nullas and hamlets were crammed with dead and dying: 'All the fallen Beloochs were of mature age, grimvisaged men, athletic forms; the carcass of a youth was not to beg found'.[13] But, 'contrary to all expectation', thirteen unwounded prisoners were taken, as against three at Miani; 'and this slight approach to mildness gave the General infinite satisfaction, for the ferocity both sides had pained him deeply.[14]

Napier continued to roar up and down. His voice became a bellow:

> 'If you come in and make your salaam, and promise fidelity to the British Government, I will restore to you your lands and former privileges, and the superintendence (*sic*) of the dawks. If you refuse, I will wait till the hot weather is gone past, and them I will carry fire and sword into your territories, and drive you and all belonging to you into the mountains; and if I catch you I will hang you as a rebel. You have now your choice. Choose!'

The chief so exhorted chose to make his salaam. But 'his barbarian pride would not bend'. He came with six attendants, and his demeanour was reported by the colonel who received him as haughty. He was accordingly told to come in again, with proper humility: 'Come here instantly. Come alone and make your submission, or I will in a week tear you from the midst of your tribe and hand you'. 'Had he hesitated, the General would have been upon him within the time specified'.

Sind was annexed the Amirs exiled; Napier received £70,000 Prize-money, and the Governor-General strained even his throat of eloquence in crowing over what had been achieved;

> 'The army of Scinde has twice beaten the bravest enemy in Asia, under circumstances which would equally have obtained for it the victory over the best troops in Europe...
>
> 'To have punished the treachery of protected Princes; to have liberated a nation from its oppressors; to have added a province, fertile as Egypt to the British empire; and to have effected these great objects by actions in war unsurpassed in brilliancy, whereof a grateful army assign the success to the ability and valour of its general; these are not ordinary achievements, nor can the ordinary language of praise convey their reward'.

Outram refused his £3000 prize-money; told Napier, for whom he cherished warm affection (which was returned): 'I am sick of *policy;* I will not say yours is the *best* but it is undoubtedly the shortest–that of *the sword*. Oh, how I wish you had drawn it in a better cause!'; and went home to plead for the Amirs. Mr. Gladstone afterwards revealed[15] that Sir Robert Peel's Cabinet, of which he and the Duke of Wellington were both members, disapproved, he believed unanimously, of the conquest. 'But the ministry were powerless, inasmuch as the mischief of retaining was less than the mischief of abandoning it, and it remains an accomplished fact', Even Napier once wrote in his Diary: 'My present position is not, however, to my liking: we had no right to come here, and are tarred with the Afghan brush'. In England, Elphinstone's contemptuous comment was:[16] 'Coming after Afghanistan, it put one in mind of a bully who has been kicked in the streets, and went home to beat his wife in revenge'. The conqueror's sardonic pun',[17] 'Peccavi' ('I have Sind'), is one of the few things in connection with British-Indian history that have lodged in the common mind. The pun, however, was not his; it was made by *Punch*.

Having conquered Sind, Napier entered on its pacification. Like many great soldiers, he regarded 'the frocks' with scorn. 'Having fixed notions of government' (as of most matters) he reflected the civilian element and its opinion, observing that

> 'the mercantile spirit weakens if it does not altogether exclude noble sentiments. . . . The bravery and devotion of the troops...have expanded the original small settlement in the Hooghly to a mighty empire; and yet on every accession of territory the soldier has been treated as unfit to govern what his sword had won; on each new acquisition a civil establishment has been fastened, incongruent with the military barbarism of the people to be governed but fulfilling the conditions of patronage and profit.... For those civil servants have much higher salaries and allowances than the military servants have....
>
> 'In this manner a vicious circle of policy is completed, and a solution furnished of that seeming paradox, that while the instruction issued by the directors for the government of the East have always been moderate and opposed to aggrandizement by war, their empire has been continually augmented by arms and little or nothing has been affected for the welfare of the people.'

The civil servants he styled 'ignorant of great principles, devoid of business habits', wasteful and greedy for jobs and ease, run by nepotism grossly overpaid and demanding swollen costly establishments. They have worn out originally vigorous appetites and feeble minds while enjoying large salaries and the adulation of black clerks. Despising and avoiding the society of the natives, they yet pretend to know the characters of those natives, and call themselves the Statesmen of India!'

He set up a cheaper administration than the bureaucracy considered proper. The Court of Directors he dismissed as 'but cunning fools, and I am a man whose daily occupation is to deal with the lives of my fellow-men'. To the administration of India generally he called 'Hands off Sind!,' and he set the model which the world-famed Punjab Tradition was to copy and amplify a few years later. To the chiefs and nobbles he restored their swords, with this stern though flattering admonition':[18]

> 'Take back your sword. You have used it with honour against me, and I esteem a brave enemy. But if forgetful of this voluntary submission you draw it again in opposition to my government, I will tear it from you and kill you as a dog.'

He had absolute powers of life and death without trial, and did a deal of hanging, justified by the region's profligacy of murder. Felons were suspended bearing labels in three languages (as in an ancient example) explaining the reason for their doom. Lord William Bentinck had abolished flogging in the native army; Napier ignored this change, flogging freely, as a sane alternative to shooting or dismissal, the penalties lavishly meted out in those hard times. He held that 'the human mind is never better disposed to gratitude and attachment than when softened by fear'; and he used to observe: 'It will not do to let their barbaric vanity gradually wipe àway the fear cast on them by the two battles'. The properly behaved were sometimes allowed to salaam to Queen Victoria's picture, which was kept 'covered with a curtain from the gaze of private men the retainers'.[19] It is no marvel that the Conqueror of Sind has been so long the hero of boys's stories, and his simple philosophy that of all those who 'know how to deal with Orientals'. His nickname with the tribes was 'Shaitan-Ke-bhai', Satan's brother'.

The civil service were chagrined, not unnaturally. Nevertheless,

> 'if we would speak true,
> Much to the man is due'.

He waged energetic war against slavery. The occasional suttees in Sind (mainly a Muslim region) were peremptorily stopped. When the Brahmins protested that burning of widows was a religious custom, he replied cheerfully that in that case they must prepare the pyre, of course. But

> 'my nation has also a custom. When men burn women alive we hang them and confiscate all their property. My carpenters shall therefore erect gibbets on which to hang all concerned when the widow is consumed. Let us all act according to national customs'.

No more widows were burnt. When a chief interceded for a man who had merely killed his wife, a trivial fault, Napier replied that she had done her husband no wrong. 'No! but he was angry! why should he not kill her?' 'Well, I am angry', said Napier. 'Why should I not kill him?'—and did kill him. There is something to be said for a despot whose hand is heavy on cowardly savagery. He did a magnificent work; and Providence, as the Sindhis were quick to note, approved him, by sending abundant showers at the very beginning of his rule.

Moreover, the moralities are mixed, Utterly indefensible as the conquest of Sind was, when the argument got away from legality and international ethics a deeper defence revealed itself (as Napier felt, and sometimes expressed in his rough, roaring fashion). The Amirs' rule was hard on minorities not of their faith; and it was as barbarous as any other of these childish Eastern administration. Napier found one wretch a prisoner in a cage, where he had been so long that he could not live in any other way. It is interesting to remember that within the last half-dozen years a similar case was discovered in Sind, the victim of an ecclesiastical sentence, whose promulgators were defended by a much admired Muslim nationalist lawyer. Outram, like Henry Lawrence, was apt to see one side only, that of native potentates who liked and trusted him and impressed him with their charm; a side of their activities one deeply diabolical, lay necessarily out of the sight of the courteous, fair-minded English gentleman to whom his own country's reputation for good faith was a passion. Napier also saw one side only, being impatient of princely rights. A time will come when the historian of British India will be able to take both sides into account.

Sind's revenues proved insufficient; but that was because a large army was kept in the province, ready for the expected Sikh War. Watching at the Punjab marches, and convinced that a Punjab War must come, Napier compared himself to Cato with his *Delenda est Carthago*'.

Towards the close of 1843 Lord Ellenborough achieved another war, the last Maratha one. This arose out of the political situation, which drove all independent and martial spirits into what was the only State, outside Nepal and the Punjab, with any genuine autonomy left. Gwalior, a scene of confusion, had an army of 40,000 men and a strong artillery fore. The Governor-General's interference was justified by expediency only, and was precipitated by his anticipation of war with the Sikhs, whose friendly Maharaja, Sher Singh, was assassinated, September, 1843. Fearing a possible junction of Sikh and Maratha troops, in a minute (November 1) he took occasion to proclaim that the British Government could not tolerate 'the existence within the territories of Sindhia of an unfriendly government nor that those territories would be without a government willing and able to maintain order.[20] He suddenly remembered that Wellesley's treaty with Sindhia in 1804 provided for a subsidiary force in Gwalior. The provision had been allowed to lapse; but the British government was about to surprise native India by discovering a tender regard for treaties. Two British armies marched on Gwalior, the Governor-General accompanying the larger one under General Sir Hugh Gough, the Commander-in-Chief. This on December 23 crossed Chambal, and thereby invaded Gwalior. Queerly enough, it was taken for grant that the matters at issue would be settled peacefully, the mere presence of British arms disposing the Marathas to kindly thoughts. The Gwalior army was not taken seriously. Lord Ellenborough, relating the event in a letter to the Duke of Wellington (January 21, 1844), begins: 'I little expected ever to have to write to you about a battle in which I had myself been present—however, so it is'.

The Marathas under cover of night moved from the place where they were known to be, and entrenched at Maharajpur, with their batteries before them. The Commander-in-Chief regarded them as a rablle, and his Adjutant-General observed that all he needed was a horse-whip. Ladies accompanied the 'promenade', on horseback and on elephants. The gay party was about to breakfast, when masked batteries opened on them; later, from the long millet and sugarcane, 'literally, batteries were put up like copies of partridges'. A hugger-mugger haphazard battle followed, of 12,000 Company's men against slightly more Marathas. The British had left their heavy guns behind, and their field pieces were soon silenced; so 'the troops were, according to the usual tactics of Sir Hugh, launched on the batteries, which were served with desperation as long as a gunner was left'.[21] The Company lost 800 killed and wounded, and the enemy about 3000. On the same day (December 29, 1843) General Grey won a battle of a less arduous kind, at Panniar.

Gwalior was not annexed, but passed under British rule for the next ten years, the prince being a minor. Gwalior Fort was put in control of a Company contingent, which in the Mutiny cast off their officers and joined the rebellion. The State army was reduced to 3000 infantry, 6000 cavalry, and thirty-two guns.

Lord Ellenborough returned, reforcing, and reached Calcutta in March. On the 15th of June, 1844, to his astonishment, he heard that the court of Directors had revoked his appointment, and dismissed him. This was their retort to his consistent contempt for them: to the absence of respect in his communications: to his gasconades and histrionics: to his scorn of the civil service and exclusive affection for the army (he often mourned that he was not a soldier): and to his military obsession generally. 'His administration presented only a succession of battles.[22] His exuberance and verbal intoxication had undone him; the man of the Gates of Somanath Proclamation, and many other only less ridiculous because less prominent, was regarded as a dangerous mountebank. The army was intensely annoyed, and emitted a number of speeches and addresses which from Indians would have been held wickedly seditious. The Fort William officers gave him a feast, which the Duke of Wellington refused to censure:

> 'I who am thus called upon to notice this affair as a serious offence against discipline and a breach of military order, have served the public now for nearly half a century, and I believe I may safely say that neither in these times nor in any other did there ever exist an officer half so feasted and "festivated", or who received half the number of testimonials from those under his common that I have'.

Lord Ellenborough had excellent qualities, a freedom from nepotism unusual in office-holders of any age and particularly of that 'patriotic distribution of his patronage', immense energy. But excitability had its usual effect of disguising genuine powers of mind. These on occasion could find conspicuously wise and independent utterance, as in his letter to Queen Victoria (January 18, 1843):

> 'The anomalous and unintelligible position of the local government of India excites great practical difficulties in our relations with native chiefs who in an empire like

ours have no natural place, and must be continually in apprehension of our design to invade their rights and to appropriate their territories. All these difficulties would be removed were your Majesty to become the nominal head of the empire. The princes and chiefs of India would be proud of their position as the feudatories of an empress; and some audicious measures calculated to gratify the feelings of a sensitive race, as well as to inspire just confidence in the intentions of their sovereign, would make the hereditary leaders of this great people cordially cooperate with the British Government in measures for the improvement of their subjects and of their dominions. 'Lord Ellenborough can see no limit to the future prosperity of India if it be governed with due respect for the feelings and even the prejudices, and with a careful regard for the interests, of the people, with the resolution to make *their* well-being the chief object of the Government, and not the pecuniary advantages of strangers to which Providence has committed the rule of this distant empire'.[23]

The measured criticism underneath those closing words should be noted; like many who came to India from outside— and this detachment is the clinching argument for having a Viceroy from England, instead of a 'man on the spot', for the best man on the spot cannot escape that strangling loop of prejudices and stock opinions which besets Anglo-India— Lord Ellenborough was disguised by tendencies which seemed to him unethical in their brutally direct selfishness.

However, the British Civilian Community viewed his supersession 'as an act of unquestionable wisdom',[24] while recognising that he had merits.

REFERENCES

1. P.E. Roberts, *History of British India*, 325.
2. Sir Charles Napier (Sir William Napier, *The Conquest of Scinde*, i. 92.)
3. Description by his brother, Sir William Napier, *op. cit* i. 22.

4. J.C. Marshman, *History of India (abridged* edition), 435,
5. *Conquest of Scinde,* i. 97, 98.
6. *James Outram,* 316.
7. P.E. Roberts, *History of British India,* 327.
8. Marshman, *History of India,* 432.
9. Sir W. Napier, *The Life and Opinions of General Sir Charles Napier,* ii. 218.
10. *James Outram* i. 298-9.
11. *The Conquest of Scinde,* ii. 311-12.
12. *Op. cit.* ii. 320-1.
13. *Op. cit.* 390.
14. *Op. cit.* ii. 407.
15. *Contemporary Review,* November, 1876.
16. Letter to Metcalfe: *Life of Elphinestone,* ii. 374.
17. Roberts, *History of British India,* 330.
18. Sir William Napier, *History of General Sir Charles Napier's Administration of Scinde,* 14.
19. *Op. cit.* 17.
20. *The Indian Administration of Lord Ellenborough, edited* by Lord Colchester, 412.
21. Marshman, *History of India,* 440.
22. *Op. cit.* 441.
23. *The Indian Administration of Lord Ellenborough,* edited by Lord Colchester, 64-5.
24. Marshman, 441. It is right to add that there was some justification for his support of the military. The civil service had an undue share of emoluments; and their resentment of Lord Ellenborough's support of the army was expressed in intrigues at the Court of Directors, which led to his dismissal. His faults would have been overlooked if he had been willing to put through 'jobs'. His subsequent career was distinguished by some actions that showed conspicuous ability to judge Indian affairs calmly and wisely, even when his countrymen were in clamour. His criticism of the European press in India is an excellent example, and still worth pondering.

5

Administrative and Social Reforms

Himself an industrious and regular worker, Sir Charles Metcalfe was a hard taskmaster and knew well how to extract work from his subordinates. The training received in his early years as Personal Secretary to Lord Wellesley, had perhaps left in Metcalfe a touch of the autocratic temper, for which Wellesley was well known. Metcalfe, therefore, insisted on the strict performance of duty by all his subordinates, and did not tolerate any laxity in this regard. He did not hesitate to reprimand even the highest placed officials, if they were guilty of any breach of duty. Thus in a letter dated the 20th April, 1835, the Hon'ble R. Cavendish, British Resident at Nagpore, was peremptorily warned that his attention "should be confined to your proper duties as Resident of Nagpore, and any interference on your part with those of Gwalior whether by advice or otherwise, is considered to be highly objectionable".[1]

Enforcing Honesty and Discipline

Sir Charles Metcalfe also laid great emphasis on the honesty of all Government officers. In order to safeguard against the clandestine and illegal acquisition of landed property by Indian Judicial Officers, he on the advice of the Court of Sudder Dewani Adalut, made it incumbent upon all such Officers to file a schedule of their landed property on assuming office, and to renew it on the occasion of further acquisition.[2] The omission to enter any portion of their property in the schedule, which was to be duly registered in the Office of the Collector concerned, was to render the Officer guilty of the omission liable to dismissal from service. He even referred for the consideration of the Law Commission the question of rendering all lands liable to forfeiture which had been purchased under fictitious names by any party, whether Indian officers of the Government or others.[3] Incidentally, the above principle introduced by Metcalfe, has not yet outlived its utility. Even today, all officers of the Government of India are obliged to submit periodical statements of their landed property; and any property, the acquisition of which cannot be satisfactorily explained, is presumed to have been acquired by illegal means.

Even in the case of European Officers of the Government, Metcalfe did not permit them to accept any gift or gratification to which they were not entitled under the rules of the service to which they belonged. On this very ground, he refused permission to a Committee of indigo planters residing within the district of Pubna, Bengal, who had addressed the Government[4] expressing their desire to present a token of their esteem to Mr. A.J.M. Mills, who had held the office of the Joint Magistrate of that district for a long time. The Committee were politely informed that the rules governing the service of Mr. Mills did not permit him to accept any gifts of any kind; but that the regard and satisfaction with which the public conduct of Mr. Mills was viewed by the "Committee would be regarded by the Government of India as an honourable and satisfactory evidence of his official merits.[5]

A strict disciplinarian, Metcalfe firmly believed that Government servants found guilty of dishonesty should not receive any indulgence at the hands of the Government. In a despatch[6] dated the 12th February, 1836 he conveyed his opinion to the Court of Directors that "it was desirable and necessary that every possible means should be used and every opportunity taken of convincing those servants, that every instance of official dishonesty will be visited with severe punishment ..." In September, 1835, the Government of Bombay recommended for the sanction of the Governor General in Council the proposal to grant a pension of Rs. 50 per annum to an individual named "Ghoolam Moideen", a Junior Indian Commissioner at Bulsar in Surat District, who had been removed from employment on being convicted of extortion. Long and excellent service and the high character of the individual till the time of his conviction, were the grounds on which Bombay Government had based their recommendation. But Metcalfe, true to his principle, withheld his consent to the recommendation made by the Government of Bombay. He remarked that the confer a pension on a person who had been convicted of gross delinquency, whatever might have been his previous merits and services, would be in every respect objectionable as it would establish a most injurious and pernicious precedent, and would certainly lead to a belief on the part of the Government servants that with the loss of their integrity they were not liable to forfeit the favour of the Government.[7]

While Metcalfe knew how to enforce discipline and extract work from his subordinates, he was not oblivious to their interests and took measures to improve their lot. He passed orders regarding the equalisation of allowances of medical officers at Civil Stations in all the Presidencies in India,[8] thus ending the unjust and invidious system of granting different allowances to medical officers posted at different stations. These orders were given effect to in the Bombay Presidency by a separate notification.[9] The Governor General also sanctioned a plan submitted by the Government of Fort St. George for modifying and equalizing the allowances of Head Assistant Collectors, Collectors and Principal Collector under the Madras Presidency.

The attention of the Board of "Revenue, Madras, had often been drawn to the defective and unsatisfactory state of the revenue administration of the Madras Presidency in general and of the Northern Circars in particular. The Board attributed the evil mainly to the absence of correct accounts, the inefficiency of the village establishment and the insufficiency of the Collectors' establishment.[10] For purposes of revenue administration, the districts of Madras Presidency had been distributed into two distinct categories, viz., the "Settled districts" where the system of permanent settlement prevailed, the "Unsettled Districts" whose revenue was assessed annually. The allowances of Collectors or settled districts were fixed at a lower scale on the presumption that their revenue duties were lighter as compared with those of Collectors of districts in which the revenues were subject to annual settlement. But certain changes which took place at that time, brought large portions of the Northern Districts under the direct management of the Collectors who had to settle their revenues annually under disadvantageous conditions, without any increase having been made in their allowances. This loss was made up to a certain extent by the commission allowed to be drawn on the net revenues of private estates under the management of the Collectors. But the remuneration from this source was fluctuating and varying. The Madras Board of Revenue, therefore, made the following recommendations to the Government of Madras in order to do away with the evils then existing in the revenue administration of that Presidency:[11]

(1) To abolish the distinction between the Collectors of "Settled" and "Unsettled" districts by allowing both to draw equal salary. The commission on the revenues of estates was in future to be credited to the Government, thus compensating the Government for the increase in salary of Collectors of "Settled" districts.

(2) To abolish the commission on the extra branches of revenue, and to apportion the average amount equally among all the Collectors by an addition to their existing salaries

(3) To reduce the number of principal Collectors to 10 and to abolish the rule which restricted the appointment of Principal Collectors only to certain particular districts.

The Governor of Madras forwarded the above recommendations to the Supreme Government for approval, with the remarks that the arrangement suggested by the Board of Revenue appeared to be "well calculated to promote the object in view, viz., the improvement of the Revenue administration especially in the Northern Circars, and generally in all the Districts under this Presidency. . . ."[12] In a letter dated the 29th February, 1836, the Secretary to the Government of India communicated to the Madras Government the sanction of the Governor General of India in Council to the arrangement submitted for modifying and equalizing the allowance of Head Assistant Collectors, Collectors and of Principal Collectors under the Presidency of Fort St. George in the manner proposed by the Madras Revenue Board.[13]

Sir Charles Metcalfe was greatly averse to interfering with the prevalent usages and practices regarding the service and allowance, etc., of Government employees. On 16th April, 1835, the Government of Bombay forwarded for the approval of the Governor General of India in Council, the draft of an Act for legalising the alienation of the emoluments and office of "Patels" under that Presidency.[14] In reply the Bombay Government was informed that 'the Governor General in Council entertains considerable doubts as to the expediency of enacting the Law suggested...". In order to enable the Governor General to take a decision in the matter, the Bombay Government was also requested to furnish information as to the usage which prevailed in the Indian States, with regard to the office and emoluments of the "Patels" and whether they were considered as alienable or otherwise.[15]

Relations with Subordinate Governments

Metcalfe also held definite views about the functions of the supreme Government of India and its relations with the local governments or the governments of the different Presidencies in India. As early as October, 1830, he, as a Member of the Governor General's Council, had recorded a Minute[16] in which he stated that "Every one who has attended to the subject, must I conceive admit, that the Supreme Government, as at present constituted, is too much occupied with the details of its own Presidency, to exercise any very effective control over the other Governments. If, therefore, it is intended by the Home Authorities, that the Supreme Government should be efficient, as a Government of Control over subordinate Presidencies, it seems indispensable, that it should be relieved from the laborious occupation of local administration". In the same Minute Metcalfe also stated that it appeared to him that the political relations of the British Government in India ought to be retained exclusively under the direction of the Supreme Government, on account of the paramount importance of those affairs, on which peace and war and consequently the safety and stability of the British Empire in India depended, and also on account of the expediency of having all political relations managed and controlled by one presiding spirit, under one uniform system of policy. He saw no advantage in interposing subordinate Governments between the Supreme Government and the Indian States, with whom the British Government had political relations.

It is, therefore, not surprising that on assuming the Office of the Governor General of India, Sir Charles Metcalfe tightened up the control of the Supreme Government over the governments of the subordinate Presidencies. On 17th May, 1835, the following Resolution was recorded by the Governor General in Council:[17]

> "The Governor General of India in Council is pleased to resolve that copies of Minutes of the Members of the Supreme Government shall not be sent to the

Subordinate Governments or Authorities on any occasion of a reference being made to them arising out of such Minutes".

It was also ordered that copies of the above Resolution should be sent to all the Departments of the Government of India, for information and guidance.[18]

The enhanced legislative powers with which the Government of India were vested under the provisions of the Charter Act of 1833, appeared to conform to the wishes of Sir Charles Metcalfe, as is evident from the following remarks of the Governor General in Council to the Court of Directors: "We entirely concur in the justice of your Hon'ble Court's remarks on the expediency of the Law whereby all Legislative functions are exclusively vested in one Central Government. We consider that such a provision would have been under any circumstances desirable. . ."[19] But Metcalfe was conscious of the great responsibility that had devolved upon him as a result of the enhanced legislative powers of the Supreme Government. He declared that he was fully aware that whatever laws might be drafted by the subordinate Governments, he was wholly responsible for every law which he might pass in his capacity as Governor General of India, and assured the Court of Directors that he would never delegate this part of his duty to those Governments, nor neglect it even in matters most strictly local.[20]

In order to guard against any misuse of the additional powers conferred by the Charter Act of 1833, the Court of Directors had instructed the Governor General of India in Council not to exercise undue interference in the affairs of the subordinate Governments. Metcalfe took the first opportunity to allay the apprehensions of the Court in this behalf, and stated that in the superintendence of the administration of the local Governments he would carefully bear in mind their observations and instructions, endeavouring to control those Governments effectually, without falling into the error of attempting to do what could only be efficiently done by them, against which the Hon'ble Court had warned the Governor General in Council.[21]

But it appears that the apprehension of the Court of Directors was not ill-founded as Metcalfe could not resist the temptation of interfering too much in the affairs of the subordinate Governments. He proposed the enactment of a law which sought to control the powers and movements of the Governors of the various Presidencies. The following were the main clauses of the proposed Act:[22]

1. "That no Governor or Presidency which has a Council, shall be absent from the Seat of Government while a Council is held, without the consent either of the Governor General of India in Council, or of the Governor in Council of the Presidency; and that no Governor of a Presidency which has a Council, shall be absent from the Seat of Government for a Calendar month, without the consent of the Governor General of India in Council".
2. "That whenever such consent as is above required, shall be given either by the Governor General of India in Council, or by the Governor in Council of the Presidency, the reasons for such consent shall be recorded".
3. "That if any Governor of such a Presidency as is aforesaid shall be absent from the Seat of Government without such consent as is above required, he shall exercise none of the powers of Governor till he shall return to the Seat of Government and in the interval, such powers shall be exercised by the Member of the Council of the Presidency who would have been entitled to exercise those powers in case of a vacancy".
4. "That if any Governor of such a Presidency as is aforesaid, shall be absent from the seat of

Government with such consent as is above required, it shall be competent to him to require the Council of the Presidency to refer to him any matter on which he may desire to vote, and his written opinion subscribed with his name, shall on all occasions be reckoned as his vote in Council, and if the votes be equal, as the casting vote".

5 "That in every such case it shall be competent to the Governor General of India in Council to authorize the Governor alone to exercise all, or any of the powers which might be exercised by the Governor in Council".

In considering the enactment of the proposed law, Lieut. Colonel Morison, Member of the Governor General's Council, recorded a Minute[23] dated the 30th November, 1835, in which he expressed his doubts both as to the competency of the Government of India to pass such an enactment, and as to the expediency of the measure itself. While disagreeing with the proposed measure, he recommended that the consideration of the question might be deferred for the time being.[24]

The observations recorded by Lieut. Colonel Morison were considered by the Governor General in Council at their meeting dated the 7th December, 1835.[25] It was decided at this meeting to call for the opinion of the Advocate General as to whether the Supreme Government was competent to define the relative powers of the Governors of the Presidencies and their Councils during the absence of the Governors from the seat of Government. The opinion of the Advocate General was also sought regarding the competence of the Governor General of India in Council, in his legislative capacity, to authorise the Governor of a subordinate Presidency to act independently of his Council, or to invest the Governor, when absent from the seat of Government of the Presidency, with power and privileges which he possessed when present at the seat of his Government.[26]

The reply[27] furnished by the Advocate General, Mr. Pearson, showed that he entertained grave doubts and objections to the course of proceeding contemplated by the Governor General in Council. In view of the above opinion of the Advocate General, Metcalfe decided to abandon the scheme of enacting a law on the subject, and referred the matter to the Court of Directors "in order that if it should appear expedient to you, measures may be taken in England to provide such a remedy as the occasion may seem to you to require".[28]

Sir Charles Metcalfe's relations with the authorities in England remained cordial during his period of Governor Generalship and the following reply to the Court of Directors regarding the legislative powers of the Governor General of India in Council, bears ample testimony to this fact:

> "We shall be cheered in the pursuit of our object by the expectation of being aided by the cordial and powerful support of your Hon'ble Court, to whom we shall never fail to communicate fully and frequently on all points connected with a duty, the importance of which has been so truly and forcibly described in the paragraph to which we are now replying".[29]

Problem of 'Sati'

In the field of social reforms, Sir Charles Metcalfe continued the work of his predecessor, Lord William Bentinck. He took measures to see that the social evils which Bentinck had taken pains to suppress were not encouraged again during his regime. When a case of Sati or widow-burning was reported to have been committed at Ahmednagar, Metcalfe insisted on the Raja of Ahmednagar signing a written promise that in future he would discourage the wicked system of widow-burning in the territories under him. Considering the weakness of the young Raja and the supreme influence of his relations and Ministers in the State the Government of Bombay had stated that a very imperfect security would be obtained by taking merely his own promise to discourage Sati in future in his State. The Bombay Government had suggested that the leading Ministers and all such relations of the Raja as formed part of his family should also be required to enter into written engagements of a similar nature.[30] But the Bombay Government was informed that the Governor General in Council could not recognise the expediency of subjecting the relations and ministers of a Chief who was not a minor to the responsibility for acts committed within his territory. Metcalfe thought that by following this course, the responsibility would become divided and consequently weakened, and it would be extremely difficult to fix the party on whom it should fall. The Governor General in Council was, therefore, of opinion that it was preferable to consider the Chief alone responsible in such cases.[31]

The above remarks show clearly the importance which Metcalfe attached to the problem of Sati. But he was also sensible to the delicacy of the question and the untoward results which undue interference on the part of the British Government with the performance of the right of "Sati" might produce on the minds of the Hindu population of India. In consequence of the circumstances attending a case of "Sati" which originated at Poona, but was actually committed at Satara, the Government of Bombay submitted for the approval of the Supreme Government the draft of an Act for the abolition of "Sati" under that Presidency.[32] But the Bombay Government were promptly informed[33] that the Governor General in Council deemed it "exceedingly desirable to avoid, if practicable, any further legislation (except what would be included in the General Code) on the delicate subject in question". It was observed that occurrences like the one referred to by the Bombay Government were happily not so frequent as to require the immediate promulgation of any enactment for their prevention. The case was, therefore, forwarded for the consideration of the Law Commission with a view to assimilating in the uniform Criminal Code under preparation, the law with regard to "Sati" at all the Presidencies, providing at the same time rules to guard against evasion.

Female Infanticide

The social evil of female infanticide also received due attention during the Governor Generalship of Sir Charles Metcalfe. There is reference to a latter dated the 18th August, 1835. From Jhareja Soorajee, a Chief of Rajkot, in which the Chief promised to abstain in future from the custom of putting to death the female children in his family, and also promised to inform the Political Agent at Rajkot beforehand about the births likely to take place in his family[34] The Chief was also asked to furnish suitable security that he would keep the above promise and also inform the British Government punctually about the occurrence of any case of infanticide within his "Talooka". Raja Chundersinghjee of Wankaneer in an agreement dated the 6th October, 1835, gave the required security on behalf of Jhareja Soorajee. He took upon himself to see that Soorajee fulfilled his promises faithfully and made himself responsible to the British Government for any breach of promise committed by Soorajee.[35]

A similar security was also obtained from the chief of Kotra Sangana.[36]

Human Sacrifice

The evil of human sacrifice appears to have become almost extinct by that time. No case of human sacrifice was reported to have been committed during the Governor Generalship of Sir Charles Metcalfe. But reference is available to a case in which four British subjects had been kidnapped for the purpose of human sacrifice as far back as 1832, with the connivance of or by the orders of the Raja of Jaintia.[37] Three of the kidnapped persons had never afterwards been heard of, but in spite of repeated efforts, the British

Government had failed to obtain any redress for the crime or the surrender of criminals who kindnapped the British subjects for the evil purpose of human sacrifice. The Raja of Jaintia was, therefore, apprised by Metcalfe that if the perpetrators of the atrocity in question were not delivered up within two months, orders would be issued for the attachment of the Gobah District of his territory, where the human sacrifice was believed to have been committed.[38] It became necessary to adopt this measure against the Chief of Jaintia in consequence of his failure to comply with the just expectations of the British Government for the surrender of the culprits, and of "his proved participation in the offence under enquiry".[39]

Suppression of 'Thugi'

In spite of the incessant war waged by Lord William Bentinck against "Thugi," the evil appears to have continued in a virulent from during the Governor Generalship of Sir Charles Metcalfe. But Metcalfe, fully alive to the seriousness as well as the enormity of the problem, spared no pains and employed all the resources of his Government to extirpate this evil. This is evident from the vigorous measures adopted by him in the various parts of the country for the suppression of the atrocious crime of Thugi, and the more extended system of operations which he pursued to round up and punish the Thugs. The Agent to the Governor General in the Saugor and Nerbudda territories reported the existence of Thug confederacies in that area, and proposed the adoption of coercive measures against the "Zamindars" in whose villages the Thugs might be arrested.[40] Metcalfe directed the Agent that "Whenever thugs have been convicted, the resident Zamindars in whose villages they were proved to have had their abode, ought to be summoned and made to execute Moochilkas (i.e., securities) binding themselves under specific penalties, to prevent the residence in their villages of any similar offenders for the future".[41]

Major N. Alves, Agent to the Governor General in Rajputana, reported the measures adopted by his Assistants, Lieutenant Trevelyan and Lieutenant Briggs, for the suppression of "Thugi" in Jodhpur and Marwar.[42] The Agent thought that the exertions of Lieut. Trevelyan were judiciously applied and persevered, and he also expected some success for Lieut. Briggs's partisan Marwar. But he was of opinion that they might meet with evasion and counteraction from causes which affected all the Rajput States, and that of Jodhpur still more than any other.[43] In the words of Lieut. Trevelyan, these causes were "the disorganised condition of Marwar generally," and "the numerous villages belonging to Charuns, Jagis and other religious sects, who set the orders of the Government and its local officers at defiance, and harbour all descriptions of offenders (many of whom are guilty of the grossest crimes) receiving a share of the profits of their atrocities, as remuneration for the shelter afforded them in their sanctuaries. . . ".[44] However, as these causes were not likely to be removed suddenly, Metcalfe directed the Agent to the Governor General in Rajputana to "exercise patience and to avoid precipitancy, without relaxing in our endeavours to effect the object in view".[45] He further remarked that it was to be hoped that by degrees the people of that quarter would be awakened to the real extent and enormity of the practice of Thugi, and that when this effect was once produced and the general opinion was favourable to the proceedings of the British Government, the speedy suppression of the crime might confidently be looked for.[46]

A proposition had been made to the King of Avadh for securing the co-operation of his Government for the suppression of Thugi in that quarter, and the rounding up of gangs of Thugs which found shelter in His majesty's territories. The King expressed his ready assent to the project, and operations were accordingly taken in hand under the superintendence of the Resident at Lucknow for the extirpating of the crime in the area.[47]

On receipt of intelligence of the murder by Thugs of six peons in charge of the safety of the Treasury in the Northern Division of Arcot, the Government of Madras was requested to issue instructions to all the Magistrates in the Districts to give immediate intimation of the occurrence of such crimes which might be reported to them.[48] The Government of Madras stated that there could be no doubt that the crime of Thugi was prevalent of a considerable extent in the District under that Presidency, especially in the carnatic, yet nothing effectual could be done for its suppression without the appointment of a special agency for that express purpose, and the prosecution of a systematic course of operation under one head.[49] The Governor General in Council, while expressing his concurrence in the opinion of the Madras Government, notified his resolution to furnish additional assistance to Captain Sleeman who had been appointed to the Office of General Superintendent of the operations for the suppression of Thugi, in order to enable him to depute one or more European Officers exclusively to the territories subject to the Presidency of Fort St. George, for the complete extirpation of Thugi from that part of the country.[50]

Slavery

The social evil of slavery that was prevalent in various Indian States at that time was divested of most of the cruel features which characterised the African slave trade. Still there existed abundant reason to justify every possible effort that could be made for its suppression, especially as the slave market was to a great extent supplied by kidnapping. Like other social evils, slavery had also attracted the attention of Lord William Bentinck. However, Bentinck realised that he could not interfere authoritatively for the suppression of slave traffic in the Indian States. But he considered that every favourable opportunity should be taken of exerting the influence of the British Government to discourage the practice, and that in the case of children or others kidnapped from the British territories, effectual means should be adopted for obtaining redress and preventing the repetition of the offence."[51]

The efforts of Lord William Bentinck in this direction were successful to such an extent that slave traffic was positively interdicted by the States of Gwalior, Kotah, Bundi, Oudh, Rewa and several of the Baghelkhand principalities.[52] The reports from the residents in other States also showed that the practice was on the decline. But the Court of Directors felt that the acquiescence of the Chiefs and States in alliance with the British power in India and under its protection, in the views and wishes of the British Government on such occasions, was in most instances the result rather of a submission to the influence of the British supremacy than of a cordial concurrence in the wisdom or expediency of what was recommended, and that little dependence could be placed on the vigilant and efficacious exertion of their authority, in permanently enforcing the prohibition of this nefarious traffic.[53] The Court of Directors, therefore, directed the Governor General in Council to instruct all the British Residents and Political Agents to keep in view the eradication of the evil of slavery, and to remonstrate against "any infringement of the prohibition when once issued or any laxity on the part of the Chiefs or their officers in giving effect to its provisions".[54]

In conformity with the above instructions from the authorities in London, Sir Charles Metcalfe continued his exertions for the suppression of slavery in the various Indian States. He even succeeded in persuading His Highness Maha Rao Sri Desulji, Rao of Cutch, to issue a proclamation dated the 6th February, 1836, abolishing the importation of slaves into his territory. The following is the text of the proclamation:[55]

"Be it known to the principal merchants of Mandvee, and every other merchant as well as trader in Kutch, whether belonging to it or only trading thereto, to all navigators of vessels, to the inhabitants of Kutch generally, that if any slaves, Negroes or Abyssinians, shall be brought for sale to any seaport in Kutch after the middle of July next, the vessel conveying them shall be confiscated, and its cargo shall become the property of this Government (Darbar). No petition for its restoration shall be listened to; and further, the offenders shall be brought to condign punishment, whether they belong to Kutch or another country. There will be no departure from the resolution. A vessel which brings slaves shall be seized, and summary punishment inflicted on those who navigate her.

> The British Government have made arrangements to suppress the trade in slaves throughout the adjacent countries, and it has instructed the officers commanding its ships to seize retain all vessels bringing slaves. I, therefore, strictly prohibit, after the date before mentioned, any more slaves being brought to this country; let all my subjects discontinue this custom, and take heed of this Proclamation, and look to their interests and welfare by attending to it."

The Government of Madras forwarded for the approval of the Supreme Government the draft of an Act intended to prohibit the importation of slaves. That Government also forwarded with the above draft copy of a letter from the Registrar of the Sudder Adalut of Madras Presidency, giving a statement of the grounds which suggested the necessity of the proposed Act.[56] However, considering the delicacy of the question, Metcalfe refrained from giving his assent to the proposed Act and referred the draft, along with connected correspondence with the Madras Government, for the consideration of the Indian Law Commission.[57]

Promotion of Learning

Sir Charles Metcalfe also tried to promote the cause of learning in India. Shortly before he took over as Governor General of India, a controversy appears to have started regarding the respective claims of the oriental learning and the European literature and science for the patronage of the Government. A difference of opinion took place in the General Committee of Public Instruction on the expediency or otherwise of promoting the acquirement of the English language and the study of European literature and science through the medium of that language at the several seminaries and colleges under their charge. There was a decided division of sentiment in the Committee. One party advocated the policy of an avowed and active preference for the propagation of European learning with English language as the medium of instruction, while the other party contended that the primary duty of the Committee was the continuance of the oriental systems of instruction.[58]

The conflicting views of the above two parties in the General Committee of public Instruction occasioned a reference to the Government of India and elicited the Resolution of the Governor General in Council dated the 7th March, 1835.[59] According to this Resolution it was decided "that the great object of the British Government" ought to be the promotion of European literature and science among the Indians, and that all the funds appropriated for the purpose of education would be best employed on English education alone. But it was stated that it was not the intention of the Governor General in Council to abolish any college or school of oriental learning while the Indian population should appear to be inclined to avail themselves of the advantages which it afforded, and necessary instructions were issued that all the existing professors and students at all the institutions under the superintendence of the Committee of Public Instruction should continue to receive their stipends.

Thus we see that although Lord William Bentinck favoured the promotion of English language and European literature, he did not want to force the Indians to adopt them against their will. But certain members of the Committee who were wholly in favour of the oriental system of learning, renewed the contest in the Asiatic Society of Calcutta, where their party was strongest.[60] A memorial[61] was, therefore, received from the Asiatic Society of Calcutta, addressed to the Court of Directors, in which the members of the Society solicited that "such reasonable sum may be supplied from the Territorial Revenues as may be sufficient for promoting amongst the natives at large the study of the ancient language and literature of their country".[62]

While forwarding the above Memorial to the Court of Directors, Sir Charles Metcalfe acquainted them of the whole controversy which led to the submission of the Memorial in question.[63] Indeed, so strong were sentiments on the matter that two of the members of the General Committee of Public Instruction, Messrs. Macnaghten and James Prinsep, resigned from the membership of the Committee.[64]

On assuming the office of the Governor General of India, Metcalfe declined to revive the above controversy[65] and decided to abide by the decision of his predecessor, Lord William Bentinck. He, therefore, approved the proposal of the General Committee of Public Instruction for providing schools with teachers of English at Patna, Dacca, Meerut, Ghazipur and Gauhati (Assam).[66] Local Committees were established at each of these places for superintending the schools and submitting periodical reports of the progress of the scholars to the Government throught the General Committee.

Metcalfe also took various other measures to provide for the educational requirements of Indians. A new medical college was established[67] at an estimated annual cost of Rs. 38,332. At the recommendation of the General Committee of Public Instruction, Metcalfe appointed an additional Professor, Dr. W.B. O'shaugnessy, M.D., for the College, to delivery lectures on Chemistry and Meteria Medica.[68] His period also saw the establishment of a big College at Hooghly with the funds of an endowment or Trust created by one

Haji Mohammed Mohsin.[69] The institution was to provide education to over a thousand students, and was to be governed by the following general principles:

1. It was to have two main Departments, English and Oriental, and the benefit of the instructions afforded by the institution was to be opened to candidates of every sect or creed who were willing to conform to the established rules of discipline.
2. The resort of students was not to be encouraged by stipends, but the inducement of honorary and pecuniary prizes was to be held out to the most proficient students.
3. No age limit to exclude the students from the institution was to be fixed, but the honorary and pecuniary rewards were to be opened only to students not exceeding 20 years in age.

The above principles were duly approved by the Governor General in Council and the College started functioning in August, 1836, with Dr. Wise as Principal.[70]

Metcalfe also resorted to novel methods of providing funds for promoting the cause of education in India. He diverted a sum of Rs. 20,000 received as "Nazrana" From Raja Rajnarain Bahadur on the grant of a title, to defray the expenses of the establishment for the new medical College.[71] Likewise, he utilised a donation of Rs. 20,000 granted by Raja Bejai Govind Singh, for the purchase of English books for the students of different schools under the control of the General Committee of Public Instruction.[72]

Thus by his many-sided reforms in the administrative and social spheres, Sir Charles Metcalfe sought to improve the material as well as moral standard of the people he governed, and in this way fulfilled the high ideals of benevolent autocracy laid down by his predecessor, Lord William Bentinck.

REFERENCES

1. For., Pol., Progs., 20th April, 1835, No. 57.
2. Leg., Letters to Court, No. 2 of 1835, dated 24th August, 1835, para. 77.
3. *Ibid.*
4. Home, Judl. (Civil), Cons., 23rd March, 1835, Nos. 8-9.
5. Home, Judl., Letters to Court, No. 13 of 1835, dated 28th September, 1835, para. 18.
6. Home, Judl., Letters to Court, No. 2 of 1836, dated 12th February, 1836, para. 24.
7. Home, Judl. (Criminal), Cins., 7th September, 1835, Nos. 7-9.
8. Home, Pub., Letters to Court, No. 27 of 1835, dated 2nd September, 1835, para. 23.
9. Home, Pub., Cons., 9th December, 1835, Nos. 6-7.
10. Home, Rev., Progs., 29th February, 1836, No. 2.
11. *Ibid.*
12. Home, Rev., progs, 29th February, 1836, No. 1.
13. *Ibid.*, No. 4.
14. Home, Rev., Progs., 4th May, 1835, No. 4.
15. *Ibid.*
16. For., Misc., No. 237 (Serial No. 61).
    This volume contains the "Civil Finance Committee Minutes" (1830-31). The Minute under reference is dated 18th October, 1830, and is signed by C.T. Metcalfe.
17. Home, Pub., Cons., 27th May, 1835, No. 6.
18. Home, Pub., Genl. Letters to Court, No. 33 of 1835, dated 16th December, 1835, para. 24.
19. Leg, Letters to Court, No. 3 of 1835, dated 31st August, 1835, para. 7.
20. *Ibid.*, para. 18.
21. *Ibid.*, para. 30.
22. Leg., Cons., 4th January, 1836, No. 1.
23. Leg., Cons., 4th January, 1836, No. 2.
24. *Ibid.*
25. *Ibid.* No. 3.
26. *Ibid.*

27. *Ibid.* No. 4.
28. Leg., Letters to Court, No. 1 of 1836, dated 25th January, 1836, para. 10.
29. Leg., Letters to Court, No. 3 of 1835, dated 31th August, 1835, para. 19.
30. For., Pol., Progs., 30th November, 1835, No. 10.
31. *Ibid.*, No. 11.
32. Leg., Cons., 18th January, 1836, Nos. 1-3.
33. *Ibid.*
34. "Collection of Treaties, Engagements and Sunnuds Relating to India", by C.U. Aitchison, Fifth Edition (1929), Volume VI, Part I (Western India States), No. CXIV, pp. 249-250.
35. *Ibid.*
36. *Ibid.*
37. For., Pol., Letters to Court, No. 14 of 1835, dated 6th April, 1835, paras. 323-328.
38. For., Pol., Letters to Court, No. 19 of 1835, dated 27th April, 1835, para. 2.
39. *Ibid., para. 3.*
40. For., Pol., Progs., 11 May, 1835, No. 80.
41. *Ibid.*
42. For., Pol., Progs., 16 May, 1835, No. 30.
43. *Ibid.*
44. *Ibid.*, No. 31.
45. *Ibid.*, No. 32.
46. *Ibid.*
47. For., Pol., Letters to Court, No. 7 of 1836, dated 29th February, 1836, para. 3.
48. For., Pol., Cons., 2nd November, 1835, Nos. 85-87.
49. For., Pol., Cons., 14th December, 1835, Nos. 1-5.
50. For., Pol., Letters to Court, No. 7 of 1836, dated 29th February, 1836, para. 14.
51. For., Pol., Letters from Court, No. 5 of 1835, dated 1st April, 1835, paras. 1-2.
52. *Ibid.*, para. 3.
53. *Ibid.*, para. 6.

54. *Ibid.*
55. "List of Treaties, Engagements and Sunnuds in the Custody of the Imperial Record Department" (now National Archives of India, Government of India), I.R.D. Treaty No. 295 (Bombay list No. 33), dated 6th February, 1836.

    Also "Collection of Treaties, Engagements and Sunnuds Relating to India" by C.U. Aitchison, Fifth Edition (1929), Vol. VI, Part I (Western India States) No. IX, page 127.
56. Leg., Cons., 7th December, 1835, Nos. 1-5.
57. Leg., Letters to Court, No. 4 of 1836, dated 29th February, 1836, paras. 32-34.
58. Home, Pub., Gen. Letters to Court, No. 29 of 1835, dated 30th paras. 3-4.
59. *Ibid.*, para. 5.
60. Home, Pub., Gen. Letters to Court, No. 28 of 1835, dated 30th September, 1835.
61. Home, Pub., Cons., 30th September, 1835, No. 12.
62. *Ibid.*
63. Home, Pub., Gen. Letters to Court, No. 28 of 1835, dated 30th September, 1835.
64. Home, Pub., Cons., 1st July, 1835, Nos. 10-13.
65. Home, Pub., Gen. Letters to Court, No. 29 of 1835, dated 30th September, 1835, para. 6.
66. *Ibid.*, para. 8.
67. *Ibid.*, para. 21.
68. Home, Pub., Cons., 5th August, 1835, Nos. 13-16.
69. Home, Pub., Cons., 5th August, 1835, Nos. 7-8.
70. Home, Pub., Cons., 17th August, 1835, No. 19.
71. Home, Pub., Genl. Letters to Court, No. 29 of 1835, dated 30th September, 1835, para. 23.
72. Home, Pub., Cons., 16th December, 1835, Nos. 2-3; and 3rd February, 1836, Nos. 11-12.

6

Revenue and Financial Policy

Political affairs alone did not monopolize the attention of Sir Charles Metcalfe. During the brief period of his Governor Generalship, he found time to look into the internal administration of the country also, and there was hardly any department of the Government which did not come under Metcalfe's minute scrutiny and which did not bear the hallmark of his administrative ability.

Abolition of Inland Custom Duty

In the field of revenue administration, perhaps the most important measure for which credit is given to Sir Charles Metcalfe is the abolition of Inland Custom Duty or the removal of internal trade barriers. In Bengal and Agra Presidencies at that time a "Transit Duty," which was in fact a trade duty, was levied on all commodities and was paid to the Government in one instalment either on the import of the commodity or on its first movement, and after franking the goods a certificate to this effect was issued to the owner. On presenting this certificate, the merchant could move his goods throughout the limits of Bengal as well as Agra without being liable to additional exactions. Thus far there was nothing wrong with the system as such. But its chief evil lay in the operation of the checks upon the evasion of this duty, which exposed the honest trader to the constant and wearisome process of the search, weighing and inspection of his goods for the purpose of verifying the certificate or the Pass under which they were being transported. The trader was subjected to this process almost at every Custom Post, and more often than not was left to the caprice of the lowest subordinates belonging to it. This forced the merchants sometimes to offer bribes to the underpaid employees of the Customs Department, who as a class were notorious for venality.

Thus the loss of time, the consequent demurrage incurred on hired conveyances, the detention from a favourable market, the lavish bribes offered to the subordinate staff of the Customs Department and the enhanced price necessarily put upon the merchandise in order to cover so much expense over cost price as well as to assure a fair rate of profit, all tended to operate against the commercial prosperity of the country. It was apprehended that the above factors would impede the healthy growth of trade in the country, injure the merchant by inducing tardy returns on the capital invested and affect materially the mass of the population as purchasers through high prices. The Government of India was, therefore, actively considering some way of reforming this deplorable state of affairs, and Lord William Bentinck had appointed[1] a Committee for revising the Customs and Post Office laws in India, although this Committee started functioning after his departure for Europe.

In his instructions to the members of the above Committee, dated the 1st April, 1835, Sir Charles Metcalfe pointed out that the "object to which your attention in the first instance seems to be most urgently called is a beneficial modification in the present system for collecting what is termed the Transit Duty......".[2] The Committee were also informed that the "present system being comparatively unproductive to the State, oppressive and vexatious to merchants, and injurious to the people at large," the best thing would be to dispense with it completely provided the

Committee could suggest some "less objectionable substitute" which might procure an equivalent amount of revenue.[3]

While the report of the Committee was still awaited, the Hon'ble Mr. A. Ross who was appointed Governor of the newly created Agra Presidency, adopted the somewhat hasty and unauthorised step of abolishing all internal custom houses established in that Presidency for the levy of Transit Duty, without reference to the Supreme Government.[4] This raised a storm of protest and the Governor of Agra was subjected to a strict censure both by the Governor General of India in Council and the Court of Directors in London. All explanations offered by Mr. Ross and his Minute dated the 27th February, 1836, in justification of the proceedings adopted by him,[5] proved to be of no avail as the Governor General in Council could not find any reason which would have necessitated the adoption by the Governor of Agra of "such extensive measures involving a reduction of the resources which the State acquires for the payment of its unavoidable expenses"[6] without previous reference to the Supreme Government. Such a change at that moment was considered specially ill timed because the Supreme Government themselves has suspended all measures on their own part for the reform of Customs, and had referred the whole question for the consideration of the Committee for the revision of Custom Laws in India, whose report was soon expected. Under the circumstances it was thought extremely inexpedient that the Government of Agra should have taken upon itself to anticipate the result of the investigation of that Committee.[7] The Court of Directors while expressing their serious disapprobation of the measures adopted by the Governor of Agra stated that "such is our sense of the extreme want of judgment manifested by Mr. Ross on this occasion, that supposing he still continued to exercise the functions of Government in the Presidency of Agra, we should have come to Resolution of cancelling his appointment.[8] The Court of Directors even instructed the Government of India that "the administration of Government of Agra be never again under any circumstances delegated to Mr. Ross".[9]

But the immediate effect of the measures adopted by the Governor of Agra was to create an anomalous position by relieving one division of the territory from all internal trade barriers, while in Bengal which was immediately contiguous to it, the Custom Laws remained in full force. Since the report of the Committee for the revision of Custom Laws was likely to take some time, the Governor General in Council was led to conclude that under the circumstances the Supreme Government was left with the alternative of either cancelling the measures adopted by the Governor of Agra by an order and reinstating the abolished custom houses, or of assimilating the system by adopting similar measure of abolition with respect to the internal custom houses of Bengal. On 2nd March, 1836, Sir Charles Metcalfe recorded a Minute[10] wherein he stated his reasons for recommending the adoption of the latter alternative without further delay. The views expressed by the Governor General were accepted by the majority of his Council, although Mr. Shakespeare recorded a Minute of dissent[11] to the measure. In consequence of the above decision of the Government of India, a public notification was issued for general information, and the Customs Committee and the Board of Customs were at the same time called upon to report on the means available for the realisation of an amount of revenue equivalent to that thus sacrificed in both the Presidencies of Agra and Bengal.[12]

Thus ended the pernicious system of internal trade barriers which was threatening the economic prosperity of British India and was a source of harassment of the traders and the people alike. But it must be said that the credit for this benevolent reform was in a way forced upon Sir Charles Metcalfe. In all fairness, the whole credit should go to Mr. Ross who, as Governor of Agra, had initiated the reform in that Presidency, and had consequently to bear the brunt of the Governor General's and the Court of Directors' anger and extreme displeasure. But for the initiative of Mr. Ross which forced Metcalfe to adopt similar measures in Bengal also in order to keep up the uniformity in the Custom Laws of the two contiguous provinces, the abolition of inland custom duty might have been indefinitely delayed.

Pensions to Dispossessed Landholders

Another benevolent measure adopted by Sir Charles Metcalfe was the award of pensions to the disseized holders of "Badshahee" grants, ousted under Section VI, Regulation 37 of 1793. There was a large class of persons holding grants of land termed "Badshahee" or Royal. The systematic and comprehensive measures which were either already in active progress, or were immediately contemplated for the effective enforcement of the Resumption Laws at that time, were likely to expose the holders of these "Badshahee" grants to "the most severe distress or even to utter destitution". Impressed with the conviction that considerations of humanity and of liberal policy alike demanded that some efficient provision should be made for the ousted individuals, the Sudder Board of Revenue suggested[13] that pensions for a certain limited term of years should be granted to the holders of the "Badshahee" tenures consequent on the resumption of their grants. On the recommendation of the Governor of Bengal,[14] Sir Charles Metcalfe as Governor General of India approved the proposition of the Sudder Board of Revenue for granting pensions to the disseized holders of "Badshahee" grants, with the modification that the life or lives of the person or persons actually ousted, and not any fixed period of years, should be the limit of each grant.[15] He also enjoined that every care was to be taken to prevent its extension beyond that limit.

Land Settlement in Agra

A controversy appears to have stated during the Governor Generalship of Sir Charles Metcalfe regarding the revenue administration of the newly created province of Agra. In a dispatch[16] dated the 28th February, 1835, Metcalfe, as Governor of that Province had solicited the sanction of the Supreme Government for making permanent settlement of lands in certain cases where its adoption appeared clearly advisable, that is to say, where the utmost proportion of the land had been brought under good cultivation, consistent with the principles of Indian farming. Lord William Bentinck in his Minute[17] dated the 19th March, 1835, had also recorded his approval of the above proposal. But Mr. A. Ross, who was afterwards appointed as Governor of Agra, recorded a Minute[18] dated the 26th March, 1835, wherein he stated his opinion that a permanent settlement ought in no instance to be formed in the Western Provinces. He based his arguments upon the principle that the rent of land was the most proper of all sources whence the money required for State purposes could be procured, and that the Government should not tie up its own hand as by limiting the amount of revenue for ever receivable from the land.

Of the other members of Governor General's Council, Mr. Prinsep supported the recommendations of Sir Charles Metcalfe for permanent settlement in Agra, while Colonel Morison declared his sentiments to be opposed to those of Metcalfe and in favour of Mr. Ross. They recorded separate Minutes[19] on the subject, setting forth the reasons for their respective views. The Governor General, Sir Charles Metcalfe, in his capacity of the Governor of Agra, had already recorded his opinion that a permanent settlement for estates in full cultivation was not likely to cause any direct or indirect loss to the land revenue, as he thought that the assessment then fixed upon lands in such estates could never be materially raised at succeeding periodical settlements. Due to this difference of opinion among the various members of the Supreme Government, all the Minutes referred to above were forwarded to the Hon'ble the Court of Directors in London for their consideration and orders.[20]

The Orders of the Court of Directors were received long after Sir Charles Metcalfe had relinquished the office of the Governor General of India.[21] The Directors considered the subject of "vast importance", and it received at their hands "that full examination and attention to which it is so justly entitled". But while anxious to promote the prosperity of the western province, they were not satisfied that the formation of permanent settlements in Agra Presidency would be beneficial either to the Government or to the country. They admitted the advantages that were to be expected to result from so defining the claims of the Government upon those interested in the soil as to create a feeling of security calculated to promote industry and consequent improvement, and earnestly desired the establishment of such a system as might ensure these desirable objects. But they were of opinion that this purpose would be served equally well by long-term settlements and, therefore, sanctioned the formation of settlements for periods not exceeding thirty years. The following sentence brings out clearly the sentiments of the Court of Directors on the subject:-

> "It appears to us that such a term (i.e., thirty years) is sufficient of inspire the holders and occupiers of the soil with those feelings of confidence which it is desirable they should possess, while it reserves to the State the power without breach of faith, of revising the settlements at the expiration of the term for which they may be made, and of participating to a reasonable and moderate degree in the increasing property of the country, a power the exercise of which may become imperatively necessary by a change in the value of the precious metals or an enhancement of the price of the necessaries of life".[22]

Revenue Officers in Bombay

An important improvement in the revenue administration of the Bombay Presidency was made during the Governor Generalship of Sir Charles Metcalfe. The jurisdiction of the "Mamlatdars",[23] who were the revenue officers in that Presidency, was too extensive, and to this cause were ascribed several disorders in the internal administration of the province resulting in great suffering to the cultivators and loss to the Government. The Ryots were sometimes obliged to undertake a journey of fifty miles in order to make their revenue payments in the Mamlatdars "Cutchehries" or Courts, and the parties concerned in "Foujdari" or criminal matters were also subjected to similar annoyance. As increasing number of Mamlatdars would have entailed a heavy additional expense, it was suggested by the Bombay Government[24] that the best plan for relieving the Mamlatdars was the introduction in Bombay of the "Mahalkaree" system then prevailing in the Konkan. Under this system the "Mahalkar"[25] with a regular police and treasury establishment was to conduct all revenue and magisterial duties of his division, acting under the general control of the "Mamlatder", just as a Sub-Collector was subordinate to a Principal Collector. The Government of Bombay also submitted[26] for the consideration of the Supreme Government the draft of a Regulation on the subject.

The Governor General in Council, being convinced of the utility of the measure proposed by the Bombay Government, approved[27] of the arrangement in principle, but made certain modifications in the draft submitted by the Government of Bombay, in order to bring out more clearly the objects desired in the proposed enactment. On the Bombay Government intimaing their concurrence to the modifications proposed by the Supreme Government, the draft was read in the Governor General's Council for the first time on the 5th October, 1835, and was finally passed on the 23rd November, as Act XX of 1835.[28]

First Uniform Currency

In the sphere of financial administration the genius of Sir Charles Metcalfe found ample scope to introduce reforms which were of an enduring nature. His most important contribution in this field was the introduction of a uniform currency throughout the British territory in India.

A great inconvenience was experienced at that time in transacting business, both Government as well as private, due to the existence of various currencies which were simultaneously in circulation in different parts of India, each having a different standard and value and bearing a different device. Thus, there were Sicca rupees, Sonat rupees, Farruckabad rupees, Arcot rupees, Madras rupees and Bombay rupees, and the compilation of their respective values involved considerable difficulty. The imperative need for some form of the currency which might put an end to the existing confusion and facilitate the transaction of business was greatly felt. The attention of Lord William Bentinck was first directed[29] to the crying need for the introduction of a uniform currency in India, but his premature departure from India left this important and arduous task to his immediate successor, Sir Charles Metcalfe.

The Calcutta Mint Committee submitted[30] for the consideration of the Governor General in Council various devices for the proposed new coin including one bearing the replica of the head of the King of England, and recommended its adoption as they considered the facial image to be much more difficult of imitation than lion or any other similar device. The Governor General in Council, therefore, resolved to give preference to this device for the general coin, and decided to take immediate measures for establishing the new coin as the general currency of all the Presidencies.[31] It was also thought that by giving the coin an impression of the likeness of the reigning sovereign of the British empire it might be possible to aid its circulation as a general colonial currency in the East, and asserting by the same act the British supremacy in India itself.[32] The reverse of the coin was to bear the words "East India Company" together with the nominal value of the coin in English, Persian and Hindi, and the ornamental devices of a lotus flower and myrtle wreath. The engraving of the specimen was executed by an Indian workman employed at the Calcutta Mint, but the Court of Directors were requested kindly to furnish matrix dies of the same device by English engravers, which were to serve as a model to the Indian workmen employed in preparing dies for the new coinage.[33]

It had also been decided by the Governor General in Council that the change in the silver coinage was to be followed up by a corresponding change in the gold and copper currency of British India, as soon as the reports and suggestions of the Calcutta Mint Committee in this respect were received.[34]

In pursuance of the above decisions for the introduction of a uniform currency for the whole of British India, the Governor General in Council in their letter[35] dated the 24th June, 1835, forwarded to the Court of Directors the draft of a proposed Act on the subject of the new Silver and Gold coinage of British India. The proposed Act was considered necessary to legalise the issue of the new coins and to regulate their weight, standard and device, and in respect of the new Rupees to fix the rate a which it was to be paid and received in discharge of sums calculated in any of the then existing legal currencies. It was deemed essential to provide for all these matter by a legislative enactment; but in regard to all other questions relating to the coining of money and the establishment or removal of mints, it was considered desirable that their direction be vested in the Governor General of India in Council in his executive capacity, and a separate Section to this effect was, therefore, introduced in the draft of the proposed Act.[36]

The main provisions of the Act were as follow:-

"i. Be it enacted, that from the first day of September 1835, he undermentioned Silver Coins only shall be coined at the Mints within the territories of the East India Company—A Rupee, to be denominated the Company's Rupee—a half Rupee—a Quarter

Rupee—and a Double Rupee; and the weight of the said Rupees shall be 180 Grains Troy, and the standard shall be as follows:

$\frac{11}{12}$ or 165 Grains of pure Silver,

$\frac{1}{12}$ or 15 Grains of Alloy,

and the other coins shall be of proportionate weight and of the same standard.

ii. And be it enacted, that these coins shall bear on the obverse the head and the name of the reigning Sovereign of the United Kingdom of Great Britain and Ireland, and on the reverse the designation of the Coin in English and Persian and the words "East India Company" in English with such embellishment as shall from time to time, be ordered by the Governor General in Council.

iii. And be it enacted, that the Company's Rupee, Half Rupee, and Double Rupee, shall be a legal tender in satisfaction of all engagements, provided the Coin shall not have lost more than two per cent in weight, and provided it shall not have been clipped, or filed, or have been defaced otherwise than by use.

iv. And be it enacted, that the said Rupee shall be received as equivalent to the Bombay, Madras, Furruckabad and Sonat Rupees, and of Fifteen-sixteenths of the Calcutta Sicca Rupee; and the Half and Double Repee respectively, shall be received as equivalent to the Half and Double of the above-mentioned Bombay, Madras, Furruckabad and Sonat Rupees, and to the Half and Double of Fifteen-sixteenths of the Calcutta Sicca Rupee.

v. And be it enacted, that the Company's Quarter Rupee shall be a legal tender only in payment of the fraction of a Rupee.

vi. Provided, that if in any contract for the payment of Calcutta Sicca Rupee it shall have been specially stipulated that if payment be maid in the Territories of the Madras, Bombay or Agra Presidency, it shall be made in the Rupee now current in those Presidencies repetitively, at a different rate from that above provided with reference to the Calcutta Sicca rupee, the contract shall be satisfied by payment within those Presidencies of Company's Rupee of the amount of Furruckabad, Madras or Bombay Rupees so especially stipulated: Provided also, that if payment of the Principal or Interests of the Public Debt be made for the convenience of Creditors at any Public Treasury other than as stipulated in the Notes and Engagement of the Government, it shall be competent to the Government to make such payments at the same exchange as heretofore.

vii. And be it enacted, that the undermentioned Gold Coins only shall henceforth be coined at the Mints within the Territories of the East India Company.

First: A Gold Mohur or Fifteen Rupee Piece of the weight of 180 grains Troy, and of the following Standard, viz.

$\frac{11}{12}$ or 165 Grains of pure Gold.

$\frac{1}{12}$ or 15 Grains of Alloy.

Second: A Five Rupee Piece equal to a Third of a Gold Mohur.

Third: A Ten Rupee Piece equal to Two-thirds of Gold Mohur.

Fourth: A Thirty Rupee Piece or Double Gold Mohur–and the three last mentioned Coins shall be of the same standard as the Gold Mohur and of proportional weight.

viii. And be it enacted, that these gold Coins shall bear on the obverse the head and name of the reigning Sovereign of the United Kingdom of Great Britain and Ireland, and on the reverse the designation of the Coin in English and Persian, and the words "East India Company" in English, with such embellishment as shall from time to time be ordered by the Governor General in Council, which shall always be different from that of the Silver Coinage.

ix. And be it enacted, that no Gold Coin shall henceforward be a legal tender of payment in any of the Territories of the East India Company.

x. And be it enacted, that it shall be competent to the Governor General in Council in his Executive capacity, to direct the coining and issuing of all Coins authorised by this Act; to prescribe the devices and inscriptions of the Copper Coins issued from the Mints in the said Territories, and to establish, regulate, and abolish Mints, any Law hitherto in force to the contrary notwithstanding."

The draft of the above Act was read in the Council of India for the first time on the 29th June, 1835,[37] and was finally passed by the Governor General of India in Council on the 17th August, 1835, as ACT XVII of 1835.[38]

Copper Currency

As regards the copper currency, some difficulty was anticipated in the beginning in introducing an entirely new copper coin for the whole of British India, due to the heavy expense involved in withdrawing the existing copper coins and substituting them by the new coin.[39] The two main copper coins then in circulation were the "Trisooli" pice and he "Calcutta pice". It was, therefore necessary to protect the new coin by a device the skilful character of which would have precluded its imitation at the Indian mints as well as by clandestine fabricators in the British territory itself. Hence, the Governor General in Council decided[40] to adopt an English device for the new copper coin. However, the general introduction of the new copper currency was not immediately contemplated. It was intended that the "Calcutta pice" should be supplied to Treasuries in the provinces so long as stores of that coin were available, and in the meantime the Mint Committee was requested to furnish specimens of an English device for the new copper currency.[41]

Subsequently, however, the Governor General in Council thought[42] that the temporary inconveniences attendant in Bengal on the tradition from the general circulation of the Sicca and other rupees to that of the new or Company's Rupee would be lessened by providing as quickly as possible a Copper currency to circulate at par with the latter, that is, at the rate of 64 pice to the Company's Rupee. It was also felt that such a measure was much desired by the mercantile community in British India, and was necessary for the protection of the people, especially those belonging to the lower classes, against loss in their transactions in copper coins.

In order to legalise the circulation of the new copper coin, a legislative enactment (Act XXI of 1835) was passed by the Government of India. The draft of this Act was originally prepared in the Financial Department, and was taken into consideration by the Governor General in Council at their meeting in the Legislative Department, dated the 7th December, 1835.[43] It was decided in that meeting that with effect from the 20th December, 1835; the following copper coins only were to be issued from any Mint within the Presidency of Bengal[44]:—

i. A Pice weighing 100 grains Troy

ii. A Double Pice weighting 200 grains Troy

iii. A Pie or one-twelfth of an Anna weighing $33\frac{1}{3}$ grains Troy.

The above coins were to have such devices as were fixed by Governor General in Council, in accordance with the provisions of Section 10 of Act XVII of 1835 (Act regarding the uniform Silver and Gold currency for the whole of British India).

The new pice was declared to be a legal tender for $\frac{1}{64}$ of the Company's Rupee the double pice for $\frac{1}{32}$ of the Company's Rupee, and the pice for $\frac{1}{192}$ of the Company's Rupee. It was at the same time provided that after the 20th December, 1835, no copper coin, in any part of the territories of the East India Company was to be legal tender, except for fractions of a rupee.[45]

Thus Sir Charles Metcalfe succeeded in introducing a uniform currency in the whole of British India—a measure calculated to increase the commercial prosperity of the country by facilitating transactions, and removed once for all the existing confusion due to the use of multiple currencies or the circulation of coins having different standards, denominations and values. It also helped in making Government disbursements, and Metcalfe even directed that all salaries, allowances and pensions payable to the servants of the East India Company, were to be audited in the new currency established under Act XVII of 1835.[46] For this purpose he fixed the rate of exchange from the Sicca rupee to the Company's rupee of 4½ per cent, i.e. 100 Sicca rupees were to be considered as equivalent to 104½. Company's rupees.[47] As the Company's rupee became more popular and the other rupees were gradually withdrawn from circulation; Metealfe ordered that all Government accounts at the different Presidencies were to be kept in the Company's rupees,[48] and thus completed the change-over to the uniform new currency.

But strangely enough this measure, full of wisdom and farsightedness as it was, did not find favour with the Court of Directors.[49] They apprehended that the prevailing confusion due to the existence of various different currencies in India would be aggravated further by the addition of one more and an entirely new currency. But their anger was mainly directed against "a change so existence and important having been determined upon" merely in anticipation of their approval and without waiting for their formal orders. However, the Court of Directors intimated to the Governor General of India in Council that "We are aware of the inconvenience and confusion which would now result from the abandonment or suspension of the plan which you have thus prematurely and inadvisably determined to adopt. We shall not therefore, at present direct any departure from it though we cannot but entertain the apprehension that the course you have pursued...may yet involve your Government in very serious embarrassment, while the alteration of the currency in which your accounts are stated will unquestionably occasion great inconvenience and confusion".[50]

Whether the fears expressed by the Court of Directors were well founded or not will be best illustrated from the results of this important reform introduced by Sir Charles Metcalfe, and this alone should be the criterion for judging Metcalfe's wisdom and administrative ability in taking this important step. It may be pointed out that the system of uniform currency, and even the denominations of most of the coins introduced by Sir Charles Metcalfe in India about one hundred and twenty years back, are in vogue even today. A reform which has stood the test of a century and a quarter should not only be above all condemnation but deserves our hearty appreciation.

Abolition of Sagar Mint

Among other financial measures adopted by Sir Charles Metcalfe, mention may be made of the abolition of the British mint at Sagar. Although for some time past the 'Sagar Mint' had been yielding considerable profit, the Calcutta Mint Committee, having been called upon by the Governor General in Council to submit a report on the subject, recommended its abolition[51] The main reason which prompted the Mint Committee to make this recommendation was their apprehension that it might be out of the power of the Sagar Mint to execute the new facial rupee intended for the whole of British India with the same accuracy as was likely to be commanded by the up-to-date machinery at the Calcutta Mint. Moreover, the regular traffic of steamers on the river Ganga which had been established at that time, had reduced the charge of conveying the coins to and from the Presidency of Bengal, even in large bulk, to a more trifle. The Mint Committee were, therefore, of opinion that this purpose would be several equally well by opening a Government depot at Allahabad o: Benares, where the new coins could be sent from the Calcutta Mint for the receipt and exchange of the coins depreciated by the establishment of the new and uniform currency under Act XVII of 1835.[52]

On receipt of the above communication from the Calcutta Mint Committee and after a mature consideration of the circumstances therein stated, the Governor General in Council resolved[53] to abolish the Sagar Mint, the establishment not being considered necessary for supplying coin of the new legal currency to that territory, and the Calcutta and Bombay Mint being deemed sufficient for providing for the whole coinage of India. Sir Charles Metcalfe also directed the Mint Committee[54] to place the building of the late Sagar Mint at the disposal of the Commissioner and Governor General's Agent for the Sagar and Nerbudda Districts, to be disposed of by sale or in such other manner as might be deemed by him most advantageous. The Mint machinery as well as the stores remaining on hand were ordered to be delivered over to the nearest Magazine, all the dies being first carefully obliterated or destroyed.[55] As regards the proposal to open a Government depot in the

Sagar and Nerbudda territories for the exchange of the old and depreciated coins with the new Company's rupee, it was decided[56] in consultation with the Agra Government that it was not necessary to establish such a depot. The Government of Agra, who had direct charge of the Sagar and Nerbudda territories, were of opinion that the new currency would automatically flow to those parts through commercial transactions, and would eventually succeed in ousting the old and obsolete coins which were no longer issued from any Mint in the whole of British India.[57]

On the recommendations of the Calcutta Mint Committee, Sir Charles Metcalfe ordered[58] the abolition of the Madras Mint also. It was, however, subsequently found that the statements on which the recommendations of the Mint Committee were based were "not only imperfect but most erroneous". Therefore, on receiving the true facts from the Government of Madras, the Court of Directors intimated their decision that they did not think it advisable to abolish the Madras Mint.[59] The Court of Directors also asked the Governor General in Council to call upon the Mint Committee for some explanation for submitting wrong statements regarding the Madras Mint.

Proposed Government Life Insurance Society

Prior to his departure for Europe, Lord William Bentinck had proposed to establish a Life Insurance Society under the safeguard of the Government, and had also appointed a Committee for that purpose.[60] After receiving the report of this Committee, on 7th March, 1835, he resolved that an office for the insurance of lives under the guarantee and on the credit of the Government be established at Calcutta, and that it was to grant policies on the lives of all classes of persons—Europeans as well as Indians.[61] Lord Bentinck also desired that if the Managers and Directors of the Private Insurance Companies then existing agreed, the business of such concerns should be incorporated with that of the proposed Government Insurance Society.[62] With this end in view, he directed the newly appointed Insurance Committee to make "free and unreserved communication" to the private institutions concerned and obtain their opinion on the subject.

On assuming the office of the Governor General of India, Sir Charles Metcalfe found that there were certain difficulties in the negotiations which the Insurance Committee was ordered to conduct with the existing Insurance Societies for their incorporation with the proposed Government Office. He, therefore, declined to sanction[63] the immediate opening of the Government Insurance Office, as recommended by the Committee, because he did not think that the arrangements with the other private societies were till then in a sufficiently advanced state to justify that measure. In his opinion, if the Government Insurance Office were prematurely opened for the issue of policies, the pre-existing institutions would be placed in a disadvantageous position for negotiating their terms by the competition of the Government guaranteed insurance.

Subsequently, however, Metcalfe received certain representations addressed to the Government of India direct by the private Life Insurance Societies then existing in Calcutta. The representations evinced that there was a decided unwillingness on the part of the private societies to merge themselves in the proposed Government Insurance Office. Therefore, after mature deliberation and in consideration of the feelings of the Private Insurance Societies, Metcalfe decided to give up the further prosecution of the scheme for the establishment of a Life Insurance Office under the guarantee of the Government, until the subject was considered in greater detail by the Court of Directors.[64] He did not accept the recommendation of the Insurance Committee to open the Government Office at once, as he thought that such a measure would have arrayed the credit of the Government on behalf of the new establishment against the credit of the pre-existing institutions. In Metcalfe's opinion, this would virtually have compromised the design of an amicable arrangement between the old societies and the new institution for the incorporations of their business: and most probably might have caused injury and injustice to individuals, which would have been "an occasion for deep regret to the Governor General in Council".[65]

The above is an excellent example of Sir Charles Metcalfe's deep concern for the welfare of the people. It shows his unwillingness to introduce any measure, however trifling, against the wishes of the people in general, although legally and constitutionally there was nothing to prevent him from doing so.

Economy in Administration

Last, but not the least, mention may be made of Sir Charles Metcalfe's efforts to introduce an all round economy in the administration. The state of finances of the East India Company was none too good at that time, and a general view of the financial prospects made it apparent that according to the most favourable calculation there was likely to be an annual deficit of one core of rupees or one million Pounds Sterling, to meet which there were no perceptible resources.[66] The Accountant General's "Financial Sketch Estimate" for the year 1835/36 also showed nearly the same result. According to this estimate, the "Indian Surplus" in round figures was about Rs. 1,28,00,000 or £ 1,280,000. Against this surplus were to be adjusted the disbursements on account of "Home charges," including notes from London, annuity funds, interest on bills, which together amounted to about £ 2,850,000, thus leaving a net deficit of about £ 1,570,000. Of this amount, it was expected that about £ 870,000 would be made up by such reductions as the Court of Directors might be able to affect in the "Home charges," and such economy as the Governor General in Council might be able to accomplish in India through his efforts. Sir Charles Metcalfe, therefore, wrote to the Court of Directors that "considering the probability of occasional extraordinary expenditure, without reference to War, it seems more likely that the deficit will be £1,000,000. The expense of War cannot of course, be estimated. But the most favourable statement which we are able to offer shows a large deficit even in peace—a state of finance which is much to be regretted and ought to be remedied".[67]

It was to remedy this deplorable state of finances of the East India Company that Metcalfe adopted various methods to bring about economy in the administration. The most important step which he took in this direction, and which indirectly saved the Government from grave loss, was to follow the policy of peace and nonintervention. War at any time is a costly affair, but at a time when the Company's finances were at such a low ebb, it would have proved simply ruinous. Due to his peaceful policy, Metcalfe was able to avoid any serious conflict with any of the Indian powers and thus saved the Government from serious economic drain.

Measures for Economy

In the internal administration of the country also Sir Charles Metcalfe cut down expenses wherever possible. Soon after assuming charges of the office of Governor General of India, he examined the question of "Durbar charges," or expenses on account of presents given to the various Indian chiefs and Princes as well as to the Missions from neighbouring countries outside India. These presents were given by many high functionaries including the Commanders-in-Chief of the Presidencies and the Residents etc. in exchange for the presents received, and were charged to the Government. In a Minute dated the 12th April, 1835 Metcalfe carefully examined the principal particulars of this head of public expenditure, and detailed his views and opinions regarding the alteration and improvement of the existing system of "Durbar charges" and the mode of affecting a substantial reduction of their amount.[68] These views were entirely approved by the members of the Governor General's Council.

Sir Charles Metcalfe was definitely against sanctioning any extra staff for Government establishments, and did not spare any pains to find out whether the existing staff was wholly and usefully employed. Thus, while scrutinising the revised statement of establishments for the office of the Resident at Mysore and that of the Commissioner for the affairs of Coorg, he desired[69] it to be conveyed to the Resident that "the Governor General in Council cannot understand for what purpose so large an Establishment is required, now that the entire administration of the Mysore country is transferred to British Officers, and you are requested to make a further reduction or if you should consider this impracticable, to state in what description of business each individual of the Establishment is employed and what is the daily average quantity of work prepared by each". It is rare to find such meticulous care for the welfare of the Government. And, Metcalfe applied the same stringent measures even to the establishments of British Residents or Envoys stationed outside India. Lieut-Colonel Burney, the British Resident in Burma, recommended the appointment of a second assistant to Ava Residency with a view to provide for the performance of the duties at Rangoon. But he was peremptorily informed[70] that as the Government of India could not sanction the expense of two assistants, the arrangement proposed could be carried into effect only by putting Mr. Bayfield, who had been deputed to look after the duties of Resident at Rangoon, on his former footing as Surgeon to the Residency at Ava and appointing a separate assistant to be stationed at Rangoon.

Metcalfe did not hesitate even in passing orders relating to the personnel staff of the Presidency Governors. If there was a tendency to increase the expenditure. A representation had been made to Lord William Bentinck as to the inadequacy of the salary allowed to the Private and Military Secretaries of the Governors of Madras, Bombay and Agra; and Bentinck had agreed to an increase in the allowances of these functionaries. Sir Charles Metcalfe, on his elevation to the post of Governor General, expressed his concurrence in the opinion of his predecessor and saw no objection to the sanctioning of allowance to the Officers, in question at the increased rates which had been proposed by Bentinck, provided the no additional expense was thereby incurred.[71] In order to ensure this object, Metcalfe proposed that the increase involved in the arrangement be conditional at each Presidency on an equal reduction in the Governor's establishment and allowance for contingencies. The members of the Governor General's Council agreed with these suggestions, and corresponding orders were, therefore, conveyed to the Governments concerned.[72]

The above measures of economy which touched almost every sphere of the administration, made Sir Charles Metcalfe a little unpopular among certain sections. But there cannot be any doubt that these measures were fully justified for the improvement of the depleted finances of the East India Company, and were prompted by a rare sense of devotion to duty.

REFERENCES

1. Home, Misc. Nos. 483-85 (Serial No. 27). These contain the Proceedings of the Committee for the Revision of the Customs and Post Office Departments in India for the period 1834-38.
2. Fin., Sep, Rev., Progs, 1st April, 1835, No. 2.
3. *Ibid.*
4. Fin., Sept Rev., Cons, 10th February, 1836, Nov. 1-11: and 2nd March, 1836, Nos. 4-5.
5. Fin., Sept. Rev, Letters to Court, No. 4 of 1838, dated 6th July, 1836, para 1.

6. Fin., Sept. Rev, Letters to Court, No. 1 of 1836, dated 2nd March 1836.
7. *Ibid.*
8. For, Pol., Letters from Court, No. 2 of 1837, dated 1st February, 1837.
   (On Lord Auckland's taking over as Governor General of India, Sir Charles Metcalfe was appointed as Lieutenant Governor of Agra in March 1836, and Mr. A Ross was reverted to his original post as a member of the Governor General's Council).
9. *Ibid.*
10. Fin., sept, Rev., Cons., 2nd March, 1836, No. 6.
11. *Ibid.*, No. 7.
12. Fin., Sept. REv., Cosn., 2nd March, 1836, Nos. 2-4 and 8.
13. Home, Rev., Cons, 8th February, 1836, No. 11.
14. *Ibid.*, No. 10.
15. *Ibid*, No. 12.
16. Home, Rev., Letters to Court, No. 7 of 1835, dated 20th July, 1835, para 1.
17. Home, Rev., Cons., 20th July 1835, No. 2.
18. *Ibid.* No. 3.
19. *Ibid.*, Nos. 4-5.
20. Home, Rev., Letters to Court, No. 7 of 1835, dated 20th July, 1835, para 7.
21. Home, Rev., Letters from Court, No. 6 of 1837, dated 12th April 1837.
22. *Ibid.*, para 3.
23. Marathi from Arabic "Muamalat" i.e., business, and Persian "dar", i.e., one who holds, from *"dashtan"* meaning to hold. Thus "Mamlatdas" means an officer appointed by the Government to hold charge of a revenue district.
24. Leg., Cons, 20th July 1835, Nos. 3-5.
25. Arabic "Mahal" i.e., division of a district or estate and Persian "Kar" i.e. doer, from "Kardan," meaning to do. Thus "Mahalkar" is an officer in charge of a part of a taluq or district, who exercises most of the powers of the "Mamladar".
26. Leg., Cons., 20th July, 1835, Nos. 3-5.

27. Leg, Cons., 5th October, 1835, Nos. 5-6.
28. *Ibid.*
29. Fin., Mint, Cons, 25th November, 1834, Nos. 1-3; and 25th January, 1835, Nos. 1-4.
30. Fin., Mint, Cons., 8th April, 1835, Nos. 1-4.
31. *Ibid.*.
32. Finl., Mint, Genl. Letters to Court, No. 10 of 1835, dated 8th April, 1835.
33. *Ibid.*, paras, 10-11.
34. *Ibid.*, para 8.
35. Fin., Mint, Genl. Letters to Court, No. 17 of 1835, dated 24th June, 1835.
36. *Ibid.*, para 3.
37. Home, Judl., (Civil), Progs., 29th June, 1835, No. 3.
38. "The Acts of the Supreme Government of India", from 1834-39, Vol. 1, Calcutta, W. Thacker & Co., St. Andrew's Library (1842).
39. Fin., Minl., Const, 20th May, 1835, Nos. 1-6.
40. Fin., Mint, Cons., Ist July, 1835, No. 1.
41. Fin., Mint, Genl. Letters to Court, No. 2 of 1836, dated 27th January 1836, para 6.
42. Fin., Mint, Cons., 2nd December, 1835, Nos. 1-2.
43. Leg., Letters to Court, No. 4 of 1836, dated 29th February, 1836, para 14.
44. Leg., Cons., 7th December, 1835, Nos. 17-20.
45. *Ibid.*
46. Fin., Gen. Letters to Court, No. 26B of 1835, dated 9th September, 1835.
47. *Ibid.*
48. Fin., Cons., 10th February, 1836, No. 1.
49. Fin., Genl. Letters from Court, No. 9 of 1836, dated 27th July, 1836; and No. 13 of 1836, dated 12th October, 1836.
50. Fin., Gen. Letters from Court, No. 9 of 1836, dated 27 July, 1836, para 5.
51. Fin., Mint, Cons., 2nd September, 1835, Nos. 1-8; and 7th October, 1835, No. 3.

52. *Ibid.*
53. Fin., Mint, Gen, Letters to Court, No. 10 of 1836, dated 29th June, 1836, para 22. (The Letters under reference reported to the Court of Directors the Proceedings of the Government of India in the Finance (Mint) Departments for the 3rd and 4th quarters of the year 1835).
54. Fin., Mint, Progs., 25th November, 1835, Nos. 6-8.
55. *Ibid.*
56. Fin., Mint, Progs., 16th December, 1835, Nos. 1-3.
57. *Ibid.*
58. Fin., Genl. Letters to Court, No. 14 of 1835, dated 17th June, 1835.
59. Fin., Genl. Letters from Court. No. 11 of 1835, dated 4th November, 1835.
60. Fin., Cons., 10th February, 1835, Nos. 1-6.
61. Fin., Cons., 7th March, 1835, Nos. 18-19.
62. Fin., Genl. Letters to Court, No. 8 of 1835, dated 8th April, 1835.
63. Fin., Genl. Letters to Court, No. 11 of 1835, dated 29th April, 1835.
64. Fin., Genl. Letters to Court, No. 13 of 1835, dated 13th May, 1835.
65. *Ibid.*
66. Fin., Genl. Letters to Court, No. 27 of 1835, dated 12th September, 1835, para 1.
67. *Ibid.*, paras, 8-9.
68. Home, Pub., Genl., Letters to Court No. 23 of 1835, dated 16th July, 1835, para 6.
69. For., Pol., Prog, 18th May, 1835, No. 123.
70. For, Pol., Cons., 12th October, 1835, Nos. 77-78.
71. Home, Pub., Genl. Letters to Court, No. 23 of 1835, dated 16th July, 1835, para 3.
72. *Ibid.*, para 4.

7

Judicial Administration

Liquidation of Arrears of Cases

At the time Sir Charles Metcalfe took over as Governor General of India, the judicial administration of British India was in a confused state. There was a huge accumulation of arrears in both the Presidencies of Bengal and Agra, and the number of judicial cases pending before the judges in the various districts literally ran into thousands. Thus in Bihar alone there were 1,560 pending cases, out of which 157 were original suits, 173 appeals and 1,230 miscellaneous cases.[1] In Chittagong the situation was still worse, there being 1,980 cases pending, out of which 334 were original suits, 574 appeals and 1,072 miscellaneous cases.[2] But the climax was reached in the district of Burdwan where there was a total number of 11,794 cases pending.[3] Of these, there were 9,049 original suits and appeals pending before Munsiffs, 1,264 before the Principal Sudder Ameen and Sudder Ameens and 1,481 before the two European judges in Burdwan District.

The above figures presented a formidable picture indeed, but Metcalfe with his usual courage and sincerity of purpose, set forth to grapple with the situation. In the first place he authorised the appointment of additional judges in the districts of Bihar and Chittagong to continue until the arrears of business were so reduced as to admit of their being disposed of within a reasonable period by the regular judicial authorities of those districts[4]. For the district of Burdwan, the Court of Sudder Dewani Adalut, Bengal, had recommended the appointment of a third European Judge. It was, however, subsequently found that out of the 1,481 cases pending before the two European judges in the district, there were 1,239 appeals from Munsiffs and Sudder Ameens, and as such could be referred to Principal Sudder Ameens. It was, therefore, thought that the arrears in a question could be reduced with equal expedition by the appointment of another Principal Sudder Ameen instead of an additional European Judge. The Court of Sudder Dewani Adalut was, therefore, asked to reconsider its proposal, and take an early opportunity of deputing a Principal Sudder Ameen from some other district to officiate at Burdwan[5]. The Governor General in Council also approved the recommendation of the Court of Sudder Dewani Adalut, Bengal, for the appointment of a second Principal Sudder Ameen to be stationed at Dacca, where the European judge had 300 pending cases, while the Principal Sudder Ameen had 555 cases pending before him[6].

On the recommendation of the Government of Bengal, Sir Charles Metcalfe sanctioned the appointment of Sudder Ameens and Munsiffs in thirteen different districts of the Lower Provinces with a view to relieve the Principal Sudder Ameens of those districts, and to enable those officers to afford greater assistance to the European judges in the disposal of appeals pending before them[7]. An additional Sudder Ameen and a Munsiff were also appointed at Bankurah district in order to obviate the difficulty experienced in the execution of the decisions passed by the Munsiffs of Jungle "Mahals", as well as to try and determine suits under the value of Rs. 1,000 within the jurisdiction of that district.[8]

Absorption of Temporary Indian Judges

Another important step taken by Metcalfe which, in addition to reducing the arrears of pending judicial cases, also had a great beneficial effect upon the Indian judges employed in the British territory, was to utilise the services of the Indian judges who were no longer required in certain districts and were, therefore, retrenched. These judges were sometimes appointed temporarily for dealing with arrears of cases, and after the arrears were liquidated, their appointments were terminated. Mr. Colvin, who was Deputy Secretary in the Judicial Department under Lord William Bentinck, had recorded a note,[9] in which he had brought out the evils of this system which, apart from resulting in extreme hardship to the retrenched Indian Judges, tended to prevent others similarly employed from exerting themselves for fear of falling in the same misfortune after their arrears were liquidated. Mr. Colvin had, therefore, suggested in his note that such Indian judges whose appointments were terminated in consequence of the reduction of arrears in the districts in which they were employed, might be temporarily attached to other districts where there were arrears of business, until they could be otherwise provided for. Sir Charles Metcalfe decided[10] to adopt Mr. Colvin's suggestion, and accordingly directed the Presidency Sudder Court to report to the Government whenever the appointment of a Sudder Ameen or Principal Sudder Ameen was abolished, so that the officer in question, if he could not immediately be otherwise provided for, might be deputed to any neighbouring district in which his services might be most urgently required. With respect to Munsiffs under like circumstances, the Sudder Court was empowered to issue its own orders for their deputation to districts in which the state of arrears might require additional assistance. A copy of the decision of the Governor General in Council on this occasion was also sent to the Government of Agra, and it was suggested to that Government to establish a similar rule under that Presidency, should the Governor of Agra see no objection to the measure.[11]

Relief to Judges

Sir Charles Metcalfe also took measures for affording relief to the "Zillah" (District) and City judges from the portion of the miscellaneous business which was brought before them, viz., the hearing and disposing of petitions for the execution of decrees and the numerous claims that invariably arise on the attachment of property.[12] The suggestion for this reform was first made by the Court of Sudder Dewani Adalut of the Presidency of Bengal, whose judges were unanimously of opinion that the Zillah and City judges should immediately be vested with the power to refer to the Principal Sudder Ameens and Sudder Ameens the execution of the decrees of their own courts and the Provincial Courts of Appeal, as well as the decrees of the Sudder Court, the Special Commissioners' Courts, and other Zillah and City Courts. The Court of Sudder Dewani Adalut were of opinion that the adoption of this arrangement would enable the Zillah and City judges to devote more of their time to cases which they were not competent to refer to the inferior tribunals. The Governor General in Council asked the Sudder Dewani Adalut to submit the draft of an Act to give effect to the above proposals. On receipt of the draft it was, with slight alterations, read in the Council of India for the first time on the 11th January, 1836, and was published on the same date for general information.[13] It was finally passed by the Governor General in Council as Act No. V of 1836, without any further alteration.

In order to put the judicial administration of the country of a sound basis and to ensure quick disposal of cases, Sir Charles Metcalfe passed an Act on 8th June, 1835 (Act No. VII of 1835), under which the local Government of Bengal and Agra were empowered to transfer criminal duties from Commissioners of Circuit to Sessions Judges, and to define the powers which were to be exercised by each respectively. But the Court of Sudder Dewani Adalut at Allahabad raised certain objections[14] to this measure adopted by the Supreme Government. The Court based their objections on the ground that the District or "Zillah" judges were already so fully employed that they needed assistance in the performance of their own duties rather than being capable of undertaking any addition to them. To the plan of transferring police duties to the Session judges, the Sudder Court were decidedly opposed under the apprehension that it would be quite impossible for them to get through the work and that the plan would eventually prove a total failure. The Court, therefore, recommended the appointment of separate officers exclusively for police duties.

In compliance with the above suggestions of the Court of Sudder Dewani Adalut, Allahabad, Metcalfe had caused the provision regarding the transfer of police duties to be omitted from the draft of the Act as originally published.[15] As regards the other objections of the Sudder Court, the Government of Agra were informed that the provisions of Act VII of 1835 to which the court objected, were merely permissive and that they were not to be carried into effect where the duties of the Session judge were so onerous as to prevent his discharging with efficiency any additional duties.[16]

Act for Contempt of Court

The Government of Fort St. George forwarded for the consideration of the Governor General of India in Council the draft of an enactment intended to limit the period of imprisonment for Contempt of Court under Section XXII, Regulation III of 1802 of the Madras Code.[17] In a letter dated the 7th October, 1835, the Registrar of the Madras Sudder Adalut had given a concise statement of the grounds which suggested the necessity of the proposed Act.[18] Metcalfe, therefore, forwarded the draft along with the correspondence to the Law Commissioners for their consideration at the proper place in the general Code which they were formulating.[19] But the Law Commissioners adverted to the possibility of persons being confined for an indefinite time under Section XXII. Regulation III of 1802 of the Madras Code, and suggested that immediate provision should be made to remedy so serious an evil, without waiting for the enactment of the general Code[20]. The Law

Commissioners also submitted the draft of an Act for giving effect to their suggestion in which they provided that no person should be kept in custody under the authority of the Section quoted above, for a term exceeding three months.

The draft of the Act received from the Law Commission was adopted by the Governor General in Council with a slight alteration as to the period of confinement, two months being substituted for three.[21] The draft originally received from the Madras Government specified two months as the period of confinement under the proposed Act, and this period also corresponded with the rules on the subject in force in the Presidency of Bengal. The draft of the Act was read for the first time[22] in the Council of India on 11th January, 1836, and was finally passed by the Governor General in Council on the 7th March, 1836, as Act No. VI of 1836.[23]

The appointment of Indian Justices of Peace in Calcutta for the first time, during the Governor Generalship of Sir Charles Metcalfe also helped in the disposal of petty cases in the city. The idea of appointing Indian Justices of Peace had been mooted by Lord William Bentinck as for back as 1833.[24] The Chief Magistrate of Calcutta, Mr. Mc Farlan, on being called upon to give his opinion on the subject, stated that respectable Indian gentleman would be useful as Justices of Peace for sitting with European Magistrates in "cases of petty assault, in the Conservancy Department and more particularly in that of assessing and enforcing payment of house tax".[25] Mr. Mc Farlan also thought that they would further be useful in legalising the proceedings of the Magistracy in many cases in which the European Magistrates were compelled to sit singly for want of adequate officers of that class, but in which the law, as it then stood, required that two judges should decide the cases. The two judges of the Supreme Court of Judicature at Calcutta, Sir Edward Ryan and Sir John Franks, on being consulted by the Government of India on the subject, stated that they anticipated "much benefit from the appointment of able, upright and intelligent Native Gentlemen to the Office of Justice of Peace", and they were both of opinion that the measure should be carried into effect immediately.[26] Lord William Bentinck, therefore, had recorded a Minute dated the 17th March, 1835, in which he mentioned a list of twelve Hindu gentlemen of Calcutta, whom he proposed for the office of Justices of Peace.[27]

On assuming the office of the Governor General of India, Sir Charles Metcalfe reconsidered the whole subject and finally determined to appoint for the time being only three individuals as Justices of Peace, and directed that their names might be included in the new Commission.[28] These three individuals were Radha Kant Deb, Dwarka Nath Tagore and Mr. James Kyd. The first two gentlemen were Hindus, while the third one was an East Indian. Metcalfe proposed to increase the list of Indian Justices of Peace as fit individuals presented themselves for the post.[29] But this was undoubtedly an important step as it was the first time any Indian was appointed as a Justice of Peace.

Act for Production of Evidence

In order to expedite the disposal of cases and to avoid unnecessary delay in referring to previous enactments while deciding cases. Sir Charles Metcalfe passed an Act (Act X of 1835), providing that the production of a Government Gazette of any Presidency containing an Act purporting to have been passed by the Governor General of India in Council, was to be held in all Courts as sufficient evidence that such an Act had been passed.[30] Mr. H.T. Prinsep, who was one of the members of the Governor General's Council, had objected to the passing of the above Act in a Minute dated the 13th June, 1835. He based his objections on the ground that a comprehensive law incorporating all the points regarding the promulgation of the Acts was necessary, and that the passing of one distinct Act to provide for one particular point only was not justified. Mr. Prinsep had also special objections to the principle of the Act itself, and though that the old rule which made the authenticity depend on the Acts issuing from the Government Printing Office, was preferable.[31]

Mr. T.B. Macaulay (afterwards Lord Macaulay), who was the Law Member of the Governor General's Council, replied to Mr. Prinsep's objections in a Minute dated the 14th June, 1835. He stated that, it being admitted that some similar law was eventually to be made on the subject, the Act under dispute served the purpose equally well, and fulfilled the immediate requirements of the Courts. As regards the objections to the Act itself, Mr. Macaulay stated that no good evidence that had existed before as to the passing of Acts, was to be rendered null and void by the proposed Act, which only sought to add one more mode of proof, and that an easy one, to the other modes existing previously.[32] The other members of the Governor Generals Council also did not concur in Mr. Prinsep's objections to the proposed Act, and agreed with the views of Mr. Macaulay as the expediency of passing such an enactment. It was, therefore, finally passed by the Governor General of India in Council on 6th July, 1835, as Act No. X of 1835.[33]

With a view to ensure the effective enforcement of the above Act, Sir Charles Metcalfe directed that all notices connected with the legislative proceedings of the Governor General of India in Council be inserted in the Official Gazettes of the subordinate Presidencies of Madras and Bombay.[34] For this purpose the Governor General in Council passed a Resolution on the 31st August, 1835, regarding the manner in which it was decided to distribute the Acts which related to the whole of British India and those which were applicable exclusively to the Presidencies of Fort St. George and Agra.[35] In communication with the Governments of Fort St. George and Bombay, it was also decided to transmit only three copies of each Act to those Presidencies, it being considered more economical to print them in the Presidencies concerned than at Calcutta. Each of the subordinate Governments was to be supplied for purposes of record and reference, with copies of all the Acts passed by the Governor General of India in Council, even when they related exclusively to different Governments.[36]

Reform of Jail Administration

As connected with the judicial administration of the country, the administration of jails also received due attention at the hands of Sir Charles Metcalfe. When Metcalfe assumed the Office of the Governor General, the condition of jails in India was far from satisfactory. The prisoners housed in these jails were treated like herds of cattle, and at certain places was followed the cruel and unwarrantable practice of chaining prisoners together during the night. There was no system of classification of convicts so as to separate prisoners convicted of the more ignominious offences from those of a less heinous character. This defeated the very objects of punishment, viz., the reformation of the offender and the benefit of the community at large.

Even the Alipore jail near Calcutta in the immediate neighbourhood of the seat of the Supreme Government of India where "the greatest quantity of European intelligence and power is concentrated," was in a shameful condition. Hundreds of the worst and most desperate criminals were assembled there, and they were all collected in one great body. They were, therefore, quite capable of overpowering any resistance put up by the persons who had their charge, when their passions were aroused.[37] And this was not a mere hypothetical supposition. Towards the middle of the year 1835, these convicts had murdered their Superintending Magistrate, and no visitor could enter the gates of the jail without danger. The condition of other jails in the interior of the country can very well be imagined by a comparison with that of the Alipore jail, which was so bear the seat of the Government in India.

The mode of employment of the convicts was also defective. They were generally employed as labourers in constructing roads, etc. Their services were also sometimes loaned to the Military department for similar purposes. There are instances where the entire inmates of certain jails were placed under the Military department. Thus on a requisition from the Military department, all the available prisoners housed in the Hansi jail, about 250 in number, were placed at the disposal of that department[38] to be employed as laboures for the improvement of the cantonment at that Station. During the period the convicts were thus employed, they were left entirely at the mercy of their Guards, who treated them most ruthlessly. The ill-treatment of these guards sometimes drove the prisoners to desperation and they either rebelled against the guards and attacked them, or tried to make good their escape. But invariably, the convicts had the worst of these encounters. Being roused by momentary passions, their plans were ill-conceived and badly executed, and almost always resulted in great bloodshed. Many convicts were killed or wounded, while only few could escape or average themselves upon their guards. To quote a typical example, out of a gang of 272 prisoners at work in a village in Hansi district, who were alleged to have attempted to escape, 52 were killed, 21 wounded and 8 effected their escape, while only two of the guards were wounded. The Court of Directors observed[39] on this occasion that there did not appear to be any premeditated scheme of rising upon the guards since the convicts neither waited for night to execute their design (though not confined in a jail, but encamped in an open space), nor selected that period of the day when the implements of labour in their hands might have served the purpose of offensive weapons. They were of opinion that the occurrence appeared to have originated at the moment due to some ill-treatment on the part of one of the guards towards one of the convicts which was resented and was instantly followed by a scene of general confusion, in which it was apprehended that the prisoners would effect their escape. The Court of Directors also observed that the obvious inference drawn from the loss of so many lives and the infliction of so much suffering on the above occasion, was that imprisonment in its practical application "is not that moderate and regulated species of punishment which might be supposed under a system of criminal justice in which it is so freely resorted to".[40]

The medical facilities available in the jail hospitals were also most unsatisfactory, with the result that the incidence of sickness and mortality was considerably high. During the period of absence of Civil Surgeons on leave, the jail hospitals were occasionally left entirely in the hands of untrained Indian doctors, whose skill and competency could hardly be relied on. The members of the Medical Board at Fort William were, therefore, compelled to suggest for the consideration of the Governor General in Council the expediency of the measure to render it imperative on medical officers attached to Civil Stations, on occasions of their obtaining leave of absence, to continue in the performance of their duties until arrangements were made by the superintending Surgeons for relieving them.[41]

The plight of the prisoners under sentences of transportation, was worse still. The prescribed punishment for such prisoners was "hard labour in Irons on the Roads or other Public Works" at the place of their transportation. That this punishment was strictly enforced is evident from a report[42] of the Sudder Faujdari Adalut of the residency of Madras, in which it was pointed out to the Supreme Government that the convicts transported from Madras to Malacca were employed in a mode altogether at variance with their sentence of hard labour, and as such operated "rather as an encouragement to, than a preventive of crime". The Governor General in Council, therefore, suggested to the Government of Madras that convicts sentenced to transportation at that Presidency might be sent to the Tenasserim Provinces, where they were more likely to meet with suitable discipline.[43] The Madras Government having adopted the above suggestion, necessary instructions were accordingly issued by the Government of India to the Commissioner in the Tenasserim Provinces to receive the Madras convicts and to make the requisite arrangements for their accommodation and safe custody.[44]

The heavy cost of transporting prisoners to places like New South Wales was another factors which presented obstacles in the way of proper execution of sentences of punishment. Moreover, considerable difficulty was experienced in procuring passage for the convicts to be transported to New South Wales. In December, 1835, the Government of Fort St. George brought to the notice of the Supreme Government that some of the convicts in the Madras jail under sentence of transportation to New South Wales, had been in confinement for more than seven months since their conviction, owing to the difficulty experienced in sending them to their destination.[45] The Madras Government, therefore, solicited the instructions of the Governor General of India in Council for the disposal of such convicts. The Governor of Madras was informed in reply that the same difficulty which existed at Madras, was also experienced at Calcutta in procuring vessels for the conveyance of convicts to New South Wales.

An important point for consideration in this connection was the inconvenience which was felt by the authorities in Van Diemen's Land, owing to the detention at that place for several weeks of convicts bound for New South Wales. The vessels in which they were conveyed, usually stopped at Van Dieman's Land on their way to New South Wales, and this necessitated the detention of the convicts at that place. In order to obviate the above difficulty, the Court of Directors in their Judicial despatch dated the 7th April, 1835, had directed the Governor General of India in Council "to take into consideration the expediency of passing a Law, authorising and directing the courts under each Presidency to pass sentence of transportation in future to such place as the Government may appoint.[46] The Governor General in Council referred the matter to the judges of the Supreme Court at Calcutta for their opinion, and added that it was deemed desirable also to provide in this connection against the inconvenience arising out of the existing state of the law relating to the commutation of sentences and the pardoning of offences. The judges were requested to state whether in their opinion there was any objection to "the enactment of a Law providing that the Governments of the several Presidencies of India should be empowered on the recommendation of the judges to commute sentences passed, and to pardon offenders convicted by the Supreme Courts".[47] In reply the judges of the Supreme Court at Calcutta stated that they thought it very expedient that the power of mitigating the severity of the laws should exist in India, but they thought that it was equally important to decide whether an Act vesting this power in the Governments of the several Presidencies would not come within the exception of the laws and regulations exempted from the authority of the Legislative Council of India, and as such, would not in any way affect the prerogative of the Crown. On these grounds the judges abstained from recommending the enactment of the law proposed by the Governor General in Council.[48]

Sir Charles Metcalfe attached great importance to this question, and conveyed his sentiments to the Court of Directors in a separate letter.[49] He stated that in his opinion "a collision of opinion between any of His Majesty's Judges and your Government is an evil to be avoided as far as practicable. We feel that it may be objectionable to qualify the exception as to our Legislative authority which provides against our interfering with the King's Prerogative...but it is obvious that so long as such an exception exists, which in necessarily not specific in its nature continual objections may be raised to the exercise of our Legislative authority, on the ground of its being at variance with the provision in question".[50] Metcalfe, therefore, pointed out to the Court of Directors the expediency of adopting measures for procuring an Act of Parliament to be passed to the effect that all Courts of Justice in India as well as His Majesty's Supreme Court of Judicature and others be required in the first instance to pay implicit obedience to any laws which may be promulgated by the authority of the Governor General of India in Council, whatever may be the legal doubts as to their validity, leaving such doubts "to be solved by the authorities to which we are in common subordinate".[51] He emphasised the point that the object of granting legislative powers to the Government of India would be frustrated to a great degree if any court in British India supposed themselves to have powers of rejecting laws enacted under its authority. Metcalfe, therefore, postponed the enactment of the proposed law regarding the commutation of sentences and the pardoning of offices until "all doubts with regard to our powers should be definitely set at rest by an authority which none can dispute.[52]

Leaving aside the legal aspect of the question, the facts enumerated in the proceedings pages regarding the condition of prisoners in India, prove conclusively that immediate reform was needed in the sphere. The ever-watchful eye of the Hon'ble T.B. Macaulay (afterwards Lord Macaulay), Law Members of the Governor General's Council, was quick to spot the trouble in keeping with his tradition, Macaulay recorded a brilliant Minute[53] dated the 14th December, 1835, in which he set forth the imperative need for the immediate reform of the jails in India. He stated that the best Criminal Code could be of very little use to a community, unless there was a good machinery for the infliction of punishment. Death was rarely inflicted in British India at that time, and the practice of flogging had been abolished. The punishment of transportation was so expensive, to say nothing of other objections, that it could be employed only in a small number of cases. Imprisonment was, therefore, the punishment which was chiefly trusted. It was probably resorted to in ninety-nine cases out of every hundred. Macaulay was, therefore, of opinion that it was extremely important to establish such regulations as would make imprisonment a terror to wrongdoers, and at the same time prevent it from being attended by any circumstances shocking to humanity. He stated that "Unless this be done, the Code, whatever credit it may do to its Authors in the opinion of European jurists, will be utterly useless to the people for whose benefit it is intended".[54]

Macaulay also pointed out in the above Minute the various evils which then existed in Indian jails, and suggested the immediate appointment of a Committee for the purpose of collecting information on the state of Indian prisons and of preparing an improved plan of prison discipline. He particularly recommended that the Committee be instructed to report on the state of the jail at Alipore, and to suggest such reforms as might make that place a model for other prisons in India.

Sir Charles Metcalfe entirely concurred in the propositions contained in Mr. Macaulay's Minute and in a Resolution[55] dated the 21st December 1835, nominated the following gentlemen to form a Committee for the purposes contemplated by Mr. Macaulay:

1. Hon'ble H. Shakespeare Esqr., President,
2. The Hon'ble Sir E. Ryan,
3. The Hon'ble T.B. Macaulay Esqr.,
4. The Hon'ble Sir J.P. Grant,
5. The Hon'ble Sir B.K. Malkin,
6. C.H. Cameron Esquire,

7. J.M. Macleod Esquire,
8. G.W. Anderson Esquire,
9. C.R. Barwell Esquire,
10. D. Mc Farlan Esquire, and
11. J.P. Grant Esquire.

Mr. J.P. Grant, who was Deputy Secretary to the Government of India in the Legislature Department, was also requested to take upon himself the duties of the Secretary to the Committee.

The above was quite a high-powered Committee as it included the Members of the Governor General's Council, the Judges of the Supreme Court at Calcutta, the Members of the newly appointed Indian Law Commission, the Chief Magistrate of Calcutta and other high functionaries. Letters were addressed to these individuals in order to obtain their consent to their nomination as members of the Prison Reforms Committee. On receiving the consent of all the members, their appointments were announced in the Calcutta Gazette.[56] The Government of India also directed all public officers to pay prompt attention to any requisition which might be made to them by the order of the Committee in connection with the object of their appointment.[57]

In furtherance of the above measures adopted by the Governor General in Council, the Government of Bengal was called upon to furnish a report as to the internal management of the Alipore jail showing the treatment of the prisoners, the nature of the labour to which they were subjected, the mode of their confinement or classification, and generally the means used is that establishment for the reformation of the offenders.[58] A statement furnished by the Medical Board of the Bengal Presidency, containing a return of the sick prisoners in the various jails throughout the Presidencies of Bengal and Agra, and exhibiting the number of persons confined, the ratio per cent of the sick to the entire number and the ratio of the number of deaths to the total strength of prisoners, was also forwarded to the Committees of Prison Reforms for their information.[59] Captain Paton, the first Assistant to the Resident at Lucknow, submitted for the consideration and orders of the Government of India a draft of rules proposed by him for the better administration of Indian jails, together with a copy of an American pamphlet on the subject. There papers were also forwarded to the Prison Reforms Committee for their consideration.

Although the result of the labours of the Committee appointed by Sir Charles Metcalfe for the improvement of jails in India could not be known during the period of his Governor Generalship, credit must certainly be given to him for taking certain concrete and constructive measures for the betterment of this important but much neglected branch of administration. These measures were not only justified, but were urgently needed on grounds of justice and humanity alike.

REFERENCES

1. Home, Judl. (Civil), Cons, 25th May, 1835, Nos. 6-12.
2. *Ibid.*
3. Home, Judl. (Civil), Cons, 11th February, 1835, No. 3.
4. Home, Judl, Letters to Court, No. 13 of 1835, dated 28th September, 1835, para, 30.
5. *Ibid.* paras, 32-34.
6. Home, Judl. (Civil), Cons, 22nd June, 1835, Nos. 8-10.
7. Home, Judl. (Civil), Cons, 8th June, 1835, Nos. 2-4.
8. Home, Judl. (Civil), Cons., Ist June, 1835, Nos. 10-12.
9. Home, Judl. Cons., 23rd January, 1835, Nos. 1-4.
10. Home, Judl., Letters to Court, No. 13 of 1835, dated 28th September, 1835, paras, 39-40.
11. *Ibid.* para 41.
12. Home, Judl, Cons, 30th November, 1835, Nos. 11-13.
13. Leg, Cons, 11th January, 1835, Nos. 1-4.

14. Home, Judl. (Criminal), Cons, 29th June, 1835, Nos. 5-8.
15. Home, Judl., Letters to Court, No. 7 of 1835, dated 20th July, 1835, paras 8-16.
16. Home, Judl, Letters to Court, No. 17 of 1835, dated 16th November, 1835, paras 95-97.
17. Leg., Cons, 7th December, 1835, Nos. 1-5.
18. *Ibid.*
19. Leg., Letters to Court, No. 4 of 1836, dated 29th February, 1836, paras 32-34.
20. Leg., Cons, 11th January, 1836, Nos. 15-18.
21. *Ibid.*
22. *Ibid.* No. 16.
23. Leg., Cons, 7th March, 1836, No. 2.
24. Home, Judl., (Criminal), Cons, 26th April, 1833. No. 11.
25. *Ibid.*, No. 13.
26. Home, Judl. (Criminal), Cons., 20th April, 1835, Nos. 1-2.
27. *Ibid.*, No. 4.
28. Home, Judl. (Criminal), Cons, 2 May, 1835, No. 20.
29. Home, Judl., Letters to Court, No. 17 of 1835, dated the 16th November, 1835, para. 18.
30. Leg., Cons., 6th July, 1835, Nos. 2-6.
31. *Ibid.*
32. Leg., Letters to Court, No. 2 of 1835, dated 24th August, 1835, para, 40.
33. *Ibid.*, para 44.
34. Leg., Cons., 20th July, 1835, Nos. 6-8; and 21st September, 1835, No. 40.
35. Leg., Cons, 31st August, 1835, No. 28.
36. Leg., Letters to Court, No. 2 of 1836, dated 1st February, 1836, para 89.
37. Leg., Progs., 21st December, 1835, No. 1.
38. Home Judl. (Criminal), Cons., 31st December, 1834, Nos. 19-20.
39. Home, Judl., Letters from Court, No. 8 of 1836, dated 30th December, 1836, para 21.

    This letter was sent to reply to Home, Judl, Letter to Court, No. 2 of 1835, dated 28 February, 1835, which contains a narrative of the Miscellaneous Judicial Proceedings having reference to the Western Provinces from 1st January to 14th November 1834, i.e., the period immediately preceding Sir Charles Metcalfe's Governor Generalship.

40. *Ibid.* para 22.
41. Home, Medical Board Proceedings, 8th February, 1836, No. 9 (Letter No. 928, dated 5th February, 1836, addressed to the Governor General of India in Council).
42. Home, Judl., Cons, 14th September, 1835, No. 1-4.
43. Home, Judl (Criminal), Cons, 30th November, 1835, Nos. 1-3.
44. Home, Judl, Letters to Court No. 2 of 1836, dated 12th February, 1836, paras, 20-21.
45. Home, Judl, Cons, 7th December, 1835, Nos. 3-4.
46. Home, Judl., Letters from Court, No. 1 of 1835, dated 7th April, 1835, para. 2.
47. Leg., Cons., 16th November, 1835, Nos. 2-5.
48. Leg., Cons., 14th December, 1835, Nos. 1-3.
49. Leg, Letters to Court, No. 3 of 1836, dated 15th February, 1836.
50. *Ibid.*, para 3.
51. *Ibid.*
52. *Ibid.*
53. Leg., Progs, 21st December, 1835, No. 1.
54. *Ibid.* The "Code" referred to was the Criminal Code which the Law Commissioners were engaged in compiling at that time.
55. *Ibid.*, No. 2
56. Leg., Cons., 25 December, 1835, Nos. 30-36.
57. Leg., Letters to Court, No. 4 of 1836, dated 29th February, 1836, para 48.
58. Home, Judl., Letters to Court, No. 3 of 1836, dated 3rd March, 1836, para. 33.
59. Home, Judl., Cons., 7th December, 1835, Nos. 9-10.

8

Ranjit Singh and the Sikh State

The Civil Administration

"Governing is an art," wrote Sir Lepel Griffin, "which may no doubt be brilliantly practised without special training by some men of exceptional genius".[1] and Ranjit Singh indeed was a monarch who could be counted as one of such men.

According to some writers, Ranjit Singh was a ruthless autocrat with all the three estates, Legislatures, Executive and Judiciary concentrated in him. But this may perhaps seem too violent an estimate of his character. That by his very nature Ranjit Singh was not well disposed towards autocracy, is proved beyond doubt when we study his habits and activities more intimately. Tradition thus says, when once the Maharaja visited the Golden Temple at Amritsar, Akali Phula Singh checked him on the way for having transgressed certain essential Sikh laws and customs. The Maharaja immediately offered his naked back to be flogged as a punishment.

The humility of Ranjit Singh is proverbial. He never appropriated to himself the high sounding titles nor did he run the government in his own name. His government was named as *Sarkar-i-Khalsa*, or the Government of the Khalsa. On his coins there was the inscription of *Nanak Sahai* or

Gobind Sahai, the word *Sahai* meaning 'protection of'. His State Seal bore the inscription *Shri Akali Sahai* or 'God, our help'. Cunningham writes of him: "Whether in walking barefooted to make his obeisance to a collateral representative of his prophets, or in rewarding a soldier distinguished by a long and ample beard, or in restraining the excesses of the fanatical Akali, or in being an army and acquiring a province, he always made it appear that everything was one for the sake of the Guru, for the advantage of the Khalsa, and in the name of Lord".[2]

Guru Gobind Singh had a drum named *Ranjit Nagara,* and Ranjit Singh used to say that he was a drum of the great Guru. He, according to Payne, "assumed few of the outward signs of royalty. His dress was invariably of simplest description, his only ornaments, even on state occasions being a string of pearls about his waist and the Kohinur on his wrist. He never wore a royal head-dress, and he never used a throne".[3] He once remarked to Baron Van Huge. "My sword is all the distinction I require".[3]

Clearly thus, Ranjit Singh did not have the disposition of an autocrat. But even if he tried to be so, circumstances were not such as to permit it. The elements of the commonwealth of Sikhs which had been so thoroughly diffused into the social fabric of this community by Guru Gobind Singh, and according to which the authority of the *Panj Piyaras,* or the 'Five Beloved Ones' was supposed to be superior even to that of the Guru himself, were too strong among the Sikhs yet to permit of any autocracy. Nor was the Maharaja, despite the efforts of his life-time, able to discipline the freebooters among the Akalis who were the armed guardians of Amritsar, the censors of the Sikh morals. The Punjab chiefs though weakened, still had the powers of which the Maharaja could not dispossess them. The instance of a powerful Dogra family at Lahore before whom the Maharaja himself sometimes felt helpless, cannot be too often quoted.

Nor was the power and freedom-loving spirit of the soldiers and the people of the Punjab themselves to be underestimated. They conquered territories not so that some personal whim of the Maharaja be satisfied, but that the name of the Khalsa and their Guru be glorified. Very often the Maharaja made conquests against his own desires, so that his soldiers be kept busy lest they should fall on him. And for the masses, particularly Sikh, everyone whether young or old, was a soldier. They had seen ages of warfare, and had not yet been disarmed. Their very character was such in the midst of which autocrats could ill-thrive.

Yet, when all this is said, it cannot be denied that Ranjit Singh was a very powerful monarch. The only thing to be remembered here is that if he was strong, he served the people and they loved him to be so. Ranjit Singh was their leader, and the famous dictum of Mr. Gandhi may here be applied for him: "Here go the people I must follow them, because I am their leader".

The Central Government

In the centre the king was the pivot of all administration and consulted whomsoever he would and did as he liked, though being careful as to what he should like and what he should dislike. He was assisted by five ministers, the Chief Minister of whom was the highest in authority, this office being occupied by persons such as Raja Dhian Singh in whom he had great confidence. Next in importance was the Foreign Minister whose office was held by Faqir Aziz-ud-din, whose advice was taken by the Maharaja even in his private affairs. Then came his Defence Minister who was the same perhaps as the Commander-in-Chief of the Maharaja's forces. Dewan Mohkam Chand, Misr Dewan Chand and Hari Singh Nalwa occupied this office. There was also a Finance Minister, Bhawani Das or Dina Nath. And then the *Sadar-i-Deori* or the Minister of the royal household who was important because he came in a closer contact with the Maharaja and therefore had a better possibility of promotions; even Raja Dhian Singh having been promoted from this office.

There were as many as twelve administrative departments in the centre, the more important among them being: (1) *Daftar-i-Abwab ul-Mal* which was in charge of the accounts of land revenue and other taxes and sources of income; (2) *Daftar-i-Tozihat* which was in charge of the royal household expenses, and which kept record of the royal harem; (3) *Daftar-i-Mawajab* was in charge of the accounts of the salaries of the military personnel and civil servants; (4) while *Daftar-i-Roznamcha kharch* kept the accounts of the daily expenses of the Maharaja.

The Local Administration

The state was divide into four provinces: Kashmir or *Janat-i-Nazir*, Multan or *Dar-ul-Aman*, Peshawar and Lahore. Besides these there were the hill principalities which paid their tribute direct to the Maharaja; and there were Sardars and Nawabs who had been dispossessed of their own states, but were granted liberal *jagirs* within which they were permitted autocratic rights.

Every province, known as Suba, was further divided into *Parganas;* the Parganas were divided into *Taluqs,* and each *Taluq* consisted of *Mauzas* the number of which varied between 50 and 100. The principles on which the divisions were made, were administrative convenience revenue-facilities and the tribal affinity of the inhabitants.

Officer incharge of every *Suba* was known as *Nazim,* and was always a person who enjoyed a very close confidence of the Maharaja. Next came *Kardar* who was the head of a division of the province, and whose office in fact was more important in being concerned with the day-to-day administration; the Nazim's office being more an appellate than of original character. The powers and duties of a *Kardar* within his division being wide, he was more truly a reflection in his division of King in the centre. In was the *Kardar* who supervised land revenue settlements and acted as a Revenue Collector. He was an accountant as well as a treasurer, judge as well as a magistrate, and Customs officer as well as an Excise officer. He supervised every branch of administration within his division, and no often did the appeals go above him to the office of the *Nazim,* he generally being the final authority within his part of the province.

Of the above mentioned four provinces, those of Lahore and Multan were better governed; while from Peshawar and Kashmir complaints of inefficiency were often received, and the Maharaja had sometimes to reprimand their officials.

According to another view, supported by Dr. Sinha[5], the country was rather divided directly into districts, and not into provinces. Three types of persons were put in the administrative charge of these districts: *firstly,* those appointed from the centre and known as *Kardars secondly,* those who were men of local influence and importance such as Dewan Sawan Mal of Multan, who occupied the office on the hereditary basis, paying an annual tribute or revenue, and seldom reporting their internal affairs to the centre; and *thirdly,* those who were military chiefs holding feudal demesnes, in return for providing a contingent of soldiers when required, their powers within their territories being unlimited.

The most important feature of the local administration was the *panchayat* or a committee fielders which existed in every *mauza* or a village, and which enjoyed wide powers within its jurisdiction. Dr. Sinha writes: "so much sanctity was attached to these panchayats that no party dared tell lies before them".[6] Every village was almost a self-sufficient unit in which land was held by its inhabitants jointly on *Bhaichara basis.*

The administration of the city of Lahore was independent of the general division of the country. It was divided into *Mohallas,* each of which was placed incharge of a locally influential man. *Kotwal* was the chief police officer who enjoyed wide powers for the maintenance of law and order, and was generally a Muslim; the most important being Mian Imam Bakhsh. For deciding the civil cases of the Muslims, a special officer known as Qazi was appointed.

The Financial Administration

The modern principles of economy could hardly be expected to have been known in the Punjab of Ranjit Singh. There was no budget system, and the money was secured as it was needed.

Land Revenue

Of the total income of the state which amounted to 3 crore rupees, 2 crores came from the Land Revenue, which therefore was an important source of income.

Several experiments were performed in the time of the Maharaja, in the methods of revenue assessment. And these methods also varied to suit a particular type of soil, and particular type of community.

Batai

This system which had been inherited by Ranjit Singh from the Mughals, continued to prevail till the year 1823. Under this system, land revenue was assessed on the threshing floor after the harvest had been gathered and the payment was received in kind. This system had a defect: a large force of officials was required to keep a watch over the cultivators from the time of sowing seeds to the time of harvesting, lest any portion of the crop should be misappropriated; and this besides being expensive, was no less cumbersome.

Kankut System

Because of its defects, the *Batai* system was replaced in 1824 by the *Kankut* system under which the revenue was assessed at the standing crop; taking its representative field and estimating the yield–of which a portion was claimed in kind. The new system was better in the respect that the assessment being made earlier, the supervision of the affairs of the cultivators, right up to the threshing floor was now no more necessary. Still, the system suffered from defects. No correct estimate of the yield could be made beforehand, nor did the basing of the calculations only on the representative field ensure the equitableness of the assessment. From 1835, therefore, the state began sometimes to follow a new practice of farming out land for 3 to 6 years to the highest bidders.

Cash Payment

The system of cash payment took the place of the *Kankut* system towards the end of Ranjit Singh's reign; and under this cash payments replaced the payments in kind. The state, however, never showed any strictness in its application, as either party could revert to the older system at any time.

Mixed System

At certain places sometimes the Mixed System was applied, under which some crops paid in kind; while others such as of sugar-cane, cotton and tobacco which defied any correct estimate of their produce, paid in cash.

The basis on which the estimates of the assessment were drawn, also varied. In certain parts of the Punjab, such as the Attock district, the estimates were drawn on the *bigha* basis, whereby an estimate on a representative *bigha* (a measurement of land) was applied to the whole of that part of the country. The estimates having been made, the price of the assessment was fixed, which the village money-lender was asked to pay in cash; he being helped by the *Kardar* in turn to collect his dues from the cultivators in kind. In certain parts, assessment was made on the basis of *plough*, where instead of taking a representative, *Bigha*, estimates were drawn on a unit of 15 acres of land which an average team of bullocks could easily cultivate. On the irrigated land on the other hand a lump sum amount was fixed on a unit of land which an average well could irrigate, and this rate was applied all over the irrigated area.

The different district settlement reports tell us that different types prevailed at different places to suit the local conditions of soil. In a major part of the country, however, *Batai* system worked in the early years of Ranjit Singh's reign, to be replaced later on by the *Kankut* and then by cash payments.

Regarding the principles of assessment, Dr. G.S. Dhillon says, the Government demand was made on the "basis of the state ownership of land," under which a cultivator was ejected if he failed to pay the rent in time. Regarding the rate of demand, the most fertile land according to Dr. Dhillon, Sinha and Chopra, paid as much as 50 per cent of its produce, while the less fertile land paid, according to Lord Lawrence; $\frac{2}{3}$ or $\frac{1}{3}$ or $\frac{1}{4}$ of the total produce. If land was held by certain state officials such as *Mukaddams* who assisted in revenue collections, the rate was still lower. Sometimes a whole *Taluq* would be leased out to a *Kardar* who made a fixed cash payment, and made his own settlement with his cultivators.

The cultivators, on the whole, writes Dr. Dhillon, paid "according to their capacity to pay and Adam Smith's famous canon of Taxation, i.e., 'equality of sacrifice,' was effectively applied".[7]

Collection and Remittance

The collection of the land revenue was made twice a year, about a month after the harvest by *Mukaddams,* helped by *Chaudhris*. The revenue thus collected was remitted to the *Kardar* who deposited it in the district treasury, from where after defraying the local expenses the balance was remitted to Lahore, in the shape of *hundis* which according to Shahmat Ali were drawn upon the bankers of Amritsar.

Customs and Excise

Besides land, Customs and Excise were the other important source of revenue, which brought to Ranjit Singh

Rs. 16,00,000 a year. The Punjab Administration Report of 1849 reported that the Sikh kingdom had been dotted over with an innumerable custom barriers, the custom lines crossing one another irregularly. All articles paid duties irrespective of their origin or destination, nor was a distinction made between articles of luxury and necessity. Even the agricultural produce which had already paid the land revenue, did not escape. And then, these articles did not pay the charges only once. As they passed from one side of the country to the other, at every place where a customs line was crossed, payment was made, so that before reaching their destination they had their original price doubled and even more.

Still, the customs could not have been too oppressive, in which case, as according to Dr. Sinha, the merchants could easily have changed their routes, and conveyed "their goods through the territory of a less exacting chief".[8] Nor could the system be judged by any contemporary European standard, or a standard of the modern times. Under the principles of economy as they then were known in India, Ranjit Sinha's system served its purpose, which is obvious from the fact that despite all its defects commerce in the country flourished.

Other Sources of Income

Yet another source of income was the *Jagirs,* which were granted for meritorious services and for gallantry in the army and which according to Shahmat Ali[9] brought an annual revenue of Rs. 87,54,590, though Princes estimated it at Rs. 1,09,28,000. The monopolies also brought their revenue. Of the eight salt mines, four were worked and the monopolies in them brought a revenue of Rs. 8,00,000. The monopolies in the distillation of spirit and in the manufacture of drugs also made their contribution.

The income from the judicial proceeds, known as *Moharana* according to Prinsep[10], added another Rs. 5,77,000 a year. While the income from *Abwabs,* which were small cesses levied with land revenue, varied between 5 and 15 per cent of the land revenue.

Then, there were the professional taxes. All the principal artisans such as weavers, blacksmiths, tanners paid one rupee per house a year, the inferior workmen or *Kamins* paid half a rupee and traders between a rupee and two.[11]

Jagirs were granted only for the life-time of a grantee and lapsed to the State after his death. And when there was a serious emergency even the State employees had to make their contributions, as for instance in 1825 when the French generals in the Maharaja's service and their regiments were asked to forego their salaries for two months.

Expenditure

The state being yet only in its territorial growth, the most important item of its expenditure was military which according to Shahmat Ali[12] claimed Rs. 1,27,96,482 a year. And then after this came the expenditure on the civil administration and other such items.

The taxation system as discussed above, may thus appear crude to the modern observer, but writes Dr. G.S. Dhillon, "allowing a due concession for the conditions under which it had to be worked out, there is scarcely any justification for such an impression.[13] The Maharaja's government in fact being a national government, money merely changed hands. If it was taken with one hand, it was returned with the other, so that the wealth of the country remained with the people of the country themselves. It was not exported abroad and therefore the system even if oppressive, was tolerable.

The Judicial Administration

There existed no written constitution or law under Ranjit Singh. Customs and usages formed the basis of justice, and religion worked behind them to supply the necessary inspiration. Whim of a judge also played its part sometimes, but it lay open to everybody to carry his appeal to the higher authorities, though not in the sense as it is done in the present times. The strange thing was that with the background of centuries of the Sikhs-Muslim strife, the Maharaja established a perfectly secular judicial system in which each community got its justice according to its own customs and prejudices, and no interference was made.

The Muslims in the country thus continued getting their justice from the Qazis who ordained marriage ceremonies, decided religious cases of the Muslims, expounded the local law and declared the recorded facts.

Justice was more local than national. And it was essentially a source of income, as no chance of securing money was missed, though effort was made to be as honest in the fact of a case as possible.

The fountain-held of justice was in the King himself, who heard appeals above the highest court of the State and intervened to see that justice in a court was properly dispensed. Next to him in authority was the *Adalat-i-Ala,* or the Central Court, the High Court, which was situated at Lahore, the headquarters of the State, and heard appeals above the courts of *Nazims* and *Kardars* before they went to the King himself. Then there were the special *Adalti* courts instituted in the cities of Amritsar and Peshawar which decided cases both civil and criminal within the respective cities.

The highest court in a province was that of the *Nazim,* the authority of which was mainly appellate and which heard the appeals above the court of the *Kardars*. The *Kardar's* court was at the head of every district, and it heard cases civil as well as criminal. Village *panchayats* administered justice in the villages in which they were accorded a special recognition and respect by the State.

Besides, there were the *Jagirdari* courts held by *Jagirdars,* whether Hindu, Muslim or Sikh, which enjoyed autocratic rights within their jurisdiction, both civil and criminal, and ordinarily the subjects of the *Jagirdars* could not bring their appeals to the regular courts of the State.

Punishments

The penal code of Ranjit Singh was not very harsh. Capital punishment was unknown except at frontier places like Peshawar, and imprisonment was rarely resorted to. In the most serious cases parts of a criminal's body were chopped off, but there was hardly a punishment which could not be commuted to fine.

In the cases dealt with by the Maharaja himself, the execution of sentences, according to Osborne: "are prompt and simple, and follow quickly on the sentence. One blow of an axe, and then some oil to immerse the stump in, and stop all effusion of blood, is all the machinery he requires for his courts of justice. He is himself accuser, judge, and jury: and five minutes is about the duration of the longest trial at Lahore".[14] In one case whereof Osborne himself was a witness, two persons were brought to the Maharaja's presence, who were said to have pilfered at the gates of his harem; the Maharaja saw them, ordered the nose of the one and the ear of the other to be cut off, and this ended the whole business.

Justice was essentially a source of income, as mentioned above. Rarely was there a punishment which could not be commuted to fine. More interesting however was the fact that the losing as well as the winning parties had to pay. The former paid as a *Jurmana* or fine, while the latter paid *Nazrana* for the favour of the case having been decided in its favour. If a case was prolonged, the victim party had to pay a special amount known as *Taikhana* for the waste of the judge's time. On the recovery of the stolen goods, ¼ of them were given to the judge as *Shukrana*. Sometimes the whole of the village near which an untraced crime had been committed, had to pay the value of the crime.

Though there were defects in the judicial system of Ranjit Singh, there were also great improvements. Charles

Mason, a traveller who passed through the Punjab wrote: "time was that a Sikh and a robber were synonymous terms, now few thefts are heard of and seldom or never those wholesale forays to which the chiefs were so much addicted".[15]

Different defects have been pointed out in Ranjit Singh's administrative system. It is said that his government was based on his personal discretion. Ranjit Singh was an autocrat whose will was the law of the land. There was abuse of his delegated authority, corruption was rife and Ranjit Sings officials exploited the ignorant and illiterate masses of the country. Ranjit Singh's taxation policy has been criticized by the *Kapurthala District Gazetteer*, according to which he "took whatever he could and whenever he could get it". According to J.M. Douie, the system of assessment was so exacting that "the villagers had to bribe the appraising officers to take less".[16] No effort was made to encourage fine arts in the country, no special emphasis was laid on the development of education, and his court did not possess even a single person of scholarly repute. His personal influence rather than an efficient government was the only hold upon the country which held the people together, and the moment this magnetic personality was removed from their midst, the centrifugal forces had their play and everything scattered away in no time.

It is hardly to be claimed that the administrative machinery of the Maharaja was perfect. Yet, perfection is a quality which only superhumans could possess, and the Maharaja never claimed himself to be anything more than an ordinary being and despite his failings and shortcomings, only a humble servant of the Khalsa. One thing however is necessary, that while drawing an estimate of the Maharaja the circumstances and age he lived in must be given a due consideration. It would be hardly reasonable to judge him by the norms and standards which are applicable only to the present times. And it is reasonable too that the majority of his critics after drawing out the defects of his system, have not ultimately failed in giving him a sympathetic consideration.

Nor could it even be asserted that there were only a few good qualities which deserve our notice. "As a military despotism the government is a mild one and as a federal union hastily patched up into a machinery, it is strong and efficient". "As things stood," Temple commented, "there have been no convulsions, no confusions of rights and properties".[17] And again, as Burnes wrote: "In a territory compactly situated he has applied himself to those improvements which spring only from great minds and here we find despotism with out its rigour, a despot without cruelty and a system of government far beyond the native institutions of the east, though far from the civilisation of Europe".[18] The thriving manufactures and trade in the country, and the increased wealth of Lahore and Amritsar as testified even by the *Administration Report of the Punjab* (1849-51), prove beyond doubt the Maharaja's love for the people and their prosperity.

While discussing the merits of his administration one cannot ignore the glimmerings of a nascent Punjabi nationalism which existed in the Sikh state founded by Maharaja Ranjit Singh. He deserves our praise for the perfect impartiality with which he chose his officers, as pointed out by Dr. Narang.[19] He had a very keen eye for merit, and when he selected his officers, it was neither religion nor race, nor was it the birth of a man that counted with him. The humblest citizen had the greatest of opportunity to rise to the highest of positions under him. None of the persons such as Mohkam Chand, Raja Dhian Singh and Hari Singh Nalwa had any claim to a greatness by birth yet they were among the most favoured servants of the State, and that was so because they possessed merit.

It is an utterly wrong interpretation of the essentials of the Sikh faith to say, as Sir Lepel Griffin does, that "the main idea of Sikhism was the destruction of Islam and it was unlawful to salute Mahommedans to associate with them or to make peace with them on any terms".[20] It was a policy which was followed neither by Guru Gobind Singh nor by Banda Bahadur, the most determined amongst the Sikh fighters against the Muslim tyranny. And much less was it believed in by Ranjit Singh under whom the Sikhs secured all the political powers in their hands and could do against the Muslims what the latter had done against them in their won days of glory. In his administration and in his selection of others the Maharaja in fact followed a policy of perfect impartiality and employed only a discerning eye for merit. The *Jats* were better as fighters than as administrators, and though the Maharaja himself was a *Jat*, perhaps none of his ministers came from this community. The Sikhs generally being warriors, they predominated in the Maharaja's military forces, while the Hindus who were generally considered to be best as financiers, supplied the Maharaja's best Finance Ministers like Dewan Bhiwani Das and Moti Ram. The Muslims began best in diplomatic and confidential matters on which depended the entire foundation of the State, no hesitation was shown in granting these jobs to them. Faqir Aziz-uddin for instance was the foreign minister of Ranjit Singh; and even the post of the head of police at Lahore, the capital of the State, was occupied by a Muslim, Mian Imam Bux. Mufti Mohammed Shah was the Maharaja's adviser in mortgages, sales and contracts; and Imammuddin held the charge of the fort of Govindgarh at Amritsar.

The Maharaja's policy of toleration was proverbial. *Sayyads* were favoured in assessment. *Ulemas* and other Muslim holy men got state-grants, and whosoever could recite the whole of the Quran from his memory, could receive a fixed reward at any time.

Then the Maharaja did not believe in the Divine Right Theory of kingship. He never appropriated any high sounding titles to himself and attributed every success to the Almighty Lord and the *Khalsa*. If despite all this the Maharaja was a despot, he was so because he carried the faith and confidence of his people with him. The State being yet in the process of formation, the dominance of military was a natural thing, yet instead of being a military despotism as put forward by some writers, if despotism it was, it was a benevolent despotism. We have instances like that of Mohkam Chand who stood before the gates of the fort at Phillore and refused to permit some Englishmen to accompany the Maharaja inside it. Mohkam Chand said, so long as he lived he would note permit this to happen, and offered himself to be beheaded before the Maharaja entered the fort. The Maharaja simply respected his servant's views and returned.

And then, though his taxation system if compared with those of his contemporary Oriental monarchs, was for better; yet if there were some defects its merit lay in the fact that no money was exported abroad. If the rate of taxation was high, the rate of payment was high likewise. Money merely changed hands. What the Maharaja took with one hand, he gave away with the other.

If no perfect legal system of the modern type was established, it was so because it was then not known. Despite all its defects, it suited the age in which it worked, and it was no wonder that he was able to evolve so much where there existed nothing but chaos and confusion.

The Maharaja kept no police to chastise the people, and passed no Arms Acts to dispossess them of arms. People manufactured and kept arms freely, and could use them against the State if they were dissatisfied. Yet rarely is there an instance where some officer or some community showed a rebellious attitude.

There was absolutely no official interference in public life. Except in cases of the realisation offend revenue and taxes there were no techicalities and red-tapism involved in state procedures. Decisions were prompt and authority was delegated to make the administration localised. The *panchayats* flourished, villages were almost self-sufficient units in administration as well as in other fields. And the people were happy.

The Maharaja's liberal policy of granting *jagirs* to the deserving hands is a fact too often quoted by his admirers, and says Sunder Sing Majithia, "even up to the present time the *jagirs* granted to religious institutions irrespective of castes and creeds show the broad-mindedness of the old chief".[21]

Nor can it be properly claimed that the Maharaja paid absolutely no attention towards the development of the arts of peace and spread of education in his country. Hindu *Dharamshalas* and *Pathshalas*, and the Muslim Mosques and *Maktabs* were given liberal endowments, as testified by his contemporaries. According to Lethbridge, the Director of Public Instructions under the British Government, there were proportionately more literate in the Punjab under the Sikh-rule than under the British. Talking of Punjab before the British, Dr. Leitner observed that troubled by invasion and civil war it ever preserved and added to educational endowments. The most unscrupulous chief, the avaricious money-lender, and even the freebooter, vied with the small land-owner in making peace with his conscience by founding schools and rewarding the learned[22]. He rather bewailed the fact that the female education which had been so popular under the Sikhs, had languished under the British.[23]

And again, if there was an abuse of the delegated authority, let us not forget that it was then a universal defect which existed because the means of communication had not yet developed to make the central hold over all parts of the country strong. The Maharaja himself left no stone unturned to see efficiency and honesty become widespread in his system. He often moved about among his people incognito and mixed freely with the peasants to knows their problems.

At the end, even if there were some defects in his administratively machinery, let us admire him that in the midst of his career of conquests, and at a place where there existed nothing but confusion, he was able to create a consolidated administrative machinery. His great service to the State, writes Gordon, was that he, "left to his successors a united kingdom, a territory larger than the present Italy".[24] And his yet greater service to the people of the Punjab was the degree of secular policy which he had evolved before he died. It is said, after his conquest of Kasur when some local Sikhs represented to him out of their narrow-mindedness against the daily Muslim call, or *Azan*, for prayer in the early morning, the Maharaja replied that it was not against the Sikh religion, and the Sikhs also could get up hearing this call and recite their *Bani*. "However, if you insist on stopping the *Azan*", he tactfully continued, "some of the leading Sikhs of your town should come forward to take up the duty of awakening the Mohammedans for the daily prayer early in the morning. After all it is not Sikh-like to obstruct the daily prayers of others".[25]

THE MILITARY ADMINISTRATION

Defining the Sikh of Guru Gobind Singh, Ibbetson wrote in the Census Report of 1881: "At Sikh means a soldier". And in 1911 Griffin explained this soldier as: "Hardy, brave, and of intelligence, too slow to understand when he is beaten, obedient to discipline, devotedly attached to his officer, he is unsurpassed as a soldier in the East".[26]

The history of this great soldier begins with that of Guru Nanak when he was created only a saint. The tragic end of the fifth Guru woke the Sikh from his spiritual meditation. The sixth Guru gave him a military discipline and he was converted into a great saint-soldier. A tradition of self-sacrifice was imbued in him by the ninth Guru, while the baptism of the tenth Guru fired the Sikh with a "burning and consuming passion for political freedom", which now converted him from Sikh into Singh, or a lion. The sacrifice of Guru Gobind Singh's four sons taught him further as to how he should sacrifice his hearth and home for a cause.

Banda Bahadur's exploits in the Punjab sharpened his taste for victories against a great power like the Mughas. He learnt the technique of guerrilla warfare from Abdali's attempts to suppress him and thus by the time Ranjit Singh ascended his throne, his tradition as "an invincible warrior, who could sacrifice his all for a cause", was fully established.

Yet, the Sikh had not learnt the discipline of an organised army. The chaos that supervened the death of Banda Bahadur had converted the Sikhs into turbulent and independent individuals "who had been accustomed to carry their swords from one leader to another as they saw the best chance of plunder, and who changed their masters as often as it suited their inclination or convenience".[27] It rested only with Ranjit Singh who proved his military genius by converting this confused mass of invincible warriors with a rich tradition of sacrifice and victories into powerful, disciplined and well-equipped army under efficient leadership.

Reorganisation under Ranjit Singh

Ranjit Singh's army as reorganised by him consisted of three different sections infantry, cavalry and artillery.

The Infantry

In the beginning the Sikhs considered infantry soldiers as inferior to the cavalryman, and he was says Griffin, in time of war left behind to garrison forts, or to look after the women.[28] But under the influence of European officers Ranjit Singh realised that the infantry was more important than the cavalry, and therefore by good pay and personal attention, and under General Ventura's introduction of strict discipline, long enduring fatigue and other qualities, the infantry soon became the most efficient standing army under Ranjit Singh.

Recruitment to the infantry forces under Ranjit Singh was entirely voluntary, but the service being attractive for the emoluments and adventures that it offered, people joined it willingly. The regular drilling system introduced by the Maharaja after the European manner, however, was not liked by the soldiers initially, and it was contemptuously termed as *Raqs Looluan*, or 'ballet steps!' Later, however, as it became a regular part of the training system, the soldiers gave in.

Composition of Infantry

Organisationally, the infantry consisted of battalions as the administrative units. The battalion consisted of 900 men, and was commanded by a commandant. The Commandant was assisted by an Adjutant and a Major. The battalion was divided into eight companies, and the company was further divided into four sections each of which consisted of 25 men who were commanded by an officer known as a *Havildar* who, in his turn, was assisted by a *Naik*.

Besides the *Havildar* and the *Naik* on the lowest rung of the ladder, the other important officers of the company, in order of seniority, were *Subedar*, *Jamadar*, and *Sarjan* (Sergeant). *Phuriya*, Bugler and a Trumpeter complete the list.

Battalion was a part of a regiment. Men lived in barracks, and each regiment carried a copy of the *Guru Granth Saheb*. The important regimental officers were the commandant, the Adjutant, the Major, the Writer, the Accountant and a *Granthi* with camp followers such as camel drivers, smiths, *Baildars*, and cooks.

The system of regular monthly salaries was introduced for the first time by Ranjit Singh. Formerly the Sikh soldiers had always dependent upon loot and plunder. But this they got only when they were on active service. Otherwise each soldier was supposed to have his own source of regular income. Under Ranjit Singh, however, the monthly salary of a General was from Rs. 400 to 460. A Commandant's pay varied between Rs. 60 and Rs. 150 and that of a sepoy between Rs. 7 and $8\frac{1}{2}$.

Commands in French: Infantry soldiers marched to the beat of the drum, and commands as introduced by the French officer, Ventura, were in French. Regiments marched swiftly and in a well organised manner. In addition to regular parades, a general parade of the entire army was held annually at the time of Dussehra in Lahore or Amritsar, which was inspected by Ranjit Singh. Their flag was of saffron colour, and their was cry *Sat Sri Akal*. Their endurance was very great, and a "whole regiment would march 30 miles a day for many days together".[29]

Commenting on their courage and aptitude, Burton, a traveller who visited the Punjab in 1831, wrote: "They are thin men with good features; they are capable of bearing the fatigue of long marches for several days in succession, so that it has become a by-word that the Punjabis have iron legs. On their marches, they encamp very regularly, and I saw 30,000 men, the army of Peshawar, moved with as much facility as a single regiment on this side (the British) of the Sutlej. No wheeled carriage is allowed, and their own bazars contain all they require."[30]

Foreign Observers' Comments: Osborne visiting the Punjab in 1839 used similar words of praise. Tall, "rather slight, but very manly looking men, with great length of limb, and broad open chests... They are hardy, far beyond the generality of natives, and seem a merry light-hearted race of people".[31] Captain Wade "could not help remarking the cheerful alacrity with which the Sikhs seemed to endure the fatigue".[32] And Baron Van Hugel was rather "surprised to find his (Ranjit Singh's) troops so proficient on European tactics".[33]

Some defects however, still persisted in this part of the Maharaja's army. "On parade," wrote Burton, "they give utterance to abusive expression, striking freely any of a rank inferior to their own. The commandant canes the adjutant, who in turn strikes the officers at the heads of *companies*, who again vent their ill-humour on the non-commissioned and privates".[34]

The drum, fife and bugle were in general use in the Sikh infantry regiments, "and in some of the favourite royal corps of Ranjit Singh, an attempts was made to introduce a band of music," writes Steinbach, "but a graft of European melody upon Punjabi discord did not produce, as may be imagined, very harmonious result".[35]

The total strength of the Maharaja's infantry in 1811 was 4,061, but in 1845, six years after his death, it was found to be 70,721. It is not clear whether the whole of this increase took place during his lifetime or after.

The Cavalry

The Cavalry of Maharaja Ranjit Singh was divided into four classes, which were as follows:

Regular Cavalry

This was a body of picked men and horses. Fine in appearance, equipment, and discipline, this body got a regular training after the European manner. It was kept under a French General, Jean Francois Allard, who had been engaged by the Maharaja in 1822. Its strength in 1811 was 1,209. In 1838 it numbered 4,090, but by 1845 it increased to 6,235.

Ghor Charah

This constituted another class of Ranjit Singh's cavalry which, unlike the regular cavalry, got no regular training. Nor was it disciplined in any military code. It was organised on the model of the Khalsa army of the *Misls* which believed rather in dash and reckless courage than in any regular procedure of offence or defence. It was paid directly by the State. The payment at first was made in Jagirs to the value of Rs. 300 to Rs. 400 a trooper per year. Later, however, cash payments became regular which varied between Rs. 250 and Rs. 300 per year. A fresh recruit who entered into this service had to make his own arrangement for a horse, but in case he was unable to do so he was provided with necessary equipment by the State against a deduction from his salary in easy instalments.

Griffin while comparing the Maharaja's infantry with his cavalry writes: "In the Maharaja's army the infantry were the pick of the youth of the country; only the handsomest and strongest were selected, while the cavalry were irregular troops, the contingents of his different Sardars, and not appointed for any consideration of bravery or strength. The *horses* were small, *weak* and *ill-bred*, and the accoutrements were of the roughest and *coarsest kind*".[36] But this was not perhaps applicable to the *Ghorcharah* cavalry where we learn that the lean and thin horses were not tolerated. Some sort of regular inspection of these horses was made, and sometimes when a horse was found to be lean, a deduction was made from the salary of its owner, as a mode of punishment or his negligence.

"By their desperate courage the Ghorcharahas," wrote Moorcroft, "had earned for themselves a name and for Ranjit Singh a kngdom".[37]

The Ghorcharah cavalry, we learn, was sub-divided into two classes: (*i*) The *Ghorcharah Khas* which comprised one regiment, its troopers being recruited from among the nobility of the province. (*ii*) The *Misaldar Sawars* who belonged originally to independent chieftains of the Punjab, on whose overthrow they transferred their services to the Maharaja.

Jagirdari Cavalry

These were the troopers maintained by *Jagirdars* who, according to the terms of their respective agreements with the Maharaja, were, when required, bound each to furnish him with a fixed number of efficient and well-equipped troopers. These *jagirdars* presented their troopers for the Maharaja's review in the general parade on every Dusehra.

The Maharaja made some strict rules against corruption in the *Jagirdari* cavalry. Every *Jagirdar* was bound to deposit a regular descriptive roll of his contingent in the State Records office, on the good condition of which depended the renewal of his *Jagir*. Even a man like Hari Singh Nalwa could not escape punishment, should he have been guilty of neglect in this matter, and he was once fined Rs. 2 lakhs for keeping less than the stipulated number of troopers.

Akalis

They were some irregular regiments of the Maharaja, "employed on any dangerous, or desperate service".[38] With naked swords, two in the hands and two in belts, with a matchlock at the back and two pairs of quoits round their turbans, they dashed about unafraid. With Akali Phula Singh as their leader, they were two to three thousand in number. They hated Europeans and Pathans, and Ranjit Singh himself, "on more than one occasion narrowly escaped assassination by them".[39] At certain places Griffin does not have very good words regarding them. "The Maharaja," he writes, "was afraid to interfere too closely with these men; for though little better than drunken savages, they were supposed by the Sikhs to possess a semisacred character, and were moreover, useful when desperate deeds were to be done, which the rank and file of the army might have declined they were identical in character and in manner of their onslaught with the Ghazis of Afghanistan and the Soudan, whose fierce and terrible attack shakes the nerve of all but the steadiest and most seasoned troops: but the Sikh soldiers of God drew their courage more from drink and maddening drugs, than from the depths of religious enthusiasm which inspires the wild children of Islam".[40] Steinbach, too, holds similar views about them.[41]

Nevertheless, these European writers seem to have erred in not understanding that these people drew their inspiration from Amritsar, a sacred tank, of which they were supposed to be custodians. A dip into this sacred tank and an Akali was no more a man, but a lion. Though he had a weakness for *bhang*, yet an Akali was a moralist who kept the torch of the Khalsa faith alight as enjoined by Guru Gobind Singh. Whenever he fought, he fought not for a material prize or for some worldly honour, but for a cause which was ever to him more than his own life.

Fauj-e-Qilajat

Besides all this the Maharaja had in his service about 10,800 men known as Fauj-i-Qilajat who garrisoned the important forts like those of Multan, Peshawar, Kangra and Attock. The average pay of garrison infantry soldier was Rs. 6 a month, the Jamadar receiving Rs. 12 or more. Every fort was placed under the charge of an officer called a Thanedar. The code of conduct for the men who garrisoned forts was very strict. None of them could be addicted to wine, nor could dancing girls be permitted inside a fort. Furthermore, to curb their immoral or lethargic habits, none of these soldiers could spend more than one-half of his monthly pay. The rest of the money had to be remitted home regularly. Nor could a garrison soldier have dishonest dealings with a shopkeeper, or a clash with any of the neighbouring civil population.

The Artillery

Ranjit Singh, wrote Osborne in 1839, "is very proud of the efficiency and admirable condition of this artillery, and justly so, for no native power has yet possessed so large and well disciplined a corps".[42]

Again, writes Lieutenant Barr about the Maharaja's gunners: "The orders were given in French. He then tried some of his fuses, which are very good. All the shot was formed of beaten iron, and cost a rupee each, and the majority of shells were composed of pewter... It is a matter almost of wonder to behold the perfection to which he (General Court) has brought his artillery".

The Maharaja's artillery was divided into four classes: (1) *Top Khana Fili,* or Elephant Batteries;; (2) *Top Khana Shutri,* or Camel Swivels, also called *Zamburaks;* (3) *Top Khana Aspi,* or Horse Batteries; (4) *Top Khana Gavi,* or Bullock Batteries.

Foreign Officers

The Sikhs before Ranjit Singh, however, were not given very much to the use of artillery. Therefore it was difficult for the Maharaja to find leaders for his artillery from among the Punjabis. Consequently, some Europeans such as Generals Court and Gardener were especially invited to officer the artillery. Later, however, men like Lehna Singh rose up and distinguished themselves in the profession. This man, according to Griffin, was an original inventor who cast many a beautiful gun. Mian Qadir Bakhsh was another important man in the line. He was sent by the Maharaja to Ludhiana at State expense, to be trained in gunnery. After this training he wrote a book on the subject.

Each of the Maharaja's guns had its own name, such as *Fateh Jung*. Some of them bore Persian inscriptions, and some the words *Sri Akal Sahai*, or 'God be our Help'. Most of the workshops for the casting of the guns were situated in Lahore, the more important of them being within the fort itself.

The total number of guns in the Maharaja's possession, writes Steinbach, was 176; the total number of swivels being 370.[43]

Manufacture of Weapons

Lahore, as mentioned earlier, was a very important seat for the manufacture of guns. Spears, swords, matchlocks and pistols were also manufactured. The best armour, including helmets, coats of mail, shields, breast-plates and gauntlets came from Multan, Jammu, Srinagar, and Amritsar. Kashmir supplied the best artisans for the purpose. But later, under the supervision of the officers as Faqir Nur-ud-din, Dr. Honigberger and Lehna Singh Majithia, the number of trained craftmen among the Punjabis themselves began to increase.

Taking an over-all view, Maharaja Ranjit Singh's army could be divided into three parts:

(1) *Fauj-i-Khas*, or special Brigade: This brigade was trained after the European pattern, and it fought generally in the frontier wars. Commanded by General Ventura, this brigade, according to Griffin, consisted of

Regular Infantry	3,176
Regular cavalry	1,667
Artillery with 34 guns	855
Total	5,698

"The infantry force," further writer Griffin, "included the *Khas* battalion, strength 820 men; a Gurkha battalion, 707 men; Deva Singh's battalion, 839 men; and the Sham Sota battalion, 810 men.

"The cavalry force was composed of a grenadier regiment, strength 730 men; a dragoon regiment, 750 men; and a troop of lifeguards, 187 men.

"The artillery was the corps known as that of Ilahi Baksh, and was commanded by a Mussalman general of that name, the best officer in the Sikh army".[44]

(2) *Fauj-i-ain* or the Regular Army: Unlike the *Akalis* and *Jagirdari* soldiers, this force was organised by the State and was regular. According to the Khalsa Darbar Records, its number in 1838 was 38,242. It consisted of the following:

Infantry	29,617
Cavalry	4,090
Artillery	4,535

(3) *Fauj-i-Beqwaid*, or Irregular Force: This consisted of *Akalis*, *Jagirdari* troops and others all of whom were irregular, as discussed above.

The total annual expenditure incurred by the Maharaja in the payment of his regular army, according to Shahmat Ali was:

	Rs
Infantry	28,09,200
Cavalry	24,53,656
Horse Artillery	3,24,864
Irregular Sowers	71,08,562
Total Rs	1,27,96,282

But, continues Shahmat Ali, "a great many deductions are made from the pay of the troops, which reduce the actual expenditure considerably".[45]

Regimental Dress

There was no infantry before Ranjit Singh, as mentioned earlier. A common trooper in the service of a *misl* chief wore a turban and a pair of short drawers. The sleeves of his shirt were usually open, and his slippers tight-fitting. Under Ranjit Singh, however, some changes took place, for a brief study of which the reader may consult the author's *History of Punjab,* second volume.

The artillery wore red turbans, black waistbands, with cross belts and scabbards ornamental in brass, long boots and white trousers. The bodyguards of the Maharaja dressed differently, in a cloth of scarlet or yellow. Yellow satin was generally used in their uniform, and shawls or scarves formed a major feature of it.

No Racial Bias

One of the cardinal features of the Maharaja's army administration was the ruler's effort to secure experts to train and command his soldiers without any racial, religious, or national bias. Besides Indians and Punjabis, the Maharaja's army included Italian, French, American, English, Anglo-Indian, Spanish, Greek and Russian officers. The total number of these European officers in the Maharaja's army, according to the British records, was 20. Carmichael Smyth's list, however, mentions 39 names, whereas Gardner gives the number as 42. At the head of these foreign officers, writes W.L. M. Gregor, "are Generals Ventura and Allard; the former is an Italian by birth, the latter a Frenchman. Both arrived in the Punjab about the same time, and they have always been on the best terms with each other".[46]

The agreement entered into by General Ventura, Allard and other European army officers, according to Grey and Garnet, was to domesticate themselves in the country by marriage, not to eat beef, not to smoke tobacco in public, to permit their beards to grow, "to take care not to offend against Sikh religion, and if required to fight against their own country".[47]

Europeans Distrusted by People

Although in the Maharaja's Army, battalions trained in the European fashion existed since 1807, regular introduction of European officers seems to have taken place much later. Allard and Ventura, according to an account, joined in 1822. The presence of these European officers was not liked by the Indian soldiers at the beginning, and even the heir-apparent Prince Kharak Singh did not look upon them with favour. Yet, as time passed the distrust of the people waned, and the European officers seem to have given a good account of their capabilities in moulding themselves according to their environments.

Towards the closing years of his life, however, Ranjit Singh's notions regarding the value of their services seemed to have changed, and according to M' Gregor, "he either fancies that he can dispense with them altogether, or, what is more probable, he grudges the pay which every gentleman resorting thither expects for his services".[48] The people at large too did not look upon them with a friendly eye. The chaos that supervened Ranjit Singh's death made their lives precarious. Col. Foulkes, an English officers, was murdered, the houses of General Court and Ventura were plundered, and they all fled the country.

Some writers of the military system of Ranjit Singh have pointed out some serious defects which the Maharaja could not remove. One defect for instance was that a part of the Maharaja's army consisted of aggregate of irregular contingents which were raised and commanded by *Jagirdars*, with the result they were more loyal to the chiefs than to the Maharaja. Nor, despite the Maharaja's strict watch upon them, did these *Jagirdars* keep their soldiers and animals in a proper condition.

The Maharaja also failed in introducing a perfect discipline in his Akali regiments. Though by his diplomacy and wisdom he was able to make a good use of them, after his death this element in his army proved to be a potent cause which hastened the decline of the Sikh power.

The army as a whole was never taught to be subservient to civil authority. The Maharaja being always busy in wars and conquests during his life-time, his military officers and leaders gathered greater importance than the civilians. The supremacy of the civil over the military authority having never been established, after his death the Sikh army to all intents and purposes became a self-governing body. Its affairs began to be conducted by its own *panchayats* representing each company, and the very existence of the civil authority was threatened.

Nor did Ranjit Singh introduce a regular system of payments. "More men were kept at hand, in particular cases, than could be easily paid for and it was his habit to stave off payment by some expedient or other". Then, as a contemporary writer comments: "No pensions were, or are, assigned to the soldiery for long service, nor is there any provision for the widows and the families of those who died, or are killed in the service of the State. Promotions, instead of being the right of the good soldier in order of seniority or the reward of merit in the various grades is frequently effected by bribery. In higher ranks, advancement is obtained by the judicious application of the donneur to the palm of the favourites at court, or the military chieftains about the person of the Sovereign".

Only the Europeans got handsome salaries. But they too began to be distrusted towards the end of Ranjit Singh's life, and some of them actually played the part of traitors against his successors. Moreover some Sardars being jealous of them, most of them had to be dismissed after Ranjit Singh's death, thus upsetting the army organisation.

Men of different nationalities and racial affiliation were recruited in the Maharaja's army, who could be kept together only under the influence of his own magnetic personality. No uniform dress was introduced. The cavalry, with the exception of the *Ghorcharas,* were "very inferior in every respect to the infantry". The Sikh artillery suffered from deficiency in gunners. "The supply system of the Sikhs, though efficient in its working, also left much to be desired.... In the matter of strategy, the Sikh leaders, like the Marathas before them, chiefly depended upon their personal experience of war. There was no treatise on this subject and no record of the military experience of the Sikh generals to provide any guidance".[49]

The Westernisation of the army, according to some writers, weakened instead of strengthening it; and that is why this army of the Sikhs, which had fought with great credit against the Imperial Mughals under Guru Gobind Singh and Banda Bahadur, failed to inspire Ranjit Singh for a war against the British.

Despite all the defects pointed out above, however, we will have to judge the merit of Ranjit Singh's army in the battle-field. Thus wrote Sir Charles Gough, the British Commander-in-Chief who fought the first British war against the Sikhs: "it has been said–and the words undoubtedly contain a general truth–that among non-European people the most successful opponents of British army have been those who, like Hyder Ali and Holkar, made no attempt to adopt alien methods of fighting... Nevertheless the struggle with the Sikhs seems to present an exception to the rule... The Sikh soldiery fought with a discipline and stubbornness unequalled in our experience of native warfare; and their doing so was largely due to the methods introduced by Ranjit Singh".[50]

Writing of the terrible carnage of the Sikh troops at Sobraon, thus wrote Sir Charles Gough: "Policy precluded me from publicly; recording my sentiments on the splendid gallantry of our fallen foe, or to record the acts of heroism displayed, not individually but almost collectively by the Sikh Sirdars and army, and I declare, were it not from a deep conviction that my country's good required the sacrifice, I could have wept to have witnessed the fearful slaughter of so devoted a body of men".[51] Thus, there is no doubt, as Sinha writes, before Ranjit Singh died, he had indeed "transformed a rabble of horsemen into the most efficient fighting machine".[52]

And but for the traitorous role played by some Lahore chiefs, the British victory over the Sikhs during the First Sikh War, should not have been an easy job.

On 27 June 1839[53], Ranjit Singh died. He had "found the Punjab a waning confederacy, a prey to the Marathas, and ready to submit to English supremacy. He consolidated the numerous petty states into a kingdom, he wrested from Kabul the fairest of its provinces, and he gave the potent English no cause for interference".[54] In the words of Jagmohan Mahajan, "He inherited mutiny and created discipline, found chaos and produced order, and succeeded by the sustained effort of a lifetime in carving out a compact kingdom for himself. But his achievement, though highly remarkable, was personal and consequently ephemeral".[55] "His rule was founded on the feelings of a people, but it involved the joint action of the necessary principles of military order and territorial extension, and when a limit had been set to Sikh dominion, and his own commanding genius was no more, the vital spirit of his race began to consume itself in domestic contentions".[56]

It seems paradoxical and ironical that the founder of an empire should be charged with the responsibility of its downfall. It was his indulgence in frequent and fiery potations which killed him before he should have died. And, also "like most men who have been distinguished in history for administrative vigour and military genius, Ranjit Singh was very susceptible to feminine influence". He married eighteen wives, "nine by the orthodox ceremonial and nine by the simpler rite of throwing the sheet" (*Chadar dalna*). But of his mistresses and concubines the chronicle is too scandalous for more than a passing reference. "When he had secured the legitimate succession in the person of his son Kharak Singh, he cared little for the discreditable intrigues of his harem. Many children were fathered upon him by these ladies, either for political objects[57] or in the hope of obtaining his special favour. To his son, Kharak Singh and to his grandson, Nau Nihal Singh, he sent several ladies of more than doubtful reputation from his own *zenana*; one of these being the beautiful Isar Kaur, who was so cruelly to commit *sati* on the death of Maharaja Kharak Singh.[58]

The result of all these activities of the Maharaja was that after the death of Nau Nihal Singh none remained with an undisputed claim to the throne. As it is well known one of the causes of the intrigues against Dalip Singh, the last of the Sikh rulers, was that his legitimacy was doubted.

No training in statecraft or in diplomacy was imparted to his numerous progeny, and even Kharak Singh, to whom there seemed no stigma of illegitimacy remained only a simpleton. Dhian Singh Dogra's[59] jealousy had always kept him away from the court, and Ranjit Singh though cautious was not wise enough to discern the court's intriguing schemes. Hugel visiting the Court of Ranjit Singh remarked, "The eldest son of the Maharaja, Kharak Singh, resides at Lahore, but is always overlooked, as his intellect is too feeble to afford any probability of his ever ruling over the scarcely united empire of the Sikhs".[60] We do not, however, know how much of this feebleness was enforced and how much was natural. Aurangzeb's attitude of suspicion towards his sons robbed them of training in kingcraft, leading finally to the consequences catastrophic to the Mughal empire. Ranjit Singh was not of suspicious character, yet his carelessness in the matter repeated this error.

Although Ranjit Singh was not of autocratic dispositions, he wielded powers which come only in the train of military dictators. Not unoften was his treasury said to be filled up only with the help of his soldiers. Everything was centralised. The Maharaja was the supreme military commander, the supreme executive head and the supreme judge of his State. Rarely was ever an initiative given to an officer in administration or in military ventures. His court, may be with a few honourable exceptions, was pack of sycophants who, though ambitious, were not yet all-round administrative and diplomatic geniuses. And the natural result was that when the Maharaja died there was misrule everywhere. Soldiers lost their commander and the people their fountain-head of justice and chief administrator.

And though the Maharaja recruited men in his service only on merit, and though it goes to his credit that in an age of religious depravity he cultivated in his court only the sane laws of religious toleration, yet the Sikhs and the Hindus on the one side, and Muslims on the other, were people not only of diverse faiths but also of contradictory traditions, which in that age placed them poles apart. Under the magnetic influence of the Maharaja they could work together, but after his death their harmonious cooperation was difficult. And this was not foreseen by Ranjit Singh.

Views differ regarding the Maharaja's financial system. "The Maharaja squeezed the last drop of blood from the peasant's veins", some would say what the Maharaja took away with one hand he gave back with the other. Every peasant family having sent a son or two in the Maharaja's army, money flowed back into the villages in the shape of their savings. Yet the way the Maharaja extorted the hard-earned money from the labour consuming lands was hardly relishing. The peasants tolerated all this because they had seen worse days, but when they learnt the better systems of the English they found it difficult to put up with the old. The changes introduced by the British were more scientific and less exacting.

Nor was the customs system of the Maharaja worth much appreciation.[61] It afforded an encouragement neither to trade nor industry. Those who studied the free flow of trade in the territories held by the British, naturally disliked a system under which scores of customs barriers ran irregularly cutting one another at irregular intervals thus making the goods brought from one end of the country to the other to be subject to customs not only once, twice, or even thrice, but many times, thus making the articles of common use dearer and more difficult to be utilised by the common man. And then the Maharaja's government was national government in which there was no need of winning the support of the privileged and moneyed classes to exploit and control the poor, as the British later on did. Ranjit Singh made every attempt to check the rich people from growing richer. These wealthy and incapable men, thus writes Cunningham, "stood rebuked before the superior genius of Ranjit Singh, and before the mysterious spirit which animated the people arrayed in arms, and they thus fondly hoped that a change would give them all they could desire".[62]

The army administration left much to be desired. Besides the irregular part of his army which was indisciplined and the Akalis who remained too undomesticated, having many a time threatened even the Maharaja's own life, the regular part of his army too was not under the practice of being commanded by the civil officers; with the result that by the time Sher Singh acceded to power in 1841, the whole army became simply a self-governing body." Its affairs" thus writes Payne, "were conducted by *Panchayats* or councils of 'five', representing each company, and elected by soldiers themselves". The principle of the commonwealth of the Khalsa which had been introduced by Guru Govind Singh and under which the authority of the 'five' was stronger than even that of the Guru himself, was misused. "To those *Panchayats* the men looked for the redress of all their grievances, and to them they made their demands for increased pay, or the dismissal of obnoxious officers. The system originated in the reign of Sher Singh, and so rapidly did the power of the councils grow that they soon acquired the complete control not only of the army, but of almost every branch of the administration". Civil supremacy in the hands of military personnel is never an authority well-placed. And it is no wonder that "In those days power was a dangerous possession. Every State official knew that to incur the displeasure of the army was equivalent to signing his own death warrant".[63] No sane statesman would dare come forward and openly challenge such a situation.

Troops rose in rebellion at Peshawar, Multan, Kashmir and newly conquered State of Mandi shortly after the Maharaja's death, and when Dhian Singh disbanded some whole regiments, "this only served to increase the general disorder, for the discharged soldiers scattering over the surrounding districts, threw in their lot with the many robber bands, who in the absence of any settled government, roamed unchecked over the countryside, blackmailing the terrified cultivators, driving off their cattle, and pillaging their farmsteads and villages".[64]

A wise conqueror as he was, Ranjit Singh failed to "breathe into the hearts of his people any noble sentiment that would have held them together after his death".[65] No common art was encouraged, no common culture developed. Nor was a common system of education founded. The people combined together only under the dominating authority of Ranjit Singh and when that unifying centre was no more, the centrifugal forces had the best of it and every thing scattered away in no time.

Although Ranjit Singh tried to whittle down the possessions of the Sardars like Hari Singh Nalwa by confiscating their *jagirs* after their death to the point even of incurring the blame of being ungrateful to his servants, yet writes G. L. Chopra, "Ranjit failed to follow consistently the policy of reducing the people of the Punjab to a more or less uniform political level; the most glaring example of such a failure was the grant of an extensive and contiguous territory to a single Dogra family".[66] And it was this Dogra family which was one of the potent causes leading to the destruction of the Sikh power. The Dogra Raja Gulab Singh, who later on carved out a separate State for himself in Kashmir, was blamed for having rebelled many times under Ranjit Singh, but he was always protected by his brother Dhian Singh, the Prime Minister of the Punjab, who never failed in prevailing upon the Maharaja to take a lenient view of the misdoings of this man of ambitions. Here was a generosity ill placed. Gulab Singh's ambitions were not misplaced, he was rather making experiments which led so unfailingly to the creation of a separate Dogra State. The sincere Sardars of the Maharaja's court were disgusted with this over patronisation of the Dogras.

Nor had the intriguers among the Dogra Rajputs failed in bringing harm to the State even during the lifetime of the Maharaja. Had Raja Dhian Singh forwarded the letter of Hari Singh Nalwa to the Maharaja in which he had requested his soldiers whom he had sent for Nau Nihal Singh's marriage to be sent back, the life of this ill-fated and hard-pressed, yet so seasoned a General, Nalwa, might have been spared at Peshawar, and he might have been of a better service to the State in the hour of its peril. Had the Dogras not kept Prince Kharak Singh away from the Maharaja's court on one pretext or the other, the prince, the heir-apparent, might have got a better training in kingcraft and saved his own life and his empire. Ranjit Singh know very well that the Dogras would not permit his children to rule peacefully after his death. "It was the aim of the Jammu brothers to bring the whole of the Punjab under their dominion, Dhian looking forward to the control of the south, and Gulab that of the north".[67] Yet he did nothing to amend the situation.

His Ministers were usually his favourites and adventurers. Selection of the Maharaja's officers was done on the basis of their outward merits, and never on the basis of their convictions. It was hardly astonishing therefore that many of them were later on found to be in correspondence with the British, paying he way for their ultimate supremacy over the Punjab.

Once while seeing the map of India in which all but the Punjab had been shown red which was the colour of the British empire, Ranjit Singh said: "*Sab lal ho jaiga,*" meaning that the time would, come when whole of this map would be marked red. In other words he knew that the British were bound to annex the Punjab after his death, and there was bound to be a war between the two powers on the score. His mistake was that he postponed this war.

The decline of the Sikh power, according to some writers, began when the Maharaja signed the Treaty of Amritsar in 1809.[68] There was no reasonable excuse, according to these writers, for his demoralised attitude towards the English after 1823. His diplomatic defeats on the question of Ferozepur,[69] on the question of Shikarpur and on that of the navigation of the Indus, were simply the signs of his cowardice.[70] That the Sikh forces were strong enough to fight and defeat the British only if their ruler had dared enter the venture, was conclusively demonstrated in the Kabul disaster of the British in the First Anglo-Afghan war, as Payne seems to agree: "British force had suffered defeat at the hands of a foe over whom the troops of the Khalsa had gained more than one decisive victory".[71] Although the Maharaja was living when the British faced their initial failure in Afghanistan and although he did see his own advantage in their failure, yet the remained unwilling or afraid to withdraw from his engagements. He against his own interests, rather sent his whole army to Peshawar under his grandson Nau Nihal Singh to act in concert with Captain Wade, leaving his Sutlej frontier, then occupied by a British division, quite unprotected. Not only this, but "the whole resources of his country in cattle, grain, etc., were thrown open to the British Government".[72]

That if he had dared he might have won a war against the British may yet further be proved when we learn that the British Governor-General became nervous when in 1838 the Maharaja sent his army to the bank of the Sutlej to check the British soldiers in case they tried to force their way through the Punjab on their march to Afghanistan.

But this boldness of the Maharaja in 1838 proved only an unfortunate event. The Khalsa army was encouraged, and they developed a confidence on their power. But this they did shortly after they lost their leader, the Maharaja himself. It was this event which later on inspired then to cross the Sutlej and it proved to be a suicide.

Bismarck used to say, a political alliance between two powers always means one rider and a horse. In the case of he Anglo-Sikh relations under Ranjit Singh "the British Government was the rider and Ranjit Singh was the horse". "He never grandly dared. He was all hesitancy and indecision".[73]

But let us not go too far in our criticism of the Maharaja lest we should be blamed of a biased attitude towards him. He was a human being after all. And as a human being he was unfortunate too, in the respect that almost all his loyal and brave Generals such as Mohkam Chand, Dewan Chand, Hari Singh Nalwa and Ram Dayal had died before he himself left this mortal world, and none remained behind except the weaklings and traitors to control the army. And again if the Maharaja failed to establish an efficient and lasting administration, let us not forget that the Maharaja was too busy in the conquest and consolidation of territories to afford enough time for other activities. Yet more, the Maharaja's time was only the medieval periods of Indian history, and traditions that he inherited were only oriental traditions. To compare his administrative works with those of the modern times or with those of his contemporary European monarchs, would simply be an anachronism and hence an injustice to the hero who was a great conqueror, yet the man who gave a forestate of secularism to the country he ruled.

REFERENCES

1. Griffin, Sir Lepel, *Ranjit Singh,* p. 129.
2. Cunningham, *History of the Sikh,* p. 233.
3. Payne, *A Short History of the Punjab,* p. 117.
4. Hugel, *Travels in Punjab and Kashmir,* p. 286.
5. Sinha, N.K. *Ranjit Singh,* p. 139.
6. *Ibid,* p. 140.
7. *Cent. Vol. of Ranjit Singh,* Amritsar, Sinha, *op. cit.,* p. 142; Chopra *op. cit.,* p. 123.
8. Sinha, *op. cit.,* p. 144.
9. Shahmat Ali, *Sikhs and Afghans,* p. 22.
10. Prinsep, *op. cit.,* p. 235.
11. *Gujranwala District Gazetteers.*

12. Shahmat Ali, *op. cit.*, p. 23.
13. *Cent. Vol. of Ranjit Singh*, ASR.
14. Osborne, *Court and Camp of Ranjit Singh*, p. 67.
15. Masson, *op. cit.*, i, p. 423.
16. Douie, *Settlement Manual.*
17. *Jullundur District Settlement Report.*
18. Burnes, *Travels*, i, p. 285.
19. Narang, G. C., *Transformation of Sikhism*, p. 179.
20. Griffin, *op. cit.*, p. 25.
21. *Cent. Vol. of Ranjit Singh*, Cawnpore.
22. Leitner, C.W., *History of Indigenous Education in Punjab since Annexation and in 1882* (1882), p. 2.
23. *Ibid.*, pp. 98-99.
24. Gordon, *op. cit.*, p. 124.
25. Prithipal Singh, *The Missionary Quarterly*, April-June 1961.
26. Griffin, *Ranjit Singh*, p. 132.
27. *Ibid*, pp. 132-33.
28. Griffin, *op. cit.*, p. 133.
29. Griffin, *op. cit.*, p. 134.
30. Burton, *First and Second Sikh Wars*, p. 11.
31. Osborne, *The Camp and Court of Ranjit Singh*, pp. 102-104.
32. Chopra, *The Punjab as a Sovereign State*, pp. 301-327.
33. Hugel, *Travels in Kashmir and Punjab*, p. 289.
34. Burton, *The First and Second Sikh Wars*, p. 11.
35. Steinbach, Lieut. Col., *The Punjab*, p. 103.
36. Griffin, *op. cit.*, p. 135.
37. Moorcraft, *Travels*, I, p. 98.
38. Osborne, *op. cit.*, p. 143.
39. Steinbach, *op. cit.*, pp. 104-105.
40. Griffin, *op. cit.*, pp. 136-137.
41. Steinbach, *op. cit.*, p. 104.
42. Osborne, *Camp & Court*. p. 144.
43. Steinbach, *op. cit.*, p. 95.

44. Griffin, *op. cit.*, pp. 141-42.
45. Shahmat Ali, *Sikhs and Afghans*, pp. 23-25.
46. M'Gregor, *History of the Sikhs*, i. pp. 254-62.
47. Grey and Garnett, *European Adventurers of Northern India*, p. 12.
48. M' Gregor, *op. cit.*, p. 143.
49. See further, Dr Fauja Singh's article, *Missionary Quarterly*, Jan-March, 1961.
50. Gough, Charles and Innes, A.D., *The Sikhs and the Sikh Wars*, p. 43.
51. *Ibid*, pp. 43-44.
52. Sinha, N. K., *Ranjit Singh*, pp. 156-172.
53. 15th of *Har, Sambat* 1896, Suri, Lala Sohan Lal, *Umdat-ut-Tawarikh*, III, (translation into English V.S. Suri), (1961), p. 695.
54. Cunningham, *History of the Punjab*, p. 200.
55. Mahajan, Jagmohan, *Circumstances Leading to Annexation of Punjab*, p. 15.
56. Cunningham, *op. cit.*, p. 200.
57. The case of his two sons through Mehtab Kaur, the senior most of his wives, is one instance. See Latif (*History of the Punjab*, p. 370) who even gives the names of the persons fron whom the two sons were procured. Sher Singh was purchased from his father Nihala, a Chintz weaver, a native of Mukerian, and Tara Singh from a Mohammedan woman, daughter of Manki, a slave girl of Mehatab Kaur.
58. Griffin, *op. cit.*, pp. 106-107.
59. Raja Dhian Singh Dogra, Ranjit Singh's Prime Minister and his relation who had their ambitions to realise after the Maharaja's death.
60. Hugel, Baron Chrles, *Travels in Kashmir and the Punjab*, London (1845), p. 287.
61. *Supra*, Civil Administration of Ranjit Singh.
62. Cunningham, *op. cit.*, p. 246; Sinha, *Ranjit Singh*, p. 138.
63. Payne, *Short History of the Sikhs* pp. 151-152, Gordon, *The Sikhs*, p. 124.
64. Payne, *op. cit.*, pp. 144-145, Gordon, p. 124.
65. Sinha, N.K., *Ranjit Singh*, pp. 136-39.
66. Chopra, G.L., *The Punjab as a Sovereign State*, p. 140.

67. Payne, *op. cit*., p. 137.
68. See volume 1 of this work, the chapter on Lord Minto.
69. Which lay on the left of the river Sutlej and over which he had decisive claims all of which however were brushed aside by the British who occupied this strategic place in 1835, and Auckland converted it into a cantonment in 1838.
70. See chapter 12 on Lord Ellenborough.
71. Payne, *Short History of the Sikhs*, pp. 133-134.
72. *Calcutta Review*, August, 1844, p. 475.
73. Sinha, N.K., *op. cit*., pp. 90-91.

9

Earl of Ellenborough, 1842-44

Annexation of Sind

The Earl of Ellenborough was born in a family which had distinguished itself in Law and Church. His father was Edward Law who later became Lord Ellenborough and was appointed Lord Chief Justice of Common Pleas. His mother was Ann, daughter of Captain George Towry. Born on 8 September 1790, he was named Edward Law till he became Earl of Ellenborough. He was educated at Eton and St. John's college. In 1813 he became M.P., and married Octavia Stewart, sister of Lord Castlereagh and daughter of 1st Marquess of Londonderry. He succeeded his father in 1818. His wife died in 1819 and he married Jane Elizabeth, daughter of Sir Henry Digby five years later. She was a versatile and very beautiful lady who proved unfaithful to him, and was divorced in 1830. Edward was appointed Lord Privy Seal in 1828, and later as the President of the Board of Control in which position he became thoroughly conversant in Indian affairs. Sir Robert Peel appointed him Governor-General of India in 1841, and he came out to blast the Afghan policy of Lord Auckland whom he succeeded. He brought the Afghan War to a close but by his impetuous and theatrical actions made himself a subject of ridicule not only in India, but also in England.[1]

The most important event during his viceroyalty in India, however, was the annexation of Sind. A country situated in the south of the Punjab, on both sides of the Indus, extending to the Arabian sea and surrounded in the east and the west by barren lands; during the Mughal times Sind acknowledged their sway. When Nadir Shah invaded India in 1739, he brought it under his submission, and after his death it remained a tributary state to the Afghans. Towards the close of the 18th century some chieftains of the Talpura tribe coming from Baluchistan occupied it, and parcelled it out among themselves. The more important of these chieftains were those of Khairpur, Mirpur and Hyderabad, the first of these claiming a suzerainty over the rest.

Past History

If we have a brief review of the past history of this country, the first contact with it was made by the British as usual through merchants in 1758 when a permission to establish a factory at Thatta was secured. In 1761 more commercial concessions were given to them, but by 1775 the English, having developed a distrust in the minds of the Amirs of Sind due to their obnoxious interference in the Sind politics, were compelled to withdraw from the country.

Another English attempt to establish some commercial interests in Sind failed in 1799. But when in 1807 the political events in Europe took a sharp turn due to Napoleon's signing the Treaty of Tilsit with the Tsar of Russia thereby developing the possibility of the French march on the eastern empire of England, the British sent a mission to Sind, as they did to the Punjab. The mission imposed a treaty on the Amirs in 1809, which was renewed in 1820 whereby an internal friendship was signed between British India and Sind, and the Amirs bound themselves not to permit any European, particularly of "the tribe of the French", or an American to settle in their country; though each would allow the settlement of the other's subjects if they conducted themselves in an orderly manner. Nothing more of importance happened in the Anglo-Sind relations till 1831.

In the meanwhile Ranjit Singh having conquered Multan in 1818, began to develop his ambitions towards Sind. In 1823 he actually led an expedition in that direction with the pretext of punishing the Balochis who he said, had attacked his troops in Multan, but with the real intention of exploring the possibility of the occupation of Shikarpur.[2] Amirs being alarmed, sent him presents, and Ranjit Singh returned. In 1824 Ranjit Singh asserted that the Afghan possessions in the Punjab having been occupied by him, he supplanted their authority, and therefore the Amirs should pay the tribute to him which of old they used to pay to the Afghans. The response naturally being negative, since the Amirs had long since stopped paying that tribute, Ranjit Singh marched his forces into Sind in 1825, but abandoned the plan of its conquest due to the severe famine that preyed upon that country. In 1826 he marched his forces once again, but Syed Ahmed having raised a standard of revolt in Peshawar, he had to return in haste.[3]

The British could not watch the rising ambitions of Ranjit Singh towards Sind unconcerned. And therefore from the year 1831 Sind entered into a period of intense diplomatic activity in which game Ranjit Singh was ultimately defeated and completely eliminated from that land. The game started with the plan of the navigation of the Indus.

Navigation of the Indus

The British had been interested in the navigation of the river Indus from the early years of the 19th century. They had been entertaining the hopes of controlling the Central Asian markets, which was very much possible through the Indus route. "The navigation of Indus" wrote William Moorcroft as early as 1809, "although little known to Europeans, as it had not been attempted by them... is perfectly practicable for boats of considerable burden".[4] There were, however, several other reasons as well which precipitated the British plan to navigate the river. By the treaty of Turkomanchai signed between Russia and Persia in February 1828, as in the words of Kaye, "Persia was delivered hand and foot bound to the court of St. Petersburgh".[5] Russia was further aspiring for the exploits not only in Afghanistan, but also in Khorassan and Herat, and according to one view, in India as well. The navigation of the Indus could develop British contacts with all these countries and thus forestall the Russian moves.

Moreover, just this time a mission from the Persian ruler Fateh Ali carrying a proposal for the marriage of his daughter, visited the Amir of Hyderabad, and the British naturally grew apprehensive that if both these countries became friendly, Russia could very easily develop her influence on Sind through Persia. And again, Russia already had commercial influence in Bokhara and the adjoining Khanates, which could be counteracted easily by similar English interests in Sind and Central Asia. Another benefit of the Indus navigation would be the development of new markets for the produce and manufactures of the European and Indian dominions of the British. And again, the British did not fail in realising the growing interests of Ranjit Singh in Sind, through the occupation of which he was aspiring to have an outlet on the Arabian sea, whereby perhaps to establish contacts with the overseas countries. The only check on Ranjit Singh toward this side, wrote Cunningham, was "to open the Indus to the navigation of the world".[6] Besides the secret purpose of the English, as confirmed by Charles Masson, was to encircle the Country of the Maharaja.[7] Lord Ellenborough's despatch of October 1842 to the Queen read: "Lord Ellenborough looks forward to the Indus superseding the gangs as the channel of communication with England, and to bringing European regiments and all military stores by that route to the North-Western Frontier".

But such a move on the part of the English, it was realised, would naturally he resented by Ranjit Singh as also by the Amirs of Sind. A very cautious plan was therefore needed, which was chalked out by the British authorities during 1827-28.

In 1827 Ranjit Singh had sent some presents to Amherst, the then Governor-General of India. The next year when Amherst retired to England, it was planned that presents should be sent in return to the Maharaja on behalf of the British crown. These presents would consist of a team of cart-horses, one stallion and 4 mares, and would be sent through the Indus, and "the authorities both in England and India contemplated that much information of political and geographical nature might be acquired in such a journey".[8] Burnes was put in charge of all these transactions, and it was planned that if the Amirs of Sind objected to his passage through Sind, he would say that there was a possibility of the carriage meant for the Maharaja being worn out if sent by road. Therefore other transition through the river was necessary.

This clearly shows the dishonesty and a treacherous diplomacy in the British game. The mission's "ulterior purpose and its being mission of espionage through Sind came to the surface later during the Afghan war," writes Dr. R.R. Sethi.[9] And Metcalfe too wrote that such a trick was 'unworthy of our Government.' Moreover we learn on the authority of Mohan Lal, that about twenty years before similar presents had already been sent to Ranjit Singh by road. The argument of the carriage being worn out, therefore, was entirely fallacious. Sir Alexander Burnes himself wrote about the scheme: "This seems to me highly objectionable. It is a trick, in my opinion, unworthy of our Government, which cannot fail, when detected, as most probably it will be, to excite the jealousy and indignation of powers on whom we play it. It may even lead to war".[10]

Amirs as it was expected, did object to the British move. And finally it was only on the threat of Ranjit Singh's forces, which incidentally were nearby in Dera-Ghazi-Khan, that the Amirs gave their permission. Besides securing the threat of the Maharaja's forces on the pretext of safe transition of the presents meant for him, the English also secured a personal intervention of the Maharaja who, it is said, called the envoy of the Amirs to his presence and reprimanded him for the behaviour. Ranjit Singh did all this because he was already out to use any pretext for his designs against Sind. But little did he know that in this case the British were playing a dog's trick on him.

Besides bringing presents, Burnes is said to have made a casual reference to the possibility of opening up the Indus and the Sutlej to navigation. Wade, the British agent at Ludhiana, who was accompanying Burnes on his visit to the Darbar, also brought with him a proposal to arrange an interview with Bentinck, the Governor-General, at Rupar where Ranjit Singh would be received with all pomp and show. The next day the Governor-General would pay a return visit to the Maharaja on the latter's side of the border.[11]

The meeting between the Governor-General and the Maharaja was arranged at Rupar on 26 October 1831. Here Ranjit Singh, according to Latif, invited the Governor-General for a joint action against Sind which could be divided between the two. But the latter refused, telling him that the British were not interested in Sind at all. Thus, while lulling the Maharaja to sleep, writes Abdul Qadir,[12] the Governor-General let him know vaguely that four days before this meeting Pottinger had already been issued the instructions to proceed to Sind and sign with the Amirs a commercial treaty.[13]

When Burnes reported favourably on the suitability of the Indus navigation, the Governor-General decided to launch his project forthwith. Pottinger was sent to the Amirs with a detailed plan for the Indus navigation. He was thoroughly educated as to how he would proceed. He would take guarantee from the Amirs against obstructions to the trade through the river. He would also make the Amirs realise how their people would flourish. And if the Amirs yet objected, Pottinger was to say that the Amirs had no right to violate the international law by depriving all the states on the Indus of trade benefits from the river, only; because they happened to occupy a small portion of it.[14]

These instructions were issued to Pottinger only four days before the meeting at Rupar. Proceeding the planned way Pottinger at long last did succeed in making the Amirs sign the treaty on 4 April 1832. The essential feature of the Treaty was that the Amirs would permit the British to carry on their trade through the Indus, but that no permission would be given for the transition of military stores, nor would they permit armed vessels through it. Further it was expressly laid down that no British merchant would be permitted to settle in Sind, and this shows how distrustful the Amirs were of the British designs. A supplement to this Treaty, signed on 22 April transferred the final powers of dividing the levy of duties on foreign goods from Amirs to the British.

All these measures, according to Gordon,[15] naturally aroused strong suspicion in the mind of the Maharaja, and it is said that when he learnt of these transactions he could not sleep for several nights. The British, however, not only soothed him, he was also prevailed upon, together with the Nawab of Bhawalpur, to open the river Sutlej as well for navigation. And thus the rivers Sutlej and Indus lay open to the British for their commercial and political games.

After opening up these rivers to navigation, the next British proposal, as it originated with Wade, was that the British officers should be stationed at several places on the line of navigation in the Indus. He argued that the Sikhs, Sindhians and Daodpotras were hostile to one another, and if the British officers were not stationed in their mist, their hostilities might hinder a smooth running of the trade. Secondly, by doing so, Ranjit Singh's intention to convert Mithankot into a mart for the produce of his own country would be foiled. Thirdly, the British purpose behind all this being political, he argued that the presence of British officers would facilitate the realisation of it. Fourthly, the line between Mithankot and Shikarpur being at the mercy of the Amirs of Sind, the British would be able to protect it. And lastly, he forwarded that Mithankot being a central place, if a British officer was stationed there he would be able to control and regulate all the trade.

But to put this proposal in the effect was not an easy job. The Amirs of Sind already apprehensive of the British designs, would not agree to the proposal that British officer should be stationed in their country. Pottinger was sent once again to handle them, but they did not budge from their position an inch. When all the appeasements and threats failed, a compromise was at last struck, and it was agreed that instead of a European, some native would be appointed as British officer in Sind. And thus was the Indus line opened up for trade.

Despite all the efforts, however, this trade route could never become popular with merchants even though so much capital had been made out of its importance. Burnes was sent to Kabul to convince the Kabul merchants of its utility, but this mission also failed and it was not long before this route had to be closed.

The reasons for its failure were quite plain. Of all the parties who signed the agreement, British alone were interested in the project. But their action too was inspired more by political motives than commercial. Ranjit Singh, Bhawal Khan of Bhawalpur and the Amirs of Sind, all showed their suspicions in the project; the Amirs detained and delayed boats passing through their territories and put all sorts of obstacles in the way of the smooth running of the trade, despite repeated threats of the British. Thus the only purpose served by opening up these rivers for navigation was that the Russian and the Sikh designs towards Sind were checked, or as Charles Masson wrote: "The results of the policy concealed under this pretext have been the introduction of troops into the countries on and beyond the river, and of some half dozen steamers on the stream itself, employed for warlike objects, not those of trade".[16] But then this was the main motive of the British, and in this they succeeded.

The Political Hold

Having thus established their commercial realisation with Sind, it was now not difficult for the English to develop their political hold. In fact, in the East, English politicians had always supplanted the English merchant, and in this Sind could be one exception. The question of Shikarpur facilitated their move.

Shikarpur, lying west of the Indus, below Mithankot, was a place known far and wide for its being an important commercial centre. Besides, it have military importance as well, for it lay on the way to the Bolan Pass, and for the protection of this Pass a military centre could best be established here. Ranjit Singh wanted to occupy the city for obvious reasons, which the English, again, would not permit.

Mazaries, a tribe of free-booters inhabiting some territory south-west of Mithankot, at a few miles distance from it, carried their incursions alike in Sind, Bhawalpur and the Lahore territories. But since they occupied the border land between Sind and Punjab, the Amirs, despite their suzerainty, could not control them. The incursions of the Mazaries in the Lahore territories increased by 1336, and Ranjit Singh decided to crush their power once and for all. Besides, taking an excuse for the losses he suffered due to their inroads, the Maharaja demanded Shikarpur from the Amirs. "The British could have no reasonable objection to his occupying it. It lay to the west of the Sutlej-Indus, and according to the treaty of 1809, they had agreed not to interfere with his affairs in tarns-Sutlej territories." the Amirs, however, appealed to the British for help and the latter were already waiting for such an opportunity. On 25 November 1836, a treaty was signed between the English and the Amirs. By this treaty, the Amirs were obliged to receive a British agent who would be a medium of communication between the Maharaja and the Amirs. The Amirs would also withdraw their *vakil* from Lahore. And in return for this the British agreed to defend the Amir's territories.

By signing this treaty, as it is obvious, the Amirs signed their own death warrants. It was now a clear writing on the wall that it would not be long before their power would be thrown in the dustbin of history and their country would be annexed. Ranjit Singh fretted and fumed, but was helpless.

The Annexation

The British imperialism in India had been known for its aggressiveness. But the policy of aggressiveness was never so nakedly followed as in Sind. The British developed their hold over this country by stages, and after what has been narrated above, the newt stage came when the British desired to send their forces into Afghanistan in support of the ex-Afghan-Amir, Shah Shuja, and Ranjit Singh did not permit the British forces to march through his country in 1839. Where might was right, there was no question of forwarding arguments. The only alternative was that the British forces should be sent through Sind, and not caring for the treaty of 1832 with the Amirs, they were simply told that "while the present exigency lasts the article of the treaty prohibiting the use of the Indus for the conveyance of military must necessarily be suspended".[17] There was no need for waiting for the Amirs's reply, and the British forces marched through Sind.

The British, however, still were not contented. And now was a demand made upon the Amirs for which there was neither any reason nor a moral ground. The Amirs were required to make a payment of their arrears of tribute to Shah Shuja, the ex-ruler of Afghanistan, now seeking refuge under the British. The Amirs argued in vain that they had not paid their tribute for thirty years, and that Shah Shuja himself had exempted them from it. Moreover, the tribute was due only to the ruler of Afghanistan, who at that time was Dost Mohammed and not Shah Shuja. But the British needed money, and no arguments. The Amirs were frankly told that "we have the ready power to crush and annihilate them, and we will not hesitate to call it into action". It is useless to criticise the British too much for such an attitude.

Still not satisfied, Sir John Keane threatened to march upon Sind, and got the Amirs to sign a new treaty on 11 March 1839. Later on, however, it was discovered that the treaty should have been different from what it actually was. And without consulting the Amirs it was arbitrarily revised and presented before them for signature. The Amirs objected, but since the British had the 'ready power' to annihilate them, they gave way. By this treaty, each Amir was placed in his own possession, and their mutual disputes were to be referred to the British for arbitration. Sind was formally placed under the British protection, and the British forces for the purpose were to be stationed at a convenient place west of the Indus. The Amirs would pay three lakhs of rupees annually to meet their expenses, and this amount would be realised from the three Amirs in proportion to their territories. Lord Auckland himself remarked on this treaty: "The confederacy of the Amirs is virtually dissolved".

During the First Afghan War, Sind was used by the British as a base for their operations. Despite chances for mischief during the British disaster in Afghanistan, the Amirs remained faithful. Still, when the war was over the Amirs were charged of disaffection and hostility. Major James Outram, the British Resident at Hyderabad, was superseded by Sir Charles Napier–a rank annexations who was put in supreme control of both civil and political affairs in Sind in September 1842. And the consequences of the political powers passing into the hands of a General were natural. Innes remarks "Sir Charles conducted his operations on the theory that the annexation of Sind would be a very beneficent piece of rascality for which it was his business to find an excuse—a robbery to be plausibly effected".

An opportunity offered itself to Napier. There was a disputed succession of Khairpur, and without considering any merit or right, Napier decided in favour of Ali Murad.[17] But when this process of the game could not bring him a speedy advantage, he declared that the charges of unfaithfulness made against the Amirs during the Afghan war had been substantiated, and therefore they deserved a severe punishment. The punishment would be in the shape of a new treaty, whereby they would cede an important territory in lieu of the tribute of three lakhs of rupees for the maintenance of the subsidiary force; would provide fuel for the English steamers navigating in the Indus; and would give up in favour of the British, the right of owning money. The money henceforward issued in Sind, would bear the "effigy of the sovereign of England". Napier declared in December 1842, that the new treaty must be signed by 20 January 1843, otherwise the unfriendly attitude of the Amirs would be proved.

The terms of the proposed new treaty were too harsh, and required of the Amirs a complete surrender of national rights. Outram called a meeting of the Amirs at Khairpur to persuade them. The Amirs of lower Sind reached in time, while those of the upper Sind were delayed by two days as a result of the machination of Ali Murad. This could not be tolerated by the hot-blooded imperious, General Napier, who took an amazing step and without declaring a war, attacked the famous fortress of Imamgarh between Khairpur and Hyderabad, and razed it to the ground; "as though the rights of the Governor-General of India, to parcel in (Sind) out at his pleasure were unquestioned".

Still, however, Outram was able to persuade the Amirs to sign the treaty so that the worst could be avoided. The Amirs warned Napier to vacate Hyderabad, lest the British should be harmed by their countrymen who could not be controlled under the circumstance. Yet the warning was not heeded, and in three days the Baluchis, excited by the high-handedness of Napier attacked Outram's residence, who after a gallant defence was able to escape to take refuge on a steamer. Now a regular war began.

On 17 February 1843 Napier gave a brilliant battle, an able general as he was, to 30,000 men of the Amirs at Miani and was able to defeat them completely and destroy 5,000 of their number by a mere force of less than 3,000 men under his command.[18] Hyderabad was occupied, on 27 March 1843 Mirpur fell, and Napier wrote to Ellenborough: "Paccavi, I have Sind". Sind was annexed, and the Amirs were exiled. Napier got £70,000 out of the plunder of Hyderabad, while Outram was offered £3,000. Which he, however, refused to keep an distributed in charity, saying "I am sick of policy".

Thus did it happen. P.E. Roberts writes: "An able and ambitious General, eager for distinction, and impatiently believing that the undoubted benefits of British rule justified almost any means of extending it, brought the rough-hewn ready-made solution of the soldiers to bear on an intricate administrative problem".[19]

The Directors themselves disapproved of Napier's Sind policy and Lord Ellenborough's silent annexation of it, though they had no courage to restore Sind to the Amirs. It is useless to repeat too often that the Amirs were innocent, that they had given absolutely no provocation to the British, and that they remained perfectly loyal to their engagements with the British during and after the Afghan war. "If the Afghan episode is the most disastrous in our Indian annals, that of Sind is morally even less excusable". Napier himself wrote in his diary: "we have no right to seize Sind, yet we shall do so and a very advantageous, useful, humane piece of rascality it will be". And commenting on this, writes Dr. Marshman, in Napier's action, "the rascality is more apparent than the advantage".[20]

Sind is the only British acquisition in India, writes Ramsay Muir, "of which it may fairly be said that it was not necessitated by circumstances and that it was, therefore, an act of aggression".[21] The conquest of Sind, at best, was only the aftermath of the Afghan disaster. "The real cause of this chastisement of the Amirs consisted in the chastisement the British had received from the Afghans".

W.A.J. Archbold agrees: "In the light of subsequent history it may even be argued that Outram's policy of trust in the Amirs would have proved less wise than Napier's policy of vigilant coercion". "And yet," Archbold comments, "the whole transaction has been thought to bear a colour of injustice which may rightly be ascribed to some of its parts, and the plea of the happiness of the people, who gained enormously by the change, has not been held sufficient to justify what happened".[22]

Truly, one may conclude with Dr. Ishwari Prasad, that the Amirs were unfortunate "victims of British imperialism; they lost their all and found no tribunal to which they could address an appeal".[23]

GWALIOR UNDER BRITISH PROTECTION

Another event of importance in the time of Ellenborough occurred in the British relations with Gwalior. Here at least, Ellenborough's attitude was based more on reason than on aggression. Sindhia had been left as the most powerful Maratha chief after the third Maratha war ending in 1818. In 1843 his throne was occupied by minor, in whose time the state's administration began to rot. The Regent of the ruler who was responsible for this, was dismissed by the young widow of the late ruler with the approval of Ellenborough, This, however, proved to be a signal for confusion which threatened a civil war in the country. The Sindhia army consisted of 40,000 men, and the greatest apprehension in the mid of Ellenborough was that the Punjab being in the midst of the most serious trouble, this formidable army might join hands with the Sikhs and thus create a serious situation. Appealing to Lord Wellesley's treaty signed with Sindhia in 1804, Ellenborough marched his forces on the Chambal, though still assuming that the matter could be settled by peaceful means. The army of Gwalior, however, was prepared to try their hands with the British, and prevented their rulers from making a peaceful settlement. Two battles were fought on 29 December 1843. One at Maharajpur where the Marathas lost 3,000 killed and wounded, while the British lost 297. British secured a victory, but at a heavy cost. The second battle was fought the same day at Paniar where General Grey won a comparatively cheap victory.

As a result of this war, though no territory of Gwalior was annexed, the state was brought under definite British protection. The ruler being a minor, for the next decade the state administration was virtually run by the British Resident. The state army was reduced to 9,000 soldiers, and a British contingent of 10,000 was raised for the state.

Hardly had Ellenborough returned with victory to Calcutta, expecting appreciation from Home, when he received the orders for his recall. The Directors had not liked his policy of naked aggression in Sind, and the tone of his despatches had offended them. This ended Ellenborough's short career in India.

Returning to England, he became G.C.B. And was created an Earl. In 1846 Sir Robert Peel appointed him First Lord of Admiralty in his Cabinet, and in 1850 he was again appointed President of the Board of Control by Lord Derby, but somehow having offended the Queen and the Parliament, he resigned from this post in 1858. After this he continued participating in Parliamentary debates, but never again occupied any post of importance. He died on 22 December 1871.

REFERENCES

1. See Chapter on Lord Auckland.
2. See for details, Prinsep, *Origin of the Sikh Power in Punjab* pp. 140; and Chhabra, G.S., *History of Punjab*, Chapter VIII.
3. Cunningham, *History of the Sikhs*, p. 165; Latif, *History of the Punjab*, p. 433.
4. Moorcroft, W., *Travels in Himalayan Provinces of Hindustan and Punjab*, II, p. 338.
5. Kaye, *History of War in Afghanistan*, I, pp. 151-56.
6. Cunningham, *op. cit.*, p. 172.
7. Masson, Charles, *Narrative of Various Journeys*, p. 432.
8. Sethi, R.R., *The Mighty and Shrewd Maharaja*, p. 78.
9. *Ibid.* p. 82.
10. Quoted by Gilliat, Edward, *Heroes of Modern India*, p. 145.
11. Ranjit Singh's Centenary Vol., published by Khalsa College, Amritsar.
12. *Ibid.*
13. Chhabra, *op. cit.*, II, Chapter VIII.
14. Punjab Govt. Records 98/181, Govt. to Pottinger, Oct. 22. 1831.
15. Gordon, *The Sikhs*, p. 31.
16. Masson, *Charles, Narrative of Various Journeys in Balochistan, Afghanistan, the Punjab and Kalat*, p. 432.
17. See for details *Cambridge History of India*, V, p. 532.
18. Napier, William, *The Conquest of Sind*.
19. Roberts, *History of British India*, p. 329.
20. Marshman, *History of India*, p. 333.
21. Ramsay Muir, *Making of British India*, p. 243.
22. *Cambridge History of India*, V, pp. 538-39.
23. Prasad and Subedar, *op. cit.*, p. 252.

10

Viscount Hardinge, 1844-48

Henry Hardinge was born on 30 March 1785. His father was Rev. Henry Hardinge, Rector of Stanhope County Durham, his Mother being "Frances, daughter of James Best of Boxley in Kent. His family came from King's Norton in Derbyshire, where an ancestor had raised a troop of horses for Charles I and had been knighted at the Restoration[1] of 1660. After getting his education at Durham, Henry joined the Queen's Rangers in Canada in 1800, was promoted Captain in the 57th Foot when he was nineteen, later got training at the Royal Military Academy and doing excellently well there, got an appointment in the Quartermaster-General's staff headed by Sir Bent Spencer. He participated in the Peninsular War, and did so well in the several battles fought in Portugal and elsewhere, that he got speedy promotions from Major to Lieutenant-Colonel, and then Brigadier-General. Henry got wounded four times and had his left arm shot off in one of the battles. Wellington rewarded him with Napoleon's sword after the Waterloo, and he got as many as ten foreign decorations.

After the War was over, he was made K.C.B. Later he entered the Parliament, and in 1821 got married in a distinguished family. The famous British statesman Castlereagh and Lord Ellenborough, the Governor-General of India during 1842-44, were his brothers-in-law. After this he got his appointment in the Cabinet as Secretary of War, later on became Chief Secretary for Ireland, declined the offer of the post of Commander-in-Chief of India in 1842, whereafter in 1844 he was appointed Governor-General of India, to succeed his own brother-in-law, Ellenborough, the Governor-General who annexed Sind.

A brave soldier and statesman, Lord Hardinge had thus distinguished himself as a man who always fully understood what he undertook. For twenty years he had been a member of the Parliament, and had also been Secretary of War, thus bringing a rich experience of soldier and politician to bear on the Indian scene.

In India, however, the soldier in Hardinge was more active than the statesman or administrator, and therefore the most important event of his Governor-Generalship was the first Sikh War, in which the great invincible Sikh soldiers for the first time met their effectual defeat, and the Sikh political edifice which had so laboriously been built by Maharaja Ranjit Singh crumbled to pieces.

Before we discuss this important event, a brief reference to his other activities may he made. In his internal administration, the foremost problem that he had to handle was to continue the work on the great scheme of irrigation, known as the Ganges Canal, which had been commenced many years before, but was not opened till 1856. He seems to have worked in this matter with proper zeal, as his son Charles Viscount Hardinge, who was his Private Secretary and biographer, wrote: "The cultivators of the Doab owe a heavy debt of gratitude to the Governor-General for his firmness in this matter".[2] The Calcutta conservancy was reformed. The transit duties between the Indian States of Central India were abolished, and the rivers Sutlej and the Indus were practically freed from these imposts. Under the superintendentship of Dr Jameson, the cultivation of tea was much encouraged, especially in Assam, where a company was also formed for this purpose.

Among his other works was has effort to abolish *sati*. In the British territories it had already been abolished by Lord Bentinck. As a result of his effort, it is said *sati* now remained only in the independent state of Nepal.

Lord Hardinge paid serious attention to the preservation of ancient monuments in India. Taj Mahal and the Agra Fort were repaired, and the unseemly grotesque ornament which had been placed on the top of Qutab Minar was removed.

More important, however, were the military reforms which he introduced after the first Sikh War. These were based on the two principles of maintaining unimpaired the strength of the European troops in India and redistributing the entire army so that the North-Western Frontier and the Punjab might be secured against any contingency. Subject to these principles, no fewer than 50,000 sepoys were disbanded, reducing thereby the strength of the Indian regiments from 1,000 to 800 men each. Despite this, however, "the army was more numerous than it had been in 1837, the last year of peace in India," writes his son and biographer.[3] Strength of artillery as regards men, was maintained, and the nine-pounders previously drawn by bullocks, were now horsed. The result of all these reforms was that no less then £1,160,000 was saved in the military budget.

At the end of the Sikh war, 12 months *bhatta* was granted to the sepoys, and pensions of the wounded men were increased from 4 to 7 rupees a month. Hutting money was disallowed, and all the wounded men received free ration in hospitals.

Among his other works was the order he issued that in future an appointment in a public service would be given only to that person who had received English education. The practice of human sacrifice among the Gonds of the hilly tracts of Orissa was suppressed. Lord Hardinge encouraged free trade, abolished many octroi duties and reduced the duty on salt. Such in brief were the peace time achievements of Lord Hardinge in India.

THE FIRST ANGLO-SIKH WAR

Ranjit Singh died in 1839, and hardly six years had passed when this war came. Much has been said regarding the causes of the First Anglo-Sikh War. On 12 December 1845 the Sikh soldiers crossed the river Sutlej, while on 13 December the Governor-General issued his historic proclamation in which he blamed the Sikhs of aggression and declared war on them. Justifying his action, he asserted among other things, that the British had faithfully observed the conditions of the treaty of Amritsar which had laid down the river Sutlej as the border line between the two governments; that despite "Many most unfriendly proceedings on the part of the Durbar, utmost forbearance was shown by the Governor-General;" and that despite "the honest British desire to remain friendly," the Sikh army marched from Lahore by the orders of the Durbar to invade the British territory, and "without a shadow of provocation, invaded the British territories". The Governor-General, thus, while declaring war also announced that all the long coveted territorial possessions of the Lahore Durbar on the left bank of the Sutlej were thereby annexed.

The above proclamation of the Governor-General has been criticised by certain Indian as well as European writers, some of whom try to put the entire blame on the British and prove that the Sikhs have done absolutely nothing that they should not have done; and there are others who say exactly the reverse. A true and impartial observer of facts, however, while blaming the British for their high-handedness, would not fail to discern certain acts of the Sikhs, which invited this catastrophe. In fact there were several factors which led of this war, and all of them must properly be scrutinised if we desire of have a true picture of the event.

The British Responsibility

The major responsibility for the first Sikh war lay on the British who had been playing an aggressive part against the Sikh's right since she signing of the Treaty of Amritsar in 1809, which itself was considered only to be an instance of Ranjit Singh's weakness. The Anglo-Sikh disputes like that of Wadni in 1823, of Ferozepur in 1835, and of Shikarpur in 1836, all prove this fact. And even before Ranjit Singh's death, after his visit to Lahore in connection which the Tripartite Treaty of 1838, Osborne had remarked in his diary that after the Maharaja's death the first British action should be to march a strong force and occupy the Punjab.

The constantly increasing military pressure of the British on the Sutlej border, before and after the death of Ranjit Singh, under the pretext that it was a precaution against troubles resulting from the possible breakdown of the machinery of the Government at Lahore after Ranjit Singh's death, was bound to provoke the Sikh nation. Yet the British paid no heed. By the treaty of 1809 the British were to withdraw the detachment of the British troops advanced to Ludhiana, but they did not do this. Yet till 1838 the British frontier troops were only one regiment at Sabathu and two at Ludhiana, with six pieces of artillery, the total number of men being a little over 2,500. Auckland raised this total to about 8,000 by adding to Ludhiana and creating a new cantonment at Ferozepur. Ellenborough created new stations at Ambala, Kasauli and Simla and raised the total thus to 14,000 with field guns numbering 48. Lord Hardinge raised the total yet further to 32,000 men and 68 field guns, besides 10,000 of the men with artillery at Meerut.

Then again, the Tripartite Treaty was signed, as we have discussed, between Ranjit Singh, the British and Shah Shuja in 1838. One of the essential terms of the Treaty was that after Shah's success, he would confer Peshawar to the Sikhs. While, despite the Sikh dissatisfaction with the general terms of the Treaty, they were preparing to give an account of their faithfulness to the agreement on the one hand, while on the other, through their agent Macnaughten, the British entered into a secret understanding with Shah Shuja, that when Ranjit Singh's line ended with his grandson, Prince

Nau Nihal's death, Shah Shuja would be helped in securing Peshawar. And writes Cunningham: "it would be idle to suppose the Lahore Government ignorant of a scheme which was discussed in official correspondence".[4]

Later, when the British plans in Afghanistan failed, and they had to fight the first Afghan war, under the terms of the Treaty, Henry Lawrence wrote to J. C. Marshman in April 1842, "while the Sikhs were only bound to employ a contingent of 6,000 men, they did the work with not less than 15,000 leaving the stipulated number in position, and withdrawing the rest to Jamrood and Peshawar, where they remained ready to support those in the pass, if necessary".[5] And writing to the Queen on 21 April the Governor-General himself said: "The Sikh army cooperated with that of India by a second pass leading to Ali Masjid, and there is no reason to doubt the good faith of the Sikh Government".[6] Yet when the Sikhs were giving so handsome an account of themselves in fulfilment of their engagements, the British were assembling a third army of "reserve at Ferozepur on the frontier of the Punjab to keep the Sikhs in check". But none among the Sikhs understood what the British wanted to check them from!

Lord Ellenborough himself had in fact commented in a letter to the Home authorities on 30 September 1843: "There does not seem to be any feeling against us (in the Punjab). They are only quarrelling amongst themselves apparently; nor do I see the least show of hostility to us anywhere". Maharaja Sher Singh had been murdered by this time, and even after that, the Governor-General wrote to the Duke of Wellington on 20 November 1843, "that no indication has been given of the least desire to provoke the resentment of the British Government". On 2 July 1844 he wrote further: "In the Punjab there is more of pacific appearance than at any time since the murder of Sher Singh".

Nor did the British leave any stone unturned in their efforts to seduce some influential officers of the Lahore Durbar. When Maharaja Sher Singh gave every cooperation in the first Afghan war, and sent Raja Gulab Singh to help the British against the Afghans in January 1842, it occurred to Henry Lawrence that "a consideration should be offered to Raja Dhian Singh and Gulab Singh, for their assistance, they alone in the Punjab being able to give". He wrote on 29 January 1842, "on the terms of efficient support we assist Raja Gulab Singh to get possession of the valley of Jallalabad and endeavour to make some arrangement to secure Peshawar to his family".[7] Similar efforts were made to seduce Tej Singh and Lal Singh, the Poorbia officers of Fort of Rohtas; and some European officers such as General Ventura. And in all this, they succeeded.

On 1 January 1844 the Lahore Durbar learnt that the British were building a fort at Ferozepur. Though this information proved to be incorrect, on 8 February, it was learnt that a magazine instead, was under construction. On 17 May the report reached that the English were buying large quantities of grain to be stored at Ferozepur, and on 1 June, it was learnt that the English commandant at Ferozepur had directed *zamindars* not to sow any land for an autumn crop as a very large army was to be assembled after the rains. Such British activities obviously perplexed the Sikhs, who could not understand the British actions.

During 1844-45 a large number of boats began to be prepared by the British at Bombay; the purpose being to construct bridges across the Sutlej, and as Lord Ellenborough wrote to the Duke of Wellington on 9 May 1844, to "convey troops up and down, and save an enormous charge on the Sutlej". The Sikhs naturally felt apprehensive regarding the British designs. But when asked for the information, the British only replied that the boats were meant to facilitate trade in the Indus and the Sutlej. The Indus navigation schemes having already failed, the British reply was hardly convincing.

The British establishment of a grand supply depot at Basian near Rajkot, strengthened the Sikh doubts. Then, the collection of ordnance and ammunition at Sakkar in Sind to equip a force of 5,000 to march towards Multan, was a subject of ordinary official correspondence. And although Charles Napier, the Governor of Sind, expressed complete ignorance about this correspondence among his subordinates when enquired about by Cunningham, it is difficult to imagine that such activities should not have come to the notice of the Sikhs and thereby caused a provocation in their minds. The character of Napier who had recently annexed Sind in a deceitful manner, was too well known to be ignored.

The British provocations did not end here. They in fact had been planning to attack the Punjab much before the war actually began. As early as 22 October 1841 Lord Ellenborough wrote to the Duke of Wellington: "At present about 12,000 men are collected near Ferozepur to watch the Sikhs, and act if necessary. What I desired, therefore, was your opinion, founded as far as it could be upon imperfect geographical information which could be given to you, as to the best mode of attacking the Punjab".

Again, at the same time, John Ludlow writes: "The British agent on the Sutlej had proposed to March on Lahore with 12,000 men to restore order. The Calcutta papers teemed with plans for conquering the Punjab".

The British designs and aggression are also clear from a letter which Duke of Wellington wrote to Lord Fitzgerald on 6 April 1842 at the time the Sikhs were rendering a good service to the British cause in Afghanistan: "I am glad to see such a good account of the Sikh Government...But this I may say, if we are to maintain our position in Afghanistan, we ought to have Peshawar, the Khyber Pass, Jallalabad and the passes between that post and Kabul".[8]

These two cases clearly demonstrate the British attitude towards a friendly power. Peshawar belonged to the Lahore Durbar, and if it was to be occupied by the British it could not be done without a war.

There are many other instances[9] of the British provocation to the Sikhs, the mention of which would make the catalogue too lengthy. Only one more instance may be quoted here. Clerk was replaced by Lieutenant-Colonel Richmond in June 1843, and the latter by Major Broadfoot in November 1841 as the British frontier agent. Such swift changes perplexed the Sikhs, yet more so when Broadfoot "avowed that he had arranged to occupy the Lahore territory, cis-Sutlej, in case anything should happen to Dalip Singh who was then ill (with small-pox). And he forbade the Durbar to send troops over for any purpose whatever". Further, as Campbell continues, "he acted as if the Lahore territories cis-Sutlej, were entirely under his control...he seems to have set up a formal claim to such a control, and asserted that this Lahore territory was just as much under his jurisdiction,' as he called it as any of the small protected States". Not only this, to give his claims a practical shape, when Lal Singh Adalati, a Lahore judge, crossed the Sutlej for some official duty in the Lahore territory at Talwandi, Broadfoot "roughly and very peremptorily ordered the Sikh party back over the river. Lal Singh, not willing to risk a collision, obeyed, returned to the river and embarked his men. But Broadfoot, not satisfied with this, followed them in person.... At least one shot was fired...the Sikh leaders were captured and detained. The shot then fired has been described as the first in the Sikh war".[10]

Carmichael Smyth wrote "Regarding the Punjab war; I am neither of the opinion that the Sikhs made unprovoked attack, nor that we have acted towards them with great forbearance...besides the Sikhs had translation of Sir Charles Napier's speech stating that we were going to war with them; and as all European powers would have done under the circumstances, the Sikhs thought it as well to be the first in the field. Moreover they were not encamped in our territory; but their own".[11]

The Other Factors

There were, however, other factors too which made their contribution to bring about the First Sikh War. British

India was a big country as compared to the Punjab, and therefore it offered greater opportunities for trade and industry. Yet more so when British India enjoyed a perfect peace, while in Punjab there was nothing but chaos after Ranjit Singh's death. Quite a few Punjab traders therefore corresponded freely with the English merchants in British India, Thus developing the British interest on the Punjab.

Nor could the irresponsible state of affairs in the Lahore Army be overlooked. The British failure against the Afghans whom the Khalsa had defeated several times, give an undue encouragement to the latter, and they were more anxious for a clash with the British than anybody else. Ranjit Singh having failed in establishing a civil supremacy over the military, the military officers became irresponsible after his death, and the Sikh army became a self-governing body by the time of Sher Singh. Its affairs began to be conducted by *panchayats*, or councils of "five" representing each company and elected by soldiers themselves. "In those days power was a dangerous possession. Every State official knew that to incur the displeasure of the army was equivalent to signing his own death warrant".[12] The "gravity of the situation," writes Gough, "was increased by the fear that the very high rate of pay which the Sikh soldiery had extracted for themselves, and the general success which had attended their insubordination, was having an injurious effect on the morale of the sepoys in the British army".[13] The Punjab authorities were themselves rather hard put to it. The military expenditure increased more than two-fold after Ranjit Singh's death, while the State income decreased. It was indeed a difficult problem for the inefficient Lahore rulers to face, and the British grew apprehensive lest they should instigate the Khalsa for a trouble in the north-east, for which in fact the British had been clamouring for long. And this is what actually happened.

The contribution made by the Lahore chiefs must also be mentioned. Moved "as much by jealousy of one another as by a common dread of the army, the chiefs of the Punjab clung to wealth and ease rather than to honour and independence". Their story after the death of Ranjit Singh is too full of treachery, cruelty and bloodshed to be repeated so often. The Dogras in the service of Ranjit Singh had been aspiring to occupy the Punjab throne even during his life time. Raja Dhian Singh,[14] the Prime Minister of the Maharaja, had made special efforts not to permit the heir-apparent Kharak Singh to get training in State craft. His candidate for the throne in fact was his own son Raja Hira Singh and to make his plan succeed he did not hesitate to use any method howsoever mean. He brought Kharak Singh to the throne after Ranjit Singh's death. But shortly after he got him killed by the slow effect of a poison. His son Nau Nihal Singh was next brought to the throne. But he too could not rule for long. A structure of the fort was made to fall upon him, from which he was seriously injured but not killed. He was then put to death. Mai Chand Kaur, the mother of Nau Nihal Singh, next came to the throne. But she refused to adopt Raja Hira Singh as her son, and was brutally beaten to death. Sher Singh, another son of Ranjit Singh, was now brought to power. But he realised the designs of Dhian Singh, and planned to get him murdered. But before he could do so, he fell victim to the gun shot of Ajit Singh Sindhanwalia, who was playing into the hands of Raja Dhian Singh. Ajit Singh, however, was loyal to neither. The very day he shot Sher Singh dead, he had Dhian Singh also done to death. And now came the turn of Hira Singh who marched on Lahore, dispatched Ajit Singh, the Sindhanwalia Sardar, and brought Dalip Singh another son of Ranjit Singh, to power, himself becoming his Wazir.

After thus capturing the power, however, Hira himself fell under the obnoxious influence of Pandit Julla Missar, a fanatic Brahmin from the mountains. As the grip of this Brahmin over the State affairs tightened, Hira Singh's popularity suffered. He tried to retain his hold by bribing the Sikh soldiery, and thus the army began to increase its political power. There was a contest for *Wuzarat* between Hira Singh, Suchet Singh his uncle and Jawahir Singh, the brother of Maharani Jindan, the mother of Dalip Singh. Similarly, there was a contest for the throne between Kashmira Singh, Peshora Singh, the other two sons of Ranjit Singh and Maharani Jindan who fought for Dalip Singh. In this each tried to win the support of the army, with the result that all except Jindan and the child Dalip Singh were killed, while the army became supreme. But the life of Jindan also was made only precarious, with the result that she, as according to some writers, inspired the soldiery to cross the river Sutlej, and accept the British challenge. Her purpose, as according to Gough, was that if the Sikh army "were shattered, the court would be rid of its master; if triumphant the court would claim the credit".[15]

Thus different factors led to the First Sikh War. The British had been following an aggressive policy towards the Sikhs from an early time. But while Ranjit Singh was wise and kept them at arm's length, his successors played into the hands of the British. The inexperience of Ranjit Singh's successors, the incapable chiefs of Lahore, the undisciplined Khalsa army, together inadequate resources and bad strategy brought their downfall.

The War

It would be unnecessary to go into the details of the war itself. The mention only of its most essential events will suffice. After crossing the Sutlej, the best course for the Sikhs should have been to attack Ferozepur where, as Lodlow wrote: "Our garrison of 8,000 men who have been destroyed and the victorious 60,000 would have fallen on Sir Henry Hardinge who had then but 8,000".[16] But instead of doing that, Lal Singh, the traitorous *wazir* of Lahore, having already been in correspondence with the British Political Agent, addressed Captain Peter Nicholson, assistant Agent at Ferozepur thus: "*I have crossed the Sikh army. You know my friendship for the British. Tell me what to do.* " To his Nicholson replied: "*Do not attack Ferozepur. Halt as many days as you can, and then march towards the Governor-General*".[17]

Under these circumstances though the army itself "was filled with a vehemently hostile feeling towards the British," with a "strong sense of self-confidence and of loyalty to the Khalsa, "[18] Gough wrote, it was impossible for them to get a victory. As thus arranged, Lal Singh stayed on till Sir Hugh Gough, the British Commander-in-Chief, brought his main army to the field. The Ambala and Ludhiana divisions of the British arrived at Mudki, 20 miles south-east of Ferozepur, and here the first battle of the Sikh War was fought on 18 December 1845. Lal Singh headed an attack against the British, but just when "the fight was doing on with great fierceness on both sides," writes Latif, "Lal Singh, in accordance with his original design, suddenly abandoned the field, leaving the Sikhs to fight as their valour might prompt". The Sikhs fought with an undiminished energy, but ultimately they were routed, and driven from post to post at the point of bayonet. Thus the British got their first victory, though at a very heavy cost.

The second battle was fought at Ferozeshah a village about ten miles both from Mudki and Ferozepur on 21 December 1845. The British had all their preparations, and the Khalsa army was again led by Lal Singh, assisted by Tej Singh. But despite this the resistance the British faced was so unexpected that they startled with astonishment, and were thrown into confusion and disorder. The night that ensued was truly designated a "night of terror". Robert Cust thus wrote in his journal on 22 December: "News came from the Governor-General that our attack of yesterday had failed, that affairs were desperate, that all State papers were to be destroyed, and that if morning attack failed, all would be over; this was kept secret by Mr. Currie and we were concerting measures to make an unconditional surrender to save the wounded, the part of the news that grieved me the most".[20]

Had the Sikhs attacked the British at night, the story of the war would have been different. But Lal Singh again played his stipulated role and disappeared all of a sudden.

On the morning of 22 December, the remnants of the Sikh forces were easily driven form their camp. But as the day advanced, the second wing of the Sikh army commanded by Tej Singh, who had been urged by his zealous soldiery to fall upon the English, approached in battle-array, "and the wearied and famished English saw before them a desperate and, perhaps useless struggle". But Tej Singh was no better than Lal Singh. "At eleven o'clock he opened fire on the left of his enemy's position, and again hesitated. Four hours later he threatened an attack on their right, and then, to the utter astonishment and intense satisfaction of the weary defenders, his whole force was seen to turn suddenly northwards and move off rapidly in the direction taken by the vanquished battalions of Lal Singh".[21]

As Lal Singh and Tej Singh were thus playing their game, Ranjodh Singh, a loyal Sikh leader, helped by Ajit Singh of Ladwa, attacked Ludhiana with 8,000 men and 70 guns, burning a portion of its cantonment. Sir Harry Smith, with a considerable body of troops, came to the town's relief, but was intercepted at Badhowal; a number of his men were killed and the whole of his baggage was captured. This happened on 21 January 1846. So heavy was the loss the British suffered at Badhowal that as in the words of Cunningham, they "looked towards the east, their home; and the brows of Englishmen themselves grew darker at the thought of struggle rather than triumphs.... the leader of the beaten brigades saw before him a tarnished name after the labour of a life".[22] Shortly after this, however, luckily for the English, Ranjodh Singh withdrew, and as he was retreating, he was attacked by the English at the village of Aliwal at a distance of 8 miles, and as Dr Andrew Adams wrote: "a few shots and the charge of a squadron or two in pursuit of a host of retreating Sikhs, were magnified into a grand combat, and thus the plain of Aliwal has been recorded as the scene of one of India's Marathons".[23]

The last battle was fought at Sobraon, where Lal Singh, Tej Singh and Gulab Singh played traitors. The appeals of the army to Maharani Jindan to supply them with ration and arms went in vain. The Khalsa army was deserted by its leaders who recrossed the Sutlej and destroyed the bridge behind them, so that the Khalsa army stranded, destroyed and drowned. And thus the British won their final victory. Sir Hugh Gough who, however, knew the truth, wrote "Policy prevented me publicly recording my sentiments of the splendid gallantry of a fallen foe, and I declare, were it not from a conviction that my country's good required the sacrifice, I could have wept to have witnessed the fearful slaughter of so devoted a body".[24]

The Treaty of Lahore

After the Sikhs were thus defeated, the British still could not gather the courage to annex the Punjab, because they knew that in that case even those of the Punjab traitors who had been helping, would turn against them, and in such a circumstance nobody knew what the consequences would be. Lord Hardinge, therefore, decided to watch for a better opportunity, and termed his policy, in the eyes of the world, as 'experimental forbearance', or in other words, it was to give the Sikhs one more chance for peace, form which if they failed, they would invite their doom.

The Treaty of Lahore was thus signed on 9 March 1846; its essential terms being (1) that all the Sikh territories lying south of the river Sutlej which the British had already annexed, would remain with them; (2) that further, the Jullundur Doab, or the territories between the Sutlej and the Beas, would also be handed over to them; (3) that the Lahore Durbar would pay an indemnity of Rs 1½ crores which, however, they being not able to pay, all the hill territories between the Beas and the Indus including Kashmir and Hazara were to be handed over to the British;[25] (4) that the Durbar would disband its army and keep only 20,000 infantry and 12,000 cavalry; (5) and that the British would be allowed a free passage through the Punjab when necessary. Dalip Singh was recognised as the minor ruler of

Lahore. Maharani Jindan was to be his Regent and Lal Singh the Prime Minister. A supplementary treaty was imposed on the Lahore Durbar soon after on 11 March 1846 whereby (1) an adequate British force was to be stationed at Lahore till December 1846, for the protection of Dalip Singh; (2) under the new set up, the bona fide right of the *jagirdars* in the Lahore territories were to be respected; and (3) and British would be at liberty to retain any part of the state property in the forts situated in the ceded territories, by paying for it a fair compensation.

The Treaty of Bhairowal

The British had bound themselves under the Treaty of Lahore to withdraw their forces from the Punjab before the end of December 1846. But before the stipulated date for the withdrawal came, the British hatched out a conspiracy to continue their stay. According to the plan, it is the Sikhs who must take the initiative and ask the British to continue the stay of their forces till Maharaja Dalip Singh became major. The Governor-General Lord Hardinge issued instructions to make certain bugs military movements: "My object is to give the Lahore Durbar a hint, that the Garrison is on the move".[26] And in the meanwhile efforts were continued to make some Lahore Chiefs to suggest that the British should stay. The efforts bore fruit, and on 15 December 1846 a conference of those Chiefs who were in favour of the British, was held from which Maharani Jindan, the Regent, was excluded, as an active opposition to the plan was feared from her. The Chiefs put forward a proposal. The British stipulated certain conditions which were all agreed to without discussion or dissent. The next morning, on 16 December the Treaty of Bhairowal was concluded.

Under the new treaty, (1) the British forces were to continue at Lahore till 4 September 1854 when Maharaja Dalip Singh would attain 16 years of age; and till that time, the Durbar would pay Rs 22 lakhs a year to meet the British expenses; (2) till Dalip Singh became a major, the British

Resident, helped by a Council of Regency consisting of 8 Sardars—in which the Resident could make any change or appoint a new man—would govern the Punjab; and (3) besides Lahore, the British forces could be put in any Sikh fortress, protection of the Maharaja's interests.

This rang the death-knell of the Sikh power, and made the "British the real master of the Punjab". In fact, Lord Hardinge, who is said to have followed the policy of experimental forbearance, had laid a heavy value even on the treaty of Lahore, as he wrote to Henry Lawrence, the British Resident at Lahore, on 23 October 1847: "By the Treaty of Lahore, March 1846 the Punjab never was intended to be an independent State... In fact, the native prince is in fetters and our protection, and must do our bidding"[27] The Treaty of Bhairowal was a great improvement on that of Lahore in this respect.

GULAB SINGH AND THE KASHMIR STATE

Gulab Singh was the instrument of the British in bringing about the end of the Sikh rule, and was given the independent state of Kashmir as a reward by the British. Writing about Gulab Singh in 1847, thus commented Major Carmichael Smyth: "Ambitious, avaricious, and cruel by nature... he deliberately committed the most horrible atrocities for the purpose of investing his name with a terror that should keep down all thoughts of resistance to his cruel sway. With all this he was courteous and polite in demeanour, and exhibited a suavity of manner and language that contrasted fearfully with the real disposition to which it formed an artfully designed but still transparent covering".[28]

"He is an eater of opium," Smyth further quotes a friend of Gulab Singh, "he tells long stories, keeps irregular hours, sleeps little, has a mind unsettled, offers little, promises less, but keeps his word, of good memory, free, humorous and intimate even with the lowest and poorest classes of his subjects... yet with all this, in reality a very leech, sucking their life's blood, the shameless slave trader of their sons and daughters, brothers, wives and families... the very jack of all trades, the usurer, the turn-penny, the briber and the bribed".[29]

Griffin remarked about Gulab Singh and his brother Dhian Singh "their splendid talents and undoubted bravery only render more conspicuous their atrocious cruelty, their treachery, their avarice, and their unscrupulous ambition".[30] Then talking of their descent, he writes of them together with their third brother Suchet Singh, "Whether of princely descent or not, they certainly, in intelligence and personal advantages, were men of great distinction, and eminently deserved their success in a community where honest virtues were ridiculous and violence and fraud could alone ensure victory".[31]

Cunningham, who was also a contemporary of Gulab Singh, while talking of his unscrupulous character, writes: "but it must not therefore be supposed that he is a man malevolently evil. He will, indeed, deceive an enemy and take his life without hesitation, and in the accumulation of money he will exercise many oppressions; but he must be judged with reference to the morality of his age and race, and to the necessities of his own position. If these allowances be made, Gulab Singh will be found an able and moderate man, who does little in an idle or wanton spirit, and who is not without some traits both of good humour and generosity of temper".[32]

Gulab Singh was born on 21 October 1792 in the house of one Kishore Singh who was a scion of the celebrated house of Dhrov Deo who ruled Jammu, and whose son Ranjit Singh Deo subdued many petty hill rajas like those of Kishtwar, Chaneni and Bhadarwah. Kishore Singh, however, was far removed from this ruling family of his collaterals, had absolutely no pretensions to richness or a position, and lived a simple life at Akhnur. His father Zorawar Singh had a jagir at Dayaun near Sambha, and it is with him that Gulab Singh spent his childhood days.[33]

Gulab Singh grew up illiterate and unlettered, though he had his share of training in the arts of horse-riding, swordsmanship and archery in which soon he was to make a mark. The opportunity came in 1808 when things at Jammu fell into a confusion under Jit Singh, the nephew and successor of Brij Lal Deo. Ranjit Singh sent his troops to annex the State. In the battle that ensued Gulab Singh appeared on the side of his collaterals, impressed his opponents with his prowess, and soon, after Jammu passed under the suzerainty of Lahore, he secured a service with the Sikh Maharaja as a *Ghorcharah* soldier. According to Smyth, "He was introduced to the Maharaja by Missr Dewan Chand who had marched the Sikh troops to Jammu, and he and his younger brother Dhian Singh were appointed at "three rupees each per diem".[34] "The two brothers were the most favoured of all Ranjit Singh's favourites; it is supposed, however, that Gollauboo (Gulab Singh) would not endure the Maharajah's intimacy as his brother did. In 1813 they, at Ranjeet's request sent for their younger brother Suchetoo (Suchet Singh), now a lad of about twelve years old; whose handsome face and graceful person immediately won for him the entire regard of the Maharajah. The Rajpoot brother were now all in all at Court".[35]

Gulab Singh played a prominent role in the Sikh expedition to Kashmir in 1814. When the Sikh forces marched to Multan in 1818, Gulab Singh accompanied them. During the siege of the fort, a favourite Sikh Sardar of Ranjit Singh fell dead at the foot of the fort wall. When none else could dare ride to the spot under the heavy cannon fire to bring back the dead body, Gulab Singh offered himself and accomplished the job which won him great appreciation from the Maharaja. Likewise he distinguished himself at many other places as for instance against Yusuf tribe at the time of the conquest of Peshawar in 1819, and went on amassing rewards in the shape of jagirs and valuable presents of cash, jewellery and other articles.

Jammu, after its conquest, had been allotted as jagir to Kharak Singh. His agents, however, could not establish law and order in the territory, particularly because some of the valiant Rajputs of the place refused to reconcile themselves to the Sikh yoke. Among them sprang up on Mian Dedo who soon became popular in the surrounding areas, revised a band of followers and spread his depredations all around. Gulab Singh offered himself for the job, and was permitted to march to the province where soon, by using force, diplomacy and cajolery, he had Dedo killed and reduced the rebellious elements to submission, in appreciation of which the territory was farmed out to him in 1820.

After this Gulab Singh began to spend most of his time at Jammu where, by his representations to the Maharaja that it was not easy to collect revenues without using force, he was permitted to raised his own troops. Dhian Singh in the meanwhile had in 1819 been appointed *Sadar-i-deori*, or Minister in charge of the royal household which gave him a considerable influence over the Maharaja. Gulab Singh therefore could rest assured that during his absence from Lahore, his brother would be able effectively to look after his interests with the Sikh ruler.

In 1821 Gulab Singh conquered Kishtawar for the Sikh Raj. He also reduced Rajouri to which he was specially asked to lead an expedition. The Rajput Raja of Rajouri who had given some special cause of enmity to Ranjit Singh, was captured. All this raised him yet further in the eyes of the Maharaja, and Gulab Singh was now given the hereditary title of Raja with the grant of Jammu as principality, to him and his successors in perpetuity. Ranjit Singh himself performed the *Raj tilak* at the Akhnur fort and granted him the *sanad* on 16 June 1822.[36]

After this Gulab Singh continued his exploits, extending his territories and helping the Lahore Durbar whenever and wherever his services were needed. Most important of his conquests was that of Ladakh in 1834 done by his General Zorawar Singh. His other brothers also steadily rose in positions and importance, with the result that before Ranjit Singh died, Dhian Singh enjoyed jagirs which brought him an annual income of about three lakh rupees. Suchet Singh's jagirs were worth slightly over three lakhs; Hira Singh's were worth 4 lakh 62 thousand rupees per annum, while those of Gulab Singh brought him an annual revenue of Rs. 7,37,287. The more important places which Gulab Singh held in jagir besides the Jammu province, were Akhnur, Parmandil Rihasi, Kishtwar, Ram Garh, Bhimber and Dera Baba Nanak.[37]

Intrigue with the British

Gulab Singh had developed an almost independent power in the Jammu province, and had sent expeditions to Ladakh and onwards in a bid to occupy Lhasa on his own which was not liked by the rulers at Lahore. His ambitions to occupy Kashmir also were not unknown. Nor was the preponderance of Dhian Singh in the Lahore Government looked on without forbidding by the other Lahore chiefs who suspected him of designs to place his own son Raja Hira Singh on the Sikh throne. Dhian Singh was blamed of having brought about the death of Hari Singh Nalwa, the famous General of Ranjit Singh, by his machination which did not permit reinforcements to reach him when he was hard-pressed on the frontiers. He with his other brothers was said to have been responsible for the lack of training in state-craft to Kharak Singh. After the death of Ranjit Singh, when Kharak Singh's closeness to Chet Singh threatened Dhian Singh's position as Chief Minister, he brought about the death of Chet Singh. The three brothers might have liquidated Kharak also but for the timely presence of Mai Chand Kaur and her son Nau Nihal Singh. The latter prince, when the came to power, tried to surround the Dogra hill dominions in a bid to finish their power, but before he could do anything substantial in this respect, an archway crumbled over his head by the hands of destiny or those of the intriguing Dogras.

Of all the Lahore chiefs, Dogras alone had been granted contiguous and vast hereditary jagirs. They therefore developed vested interests not only on lands but also on positions. Gulab Singh's strength in Jammu, strengthened Dhian Singh in his office at Lahore, while the latter's influence as Chief Minister gave security to the former's dominion in the hill province. They therefore could afford to lose neither one nor the other. They considered their claims to offices and jagirs as matter of fact as the royal family its royalty. Both were based only on force and fraud.

It was only for a short while that the events placed Gulab Singh and Dhian Singh in opposite camps when the former supported Chand Kaur and defended her against the troops of Sher Singh who had invaded Lahore under the inspiration of the latter.[38] Peace was restored when Dhian Singh arrived from Jammu and the immense wealth which Gulab Singh took away from the royal treasury could be done neither without an active connivance of the former, nor without leaving a bitter taste in the mouth of Sher Singh who found no wherewithal to clear the arrears of pay of the Khalsa soldiery who because of that became turbulent and brought about an ultimate ruin of the Sikhs. Had Sher Singh lived a little longer, he would definitely have brought about an end to Gulab Singh's power in Jammu, just as he wanted to get rid of Dhian Singh at Lahore. Efforts of one succeeding prince after another at Lahore to destroy the Dogras, and those of the Dogras to have them poisoned, crushed under the archway, beaten to death or shot from a double barrel gun could therefore be considered only compensatory to each other.

Little wonder under these circumstances Gulab Singh found it necessary to intrigue with the Afghans on the frontiers and the British in India to safeguard his own interests and to carve out an independent kingdom for himself in the hills. The end of the Lahore kingdom prompted him to do so. Dhian Singh was murdered and Suchet Singh was killed while trying to snatch away the Chief Ministership from his brother's son Hira Singh. The British schemes of establishing independent principality of Gulab Singh at Jallalabad were not unknown to the Khalsa army. They should have had him also murdered if it had materialised. This did not happen. Yet Gulab Singh was not safe. He clashed with Raja Hira Singh on the treasures left by Suchet Singh, and the who could have peace only after exchanging hostages. Smyth however found these differences between uncle and nephew only feigned, for crafty Gulab Singh wanted to safeguard the ultimate Dogra interests behind this smoke screen.[39] Yet no one could deny that Gulab Singh's position, as also his life, was in danger, and as "ambitious and avaricious" man as he was, he tried to save his skin simultaneously with an effort to get Chief Ministership at Lahore when he was brought there after the murder of Hira Singh by the orders of Jindan.[40] He could not pay a fine of three crore rupees, he came to Lahore surrounded by the Khalsa whom he had won over only by cajolery, as also by bribes.[41] He was half in despair, yet half in hope to succeed his nephew as Chief Minister. He was received well by Jindan, but Rani's brother Jawahir Singh foiled his hopes for the office, and he retired again to Jammu disillusioned and only with a promise to pay a fine of 65 lakh rupees to the Durbar. After Jawahir Singh, another opportunist, Lal Singh occupied the office of Chief Minister. The things deteriorated and the Sikh forces crossed the Sutlej which brought about a clash with the British. As the war started going against the Durbar, everybody thought that Gulab Singh alone could save the situation. He was summoned, appointed Chief Minister, and asked to negotiate peace. But he knew the moment peace was established, Lal Singh, the paramour of Jindan, would again have an upper hand, and he would lose once again, not only his office at Lahore, but also his estates in Jammu. Little wonder, when he met the Governor-General to sign a peace treaty, his intention was not to bring out the Lahore Durbar unscathed. While intending to reduce the military strength of the Durbar which should no more be a menace to anybody even under ambitious and crafty

Lal Singh, "he suddenly perplexed the Governor-General by asking what he was to get for all he had done to bring about a speedy peace and to render the army an easy prey".[42]

Gulab Singh has been criticised by the apologists of the Sikh rule, and the pseudo moralists both Indian and European for his treachery against the Lahore Durbar and illicit connections with the British which he tried early to develop in order to have his independence in his hill State recognised. He is said to have misappropriated the revenues due to the Lahore Government, and had usurped half of the tributary hill States of the Sikhs. Since 1836, he had been attempting to seize Kashmir.[43] He intrigued against the Lahore Durbar "which produced a *jehad* in Muzaffarbad and the other hill States bordering Kashmir". In 1844 he approached the British offering to help them develop their hold on Punjab if they recognised "his independent sovereignty in the hills".[44] He did so again in 1845, and "agreed to aid the British with his hill levies if they attempted to take possession of the Punjab". This he did in February, and in August again he "offered to destroy the Sikh army with 50,000 hill levies and facilitate the British occupation of Lahore". "As a general commanding two divisions of the Sikh army, and a feudatory vassal of the Lahore Government, he had defied the orders of the Durbar and sent evasive answers, when after Mudki and Ferozeshah, he was ordered to reinforce the Sikh armies on the Sutlej".[45] After Aliwal when pressed by the Durbar to take charge as Wazir, he arrived at Lahore and he immediately communicated "with the British authorities, assuring them of his loyalty and supplying them information". After the defeat at Sobraon, "Overawed by the skilful knavery of their Vazir, the Rani and the chiefs signed a Declaration on 15 February 1846, signifying to abide by whatever terms Gulab Singh might determine with the British". He met the Governor-General on behalf of the Durbar to sign peace, but bluntly demanded "what he was to get for all he had done".

"On 18 February, the young Maharaja was brought to the Governor-General's camp at Kasur for the ratification of the treaty. Gulab Singh suggested that the Maharaja should not be allowed to return to the Rani, intimating plainly, that it was for the Governor-General to dispose of the young chief as he pleased. Hardinge credulously looked at the functionary of the Sikh Government, he praised him for his neutrality, but discreetly ignored his ignominous suggestion".[46]

All this lengthy record of intrigues on the part of Gulab Singh should indeed earn him an unequivocal censure of history. His last act whereby he proposed even the deceitful detention of the Maharaja as custodian of whose interests he met the Governor-General, may well fit him into the title of a crafty, brazen-faced hypocrite, yet he is to be considered in light of all the murders of the members of his family at Lahore, in the light of the serious dangers to which his own position and life were exposed, and in the light of the character of the shameless, egocentric, opportunist and irresponsible forces that the Khalsa army, the ruling princes, the Ranis and their Wazirs at Lahore had become.

Be that as it may, Gulab Singh was instrumental in the conclusion of the Treaty of Lahore on 9 March 1846 which for obvious reasons he himself did not sign. Under this treaty, in lieu of a part of indemnity, the Lahore Government handed to the British all the hill territories between the rivers Indus and Beas, including Kashmir and Hazara. Kashmir was sold away, in reward for valuable services, to Gulab Singh under a separate Treaty of Amritsar signed with him on 15 March 1846, against a payment of one crore rupees which was later reduced and made further easy of liquidation.

An Independent Ruler

The Treaty of Amritsar said: "The British Government transfers and makes over for ever in independent possession to Maharajah Gulab Singh and the heirs male of his body all the hilly or mountainous country with its dependencies situated to the east of the River Indus and the west of the River Ravi including Chamba and excluding Lahul, being part of the territories ceded to the British Government by the Lahore State". The eastern boundary of this territory was to be laid down by a commission appointed by the British and Gulab Singh. In return the Maharaja was to submit his disputes with the neighbouring States for arbitration to the British, was to help the British with his troops when required, was never to employ a European or an American without the British consent, and acknowledged the British supremacy in token of which he would annually present "one horse, twelve shawl goats of approved breed (six male and six female) and three pairs of Cashmere shawls".[47]

Thus was the present State of Jammu and Kashmir created. Gulab Singh had at initial stages to face some trouble when under instigation of Lal Singh, the Chief Minister of Punjab, the Sikh Governor of Kashmir refused to surrender the valley. The British helped him to get it, while Lal Singh was tried, condemned, removed from office, and banished from Punjab.

Gulab Singh slowly consolidated his possessions and introduced several reforms in the Kashmir administration. Shawl industry was reorganised; *begar* or forced labour, was removed; and several rebellions on the frontiers were suppressed. Towards the later years of his life, Gulab Singh suffered from dropsy. In February 1856 he formally installed his only surviving son, Ranbir Singh on the throne and accepting the position of Governor of Kashmir, himself retired to the valley. He was on his deathbed when the Indian Mutiny broke out in 1857. He ordered Dogra troops to march to Delhi where they helped the British to get back its possession. He died in August 1858 at the age of sixty-six.

Coming back to the Treaty of Amritsar under which the State of Jammu and Kashmir was transferred by Hardinge to Gulab Singh for one crore rupees, it may be mentioned that a part of this money was paid by him from the treasury of Kashmir which, Kashmir being a part of the Lahore kingdom, belonged in fact to Maharaja Dalip Singh. Commenting on this Cunningham wrote the "transaction scarcely seems worthy of the British name and greatness, and the objections become stronger when it is considered that Gulab Singh had agreed to pay sixty lakhs of rupees (£680,000), as a fine to his paramount (Lahore Durbar), before the war broke out, and the custom of the East as well as of the West requires the feudatory to aid his lord in foreign war and domestic strife. Gulab Singh ought thus to have paid the deficient million of the money as a Lahore subject, instead of being put in possession of Lahore provinces as an independent prince". Later on Cunningham writes "payments required from him were reduced by a fourth, and they were rendered still more easy of liquidation by considering him to be the heir to the money which his brother Suchet Singh had buried in Ferozepur".[48] Gordon writes that it was indeed, "a very bad bargain for the Government, which unfortunately was rendered necessary by the political exigency of the moment.[49]

Almost immediately after Kashmir was transferred to Gulab Singh, some critics of Hardinge began to term it a 'political mistake'. It was suggested that with its congenial climate and fertile lands, the valley could easily be colonised by the Englishmen and developed into a 'miniature England in the heart of Asia.'[50]

But Hardinge had some strong reasons in 1846 when the valley was transferred. It must be remembered that the Punjab was not annexed after the First Sikh War, and Hardinge had hoped that with the British help it would be established as a strong and independent buffer state which would be able to absorb any hostile thrusts against the British in the north-west. As such, the annexation of Kashmir should have involved the maintenance of a long line of communication from the Sutlej, at a distance of 300 miles through the lands of people the character of whom was not yet fully understood. Not was Hardinge anxious by annexing Kashmir, to come into collision with the powerful frontier tribes, particularly after the experience the British had gained from the First Afghan War. He thought it prudent therefore to keep it independent, so that this state and the Punjab would keep the frontier tribes in check; and besides, it would establish itself as a counterpoise to the Sikhs, thus keeping the British frontier on the Sutlej peaceful and safe. Hardinge also wanted to show to the princes and other chiefs of India, the advantages that could accrue from a faithful adherence to the British interest.

But the situation soon changed when the non-annexation of the Punjab itself after the First Sikh War, began to be considered a mistake. New pretexts were raised to perpetuate the British presence in the Punjab, and simultaneously to interfere in the Kashmir State and develop the British hold thereon. The excuse of the oppressive and inefficient administration of Gulab Singh became handy, and Hardinge wrote to the Maharaja in 1848: British "are bound by no obligation to force the people to submit to a Ruler who has deprived himself of their allegiance by his misconduct". And he declared, that a "direct interference must be resorted to"[51] where the ruler has failed.

The enquiries held, however, failed to prove the charges of oppression against the Maharaja, and in the meanwhile, Hardinge retired. His successors, Lord Dalhousie, was a rank annexationist. If there was no cause to interfere in the internal affairs of Kashmir, he was anxious to create one. Every summer a number of Europeans began to visit the valley, and often misbehaved. The Maharaja complained to this effect to the British. Dalhousie jumped at the opportunity, and proposed that a British officer may be appointed in the valley to control their conduct. The Maharaja was alarmed, and was sure that any such appointment would surely be a prelude to the imposition of a Resident on the State. He tried to argue himself out of the situation, but the Governor-General would not allow him to escape. In 1852, therefore, the Maharaja had to agree to the appointment of such an officer who would be known as the "officer on Special Duty in Kashmir," and who would return when the European visitors left the valley after the summer months were over.

The Treaty of Amritsar had given Kashmir a special status as compared to the other Indian principalities. It was almost to be an independent state, with no British Resident to interfere in its internal affairs. But the appointment of the "Officer on Special Duty compromised that special status of Kashmir, and a beginning was made towards bringing it completely under the British as we shall subsequently see.

Lord Hardinge personally took part in the Sikh War, and his greatness lay in the fact that he insisted on working for this purpose under his own Commander-in-Chief, Gough. In 1848 he retired from his office in India as his own request. Back in England, he was made Commander-in-Chief of the English army in 1852. The Crimean War that followed shortly after, however, proved too heavy a burden on his advanced age. He became Field Marshal in 1855, but the very next year he was attacked by paralysis and died on 24 September 1856 at the ripe age of seventy-one. Lord Hardinge of Penshurst who became the Viceroy of India after fifty-four years of his death, was his grandson.

REFERENCES

1. Mersey, V., *op. cit.*, p. 63.
2. Charles Viscount Hardinge, *Viscount Hardinge,* p. 164.
3. Hardinge, *op. cit.*, p. 166.
4. Cunningham, *History of the Sikhs*, pp. 250-51.
5. Edwards and Merivale, *The Life of Henry Lawrence,* i., p. 363.
6. *Ibid,* p. 407.
7. Edwards, Major-General Herbert, *Biography of Lawrence,* pp. 396-7.
8. Chhabra, *History of Punjab,* 11, Chapter X.
9. *Ibid,* Chapter 11, 14-15.
10. Campbell, *Memoirs* 1, pp. 75-77.

11. Smyth, Carmichael, *A History of the Reigning Family of Lahore,* p. 241.
12. Payne, *Short History of the Sikhs,* p. 151; see also supra, Chap. 11.
13. Gough and Innes, *The Sikhs and the Sikhs Wars,* (1897), p. 59.
14. Chhabra, *op. cit.,* chapters 13 and 14.
15. Gough and Innes, *op. cit.,* p. 57.
16. Ludlow, *British India,* 11, p. 142.
17. Kohli S.R., *Sunset of the Sikh Empire,* p. 121.
18. Gough, *op. cit.,* p. 66.
19. Latif, *op. cit.,* p. 569.
20. Cust, Robert, *Linguistic and Oriental Essays,* VI, p. 43.
21. Payne, *op. cit.,* p. 175.
22. Cunningham, *History of the Sikhs,* p. 274.
23. Adams, Dr. Andrew, *Wanderings of Naturalist in India,* pp. 60-61.
24. Gough, *op. cit.,* p. 138.
25. And of this, the British sold away Kashmir at a small price to Gulab Singh, as a reward for the support he had given them during the war. See the following chapter.
26. Edwards and Merivale, *Life of Sir Henry Lawrence,* (London, 1872), 11, pp. 100-101.
27. *Ibid.*
28. Smyth, *Reigning Family of Lahore,* p. 257.
29. *Ibid,* p. 258.
30. Griffin Sir Lepel, *Ranjit Singh,* p. 127.
31. *Ibid.,* p. 190.
32. Cunningham, *History of the Sikhs,* p. 289.
33. Gulab Singh's mother was Mahadevi, the daughter of Rana Kishan Pal of Maharta near Basohli, who was said to have been buried alive after her birth, as her parents did not want to suffer the shame of a female child, but was later dug up and found alive. See Narsingh Das Nargis, *Dewan Gulab Singh,* pp. 1-5.
34. Smyth, *op. cit.,* p. 250; according to Shahmat Ali, *Sikhs and Afghans,* p. 92, Gulab Singh was entertained at Rs. 2 a day, *Gulbnama* of Kirpa Ram, however, asserts that he was immediately taken as commander of a regiment at Rs. 275 per month, and K.M. Panikkar, *The Founding of the Kashmir State,* p. 19, believes this.

35. Smyth, pp. 250-51.
36. Panikkar, K.M., *op., cit.*, pp. 32-34.
37. Shahmat Ali, *Sikhs and Afghans*, pp. 103-06.
38. *Supra*, Mai Chand Kaur.
39. Smyth, C., *op. cit.*, pp. 121-22.
40. *Supra, Causes of First Anglo-Sikh War*.
41. Smyth relates how, when Gulab Singh was surrounded by the Khalsa army at Jammu, he saved his life by pleading that he was the last of the Dogra family who knew where the treasures lay buried. "To enforce and illustrate the declaration, he would direct the Seiks to repair to certain places around Jummoo, where, by attending to the marks and signs which he gave them, they found large sums of buried money, fifteen, twenty, and even forty thousand rupees in one place, and which but for Gulab's disclosure might have lain hid for ever. It was thus that the Rajah gained the title which the soldiers bestowed on him of the *Soona Ki Kookoree*, or the Golden Hen." Smyth, *op. cit.*, p. 136.
42. Cunningham, *op., cit.*, p. 287.
43. Hasrat, Bikrama Jit, *Anglo-Sikh Relations*, p. 19.
44. *Ibid.*, p. 237, quoting contemporary British records.
45. *Ibid.*, pp. 243, 254, 255, 284, 385, quoting.
46. *Ibid.*, p. 286, quoting records.
47. Panikkar, *op.*, pp. 111-15.
48. Cunningham, *op. cit.*, p. 288.
49. Gordon, *op. cit.*, p. 164.
50. Wakefield, W., *The Happy Valley* (1879) pp. 85-86, quoted by Kanpur, M.L., *Kashmir Sold and Snatched* (1968), pp. 9-10.
51. Quoted, Kapur, M.L., *op, cit.*, pp. 22, 23.

11

Internal Feuds and British Policy

The death of Ranjit Singh in June 1839 ushered in a period of great political instability for the state. In less than seven years' time from 1839 to 1845 there were seven changes of government, six of which were accompanied by violence and bloodshed. Both internal and external factors were responsible for this sorry state of affairs. Internally, the state was rocked by feuds arising from the conflicting ambitions of rival groups in the governing class and the inability of the rulers to control their intrigues and counter-intrigues. Externally, the threats came from the British who felt tempted to fish in the troubled waters to advance their imperial interests. The state was plunged into a most critical situation when towards the end of this period the contenders for power within the country agreed to join hands with the external imperialists to the detriment of the interests of their own state. It was then left for the Khalsa army to make a patriotic bid in defence of the imperilled independence and integrity of the state. There are thus four important aspects which need to be examined. This chapter is intended to deal with the first of these: internal feuds. The next three chapters will be devoted respectively to external peril, emergence of Khalsa army as a predominant political force, and the patriotic role of the army in meeting foreign aggression against their country.

I

The immediate successor of Maharaja Ranjit Singh was his eldest son Kharak Singh[1]. He was a good man, no doubt, but was awfully lacking in the qualities which were demanded by the difficult tasks facing him. He was simple-minded, gullible, and mentally indolent. As prince, he had been admonished by his father a number of times for not taking sufficient interest in the management of his estates and leaving everything to the care of his *mukhtar* Bhaia Ram Singh, but in vain. In the estimate of Waheeduddin[2] he was utterly lacking in ambition and worldly sense. His real interest lay in praying, residing the Granth and sitting with legs folded and head bowed in the company of holy men–'a saint manque' indeed. Not only was he terribly deficient in practical sense, he was also deplorably weak in intellect. He has been described as imbecile by many contemporary observers[3]. He had neither the will nor the capacity to handle the affairs of the state intelligently and firmly.

But the problems which he was required to deal with were tremendous. Of them his relationship with rival groups of the ruling elite was a matter of the utmost importance. His father had taken the existence of such groups to be an asset rather than a liability. He had valued it as a useful device to maintain balance in the ranks of the nobility. No doubt, his partiality towards the Dogras had boosted them to a position of predominance among the chiefs towards the end of his reign. Still so long as the Maharaja was alive, the balance was well maintained. The interests of other groups were adequately protected and the predominance of the Dogras was not allowed to cause any harm to the legitimate interests of the non-Dogra groups. Obviously it was a very difficult task. If Ranjit could accomplish it, it was because, (i) he was a master mind, (ii) he was a strong ruler, and (iii) all groups owed their positions to his favours. Unfortunately his son and successor Kharak Singh did not possess any of these advantages. For him the best course was the one which had been recommended by his dying father. While nominating Kharak Singh his successor he had appointed Raja Dhian Singh his *Wazir* and giving the Prince's hand in the hand of the Raja had enjoined them to work together as a team[4]. To this effect both had given solemn pledges. They again pledged themselves when the pyre of the great Maharaja was lit[5]. But all these pledges were soon forgotten and the administrative arrangement which might have stood the state in good stead was cast away thoughtlessly. The blame for this entirely attaches to the new Maharaja. So far as Raja Dhian Singh is concerned, he seems to be sincerely attached to the interests of Kharak Singh. He had his mental reservations about his ability no doubt but he knew that a weak king like him would suit his interests all the more. But Kharak Singh failed to understand this. He also failed to comprehend that Dhian Singh with his great ability and influence would be able not only to run the administration of the stare smoothly and efficiently but also to carry the other groups along with him or at least maintain a working balance between them[6]. It is said that at the time Kanwar Nau Nihal Singh was not favourably disposed towards the ministership of the Raja, but the Raja had the capacity to win him over and given time would have done so.

Still if Kharak Singh did not like to have the Raja as his minister for one reason or another, the next best course for him would have been to have his own son Nau Nihal Singh as his principal counsellor. The young prince was a man of parts. He was able, courageous and cautious, and had immense administrative and military experience at his command. He was keen to give a helping hand to his father in the running of the state administration[7]. He was opposed to the ascendancy of the Dogra brothers but favoured the maintenance of a working balance among the rival groups of the nobility. With his great qualities of head and heart he would have proved a great cementing force for the various rival forces working in the country. But Kharak Singh cared for neither of these two courses. Instead, he lent his ear to the anti-Dogra elements and reposing his confidence in their friendship and support decided to replace Dhian Singh to all intents and purposes by his favourite and close relative Chet Singh Bajwa[8]. The new arrangement was a great blunder because it was welcomed by none. The Dogras were angry because Raja Dhian Singh had been degraded. Kanwar Nau Nihal Singh was displeased because his claim had been disregarded. The other groups—Sandhanwalias, Atariwalas, Majithias, many other Sardar families, etc., were offended because an obscure person, a nonentity, had been appointed to such a privileged and important position. Misr Beli Ram and Bhai Ram Singh and Gobind Ram were perhaps the only people who supported the action. The result was that Maharaja Kharak Singh was almost completely isolated. Still worse was the fact that shared resentment against the new appointment brought the discordant elements together and gave rise to a united front against the Maharaja and his new minister[9].

Another factor which turned the scales against Maharaja Kharak Singh was his policy towards the British. He was accused of being too soft or lenient towards the British. It was said that he yielded to every demand of theirs, whether reasonable or unreasonable[10]. Particularly there was resentment against his depending too much on the British Agent, Col. Wade, who had become unpopular with the Sikhs after Ranjit Singh's death. For instance, when differences between General Ventura and Col. Wade were reported to the Maharaja, the General was "advised to make up matters with Col. Wade, if possible, otherwise to remain with Kanwar Nau Nihal Singh[11]".

Seeing that there was a growing dissatisfaction with the way affairs were conducted at the court, Raja Dhian Singh secretly informed about it Kanwar Nau Nihal Singh and his brother Raja Gulab Singh who was also at Peshawar. The Kanwar left for Lahore when he heard that a date had been fixed for the coronation (*raj tilak*) of his father. He arrived in the capital along with Raja Gulab Singh in the month of September. He was much incensed to learn that the coronation had been hastened and performed in his absence when it was definitely known that he was already on his way to Lahore[12]. Soon after that, efforts were begun to find a peaceful solution of the Chet Singh issue. Raja Dhian Singh, Raja Hira Singh, Raja Gulab Singh, Fateh Singh Mann, Fakir Azizuddin and a few other important courtiers, one after another, implored the Maharaja to keep Chet Singh away from him and not to give so much prominence to him. But here was no effect on the mind of Kharak Singh who said that he would be prepared to do anything for them but could not accept this demand. The obduracy of the Maharaja compelled the Kanwar and his supporters to think of other means. A secret meeting was held at which, besides the Kanwar and the Dogra Rajas, were present the Sandhanwalia's Sardars—Attar Singh, Kehar Singh, Lehna Singh and Ajit Singh—Rani Chand Kaur, Rai Kesri Singh and a few other prominent people[13]. Raja Dhian Singh showed to those present two letters written by Chet Sing and bearing the seal of Maharaja Kharak Singh. The letters stated that the Maharaja wanted British help and for it was willing to pawn his kingdom at 38% of the revenues[14]. In all probability these were forged letters but so much was the atmosphere fraught with suspicion at that time that they were believed and accepted as genuine and a decision was made immediately to assassinate the new counsellor Chet Singh, to deprive the Maharaja of all power and to invests Kanwar Nau Nihal Singh with responsibility to run the administration. The decision was carried out in full on the 8th of October 1839[15]. From now onwards Kharak Singh was the king only in name because all power now passed into the hands of Nau Nihal Singh who reinstated Raja Dhian Singh as *Wazir*.

II

Nau Nihal Singh proved a strong and competent ruler. Whatever damage had been caused by the weak rule of his father and the unscrupulousness of the artful and ambitious people surrounding him was undone under Nau Nihal Singh. Rather, there was a general feeling that he had restored the glory of the good old days of his grandfather. The fictional rivalries of the nobility almost disappeared and no chief or group of chiefs had the courage of openly indulging in petty party politics[16]. The most powerful Jamwal group also felt the strong hand of the Kanwar. Although they still enjoyed considerable political influence and power in the country, they no longer enjoyed supremacy. Their position was no better, if no worse, than what it was under Maharaja Ranjit Singh. As Minister Raja Dhian Singh had to bear a heavy burden and was usually busy from morn till eve with government work. He was also the principal adviser to the Kanwar in state matters. But the power really belonged to, and was exercised by the Kanwar who did not always depend upon his Minister for help. Often enough he would hold consultations with Bhai Ram Singh, Bhai Gobind Ram and Jamadar Khushal Singh[17]. The Kanwar had "all[18] the energy and talents of his grandfather, though with less tact and caution". He was confronted with many difficult and complex problems when he began. The relations with the British were far from satisfactory. He was suspected of giving secret encouragement to the enemies of the British and their nominee Shah Shuja, particularly the deposed Amir of Kabul, Dost Mohammad Khan, and the Gilzai rebels[19]. But he successfully removed all British fears on this account. The British needed the Khalsa Darbar's permission for the transmission of their troops and military supplies to and from Afghanistan. He was able to meet their demand without, however, compromising the dignity of the state in any way. He insisted on the removal of the British Agent Col. Wade from his post and his plea had to be conceded. A few feudatory chiefs like the Raja of Mandi were showing dilatoriness in paying the arrears of their tribute. A big army under General Ventura and Ajit Singh Sandhanwalias was sent against the hill Raja. The Raja was captured and brought a captive to the capital and his whole territory was annexed along with 200 forts belonging to various hills chiefs. The concentration of Khalsa troops in the hills between the rivers Beas and Ravi incidentally also served the purpose of intimidating the Dogra Raja Gulab Singh of Jammu who of late had been augmenting his power by fresh conquests in Ladakh and Little Tibet.

Encouraged by the party politics at the Sikh court some attempts at disturbance of peace were made in the areas of Attock, Hassan Abdal and Hazara. But they were promptly suppressed by the Kanwar[20].

The demise of Maharaja Kharak Singh, his father, on 5 November 1840 transferred the authority, in all its plenitude, to the hands of the Kanwar. It was now thought that this would enable him to work free from the kind embarrassments which on many occasions in the past he used to suffer at the hands of his father. His rule hitherto had been a grand success. He was "popular amongst all classes, especially the military", and it was anticipated that his reign "would[21] shed an additional lustre upon the Sikh nation".

But this was not to be. The Kanwar met a fatal accident on the very day his father was cremated. He was returning from the obsequies of his father. On the way back when he was passing under a gateway of the fort, all of a sudden a portion of the arch above fell on his head and smashed his skull. Mian Udham Singh, son of Raja Gulab Singh, who was with him was killed on the spot. Raja Dhian Singh, the two Bhais, and Dewan Dina Nath who were just behind were also injured but not seriously. The Kanwar did not regain his consciousness and died during the night.

A careful inquiry into the circumstances of the accident shows that there was no intriguing hand lurking behind it. J.D. Cunningham[22] holds it to be an accident in the absence of any positive evidence to the contrary. Sohan Lal[23] does not cast the slightest doubt on any body being responsible for it. Rather, his account of the accident leaves little ground for Raja Dhian Singh or anybody else doing any mischief at any stage. Besides the Raja, the Sandhanwalia Sardars, the two Bhais, Jamadar Khushal Singh and Fakir Azizuddin were constantly in attendance upon the Kanwar from the time of the accident until he expired at night. The statements of Capt. Gardner and Major Smyth fail to provide a convincing proof that the accident was deliberately caused by the Dogras to get rid of the Kanwar or that the Kanwar was not killed by the accident by was later secretly done to death by Dhian Singh[24]. Some recent writers like Sita Ram Kohli, Hari Ram Gupta and Khushwant Singh have come to the conclusion after thorough investigation that the death of Nau Nihal Singh was the result of an unfortunate tragic accident rather than the outcome of a deep-laid plot hatched by the Dogras.

III

The sudden disappearance of Nau Nihal Singh from the scene created a most critical situation for the state. Party strife now came into play as it had never done before. The reason was that after the death of Nau Nihal Singh there was no male member in the direct line of Maharaja Kharak Singh who could be installed on the throne. In this situation the obvious choice was Kanwar Sher Singh, second son of Ranjit Singh[25]. So, Raja Dhian Singh sent an urgent message to him to reach Lahore expeditiously. In the beginning all other leading courtiers were agreeable to this proposal. Hence, a public proclamation was made to that effect and homage paid to Sher Singh by the chiefs on 9 November 1840. However, the old enmity between the houses of the Princes, Kharak Singh and Sher Singh, came in the way and stood like and insurmountable barrier. Rather than agree to have Sher Singh as the next ruler, Rani Chand Kaur, Nau Nihal Singh's mother, staked a claim of her own. She gave out that a wife of the late Nau Nihal Singh was pregnant and was already in third month with the child. On this basis she demanded that she be accepted as ruler until her daughter-in-law was delivered of the child. In this respect she was supported by the Sandhanwalia Sardars and many other chiefs including Bhai Ram Singh, Bhai Gobind Ram, Jamadar Khushal Singh and his nephew Tej Singh, Fateh Singh Mann, Gulab Singh Povindia and Shaikh Ghulam Mohi-ud-din. Others[26] led by Raja Dhian Singh while accepting in principle that the prospective child of Nau Nihal Singh had a superior claim to the *raj gaddi* than Sher Singh, strongly urged that it would be highly inadvisable to have a woman at the helm of affairs at a time when the country was faced with formidable problems. Rani Chand Kaur and her supporters, on the other hand, insisted that the interests of the unborn child would not be safe in the hands of Sher Singh. To resolve the deadlock, Raja Dhian Singh tried to induce the Rani to agree to marry Sher Singh but the proposal was pooh-poohed. She poured utter scorn on Sher Singh calling him a dyer's offspring. Still Dhian Singh and his supporters persisted in their efforts to bring about a compromise between the two and save the state from the impending catastrophe. One after the other a number of solutions[27] were suggested but none of them was found acceptable by the Rani. Ultimately it was decided that Sher Singh should retire to his *jagir* leaving his son Partap Singh behind as his representative on the Council which was to consist of Dhian Singh, Attar Singh Sandhanwalia, Lehna Singh Majithia, Jamadar Khushal Singh and Prince Partap Singh.

The withdrawal of Kanwar Sher Singh from the contest for power, however, brought about no improvement in the situation. The Rani had no experience, no knowledge and no administrative ability. She was further handicapped by her sex. She conducted the proceedings of her daily *darbars* from behind the curtain. Again, some people were prejudiced against her because they did not like to be ruled by a woman. It was unfortunate that what she lacked could not be made up by her supporters. They were all power-hungry but had no firm grip on administrative problems. Raja Dhian Singh who had the requisite ability and experience was not trusted. Though he had been frustrated in his efforts to solve the problem of succession amicably, he was willing to extend his support to the new administration provided his help was invited and valued. But as it happened, the Sandhanwalias and other supporters of the Rani were jealous of him and would not allow him to function. Instead of co-operating with him they constantly obstructed him. Feeling disgusted over this, the Raja withdrew himself from the court for five weeks. When still nobody cared for him, he applied for leave to go to Jammu, which was readily granted. He was now convinced that a change in the government was urgently called for. He decided to espouse the cause of Kanwar Sher Singh. "While leaving Lahore", writes Sohan Lal[28], "he sent a secret message to Kanwar Sher Singh to hold himself in readiness and also advised the officers of the army in whom he had confidence to join the Prince when the call came. They were given hopes of increased pay and emoluments and also some additional money gifts".

After the departure of Raja Dhian Singh things further deteriorated at Lahore. In her helplessness the Rani sent urgent messages to him to return forthwith promising that she would value his advice in future. The Raja did not pay any heed to these promises. He was now determined to end her weak rule and put Sher Singh into power. He sent word to Sher Singh at Batala to proceed immediately to Lahore. The Kanwar wasted no time and within two days of his arrival in Lahore won over almost the entire army stationed at Lahore. Now a mini civil war started. Supported by a force of 26000 infantry, 8000 cavalry and 45 guns he started his operation for the forcible occupation of the city as well as the fort. He was able to occupy the city without any difficulty but the fort defined him. Without waiting for Dhian Singh to arrive from Jammu he decided (on the advice of Jwala Singh who was opposed to Raja Dhian Singh and who was an aspirant for the post of *Wazir*)[29] to bombard the fort. Raja Gulab Singh, Attar Singh Sandhanwalia and Tej Singh from within the fort offered stiff resistance. All efforts of Sher Singh to storm the fort proved abortive and he was compelled to wait until Dhian Singh arrived on 18th January 1841. A settlement was at last reached which stated that Chand Kaur should renounce all claim to the throne and be given a *jagir* of Rs. 900,000 per annum, Raja Gulab Singh and his troops be granted a safe conduct[29a] out of the fort, Sher Singh be recognized as Maharaja and Dhian Singh as Prime Minister.

The civil war was now happily ended but before this happened it had caused an irretrievable damage to the state. The military discipline was no longer what it used to be in the past. The city of Lahore had experienced a terrible time due to the riots and plunder indulged in by uncontrolled soldiers. The state treasury had suffered even more. A great deal of its wealth had been taken away by the outgoing Dogra soldiers under cover of safe conduct. Still other serious damage was that the gulf between the Dogra and Sandhanwalia parties had become wider and almost unbridgable.

The extent to which personal interests got precedence over the interests of the state may be judged from how both Sher Singh and Chand Kaur behaved at this juncture. Both of them approached the British for help. Sher Singh promised that whatever aid might be afforded him would be rewarded by a grant of all the Sikh possessions on the left bank of the Sutlej[30]. Similarly Chand Kaur requested the British for help against Sher Singh and in return for that promised to alienate a portion of Punjab's revenues in their favour[31]. Needless to say, such selfish and unpatriotic offers only served to expose the security of the kingdom to the people who were not unwilling to exploit the situation to their advantage.

IV

When Sher Singh became king, all the chiefs with the exception of the Sandhanwalias made their obeisance to him. The Sandhanwalia were afraid that they would be penalized for their having opposed Sher Singh. Hence they sought safety in fleeing the country. Ajit Singh Sandhanwalia and left even before Chand Kaur fell from power. The Rani herself had sent him to meet the British Agent at Ludhiana to plead her cause. When Mr. Clerk refused to see Ajit Singh he proceeded to Calcutta to seek interview with the Governor-General. Attar Singh effected his escape later and like Ajit Singh took shelter in the British territory across the Sutlej. Lehna Singh and Kehar Singh Sandhanwalias, however, did not escape. They were arrested and put in chains. The entire property of the Sandhanwalias, which ran into several lakhs, was confiscated by Sher Singh. There was thus no immediate fear from the Sandhanwalias.

Sher Singh's first difficulties came not from any rival group of chiefs but from the rank and file of the army. The trouble started when the Kanwar led a massive body of troops into Lahore but failed to prevent them from acts of loot and plunder. It assumed a more serious form when the new Maharaja and his minister failed to honour the promises they had held out of the troops. While seeking their support they had promised to give them gifts and raise their salaries. But there was not enough money in the *toshakhana*, thanks to Gulab Singh Dogra and Rani Chand Kaur. So, it was a real problem to give full satisfaction to them. Charging the government with bad faith the soldiers went on rampage. For 8 to 10 weeks the city of Lahore was turned into a veritable hell[32]. There was no security of life and property. Even important people were not spared[33]. The corrupt accountants attached to military units were made special targets, and officers who tried to check them were ridiculed and some of them saved their lives with great difficulty. General Court's housed was pillaged and he had to seek refuge in British territory. General Ventura would have been killed but for the timely help rendered by the Maharaja's personal guards. Jamadar Khushal Singh could be saved with much difficulty. Gradually; the trouble spread to the *mofussil* areas[34]. Commandant Foulkes was killed in

Mandi in March 1841. Major Ford was slain in Hazara a month later. Sobha Singh, the garrison commander at Amritsar, and Col. Mehan Singh, the governor of Kashmir, were also brutally murdered. Avitable felt shaky at Peshawar and wanted to seek shelter at Jalalabad. Dewan Sawan Mal was able to escape the wrath of his soldierly by a clever ruse.

Sher Singh and Dhian Singh had to struggle very hard to restore normalcy. They called a meeting of the soldiers' representatives (*panchas*) and appealed to them to end their disturbances. They accepted some of their urgent demands, such as increase in salaries and dismissal of corrupt accountants but they declined to concede their demand for the transfer of military officers they did not like. Hence, the mutiny continued. Thereafter, the Darbar, too, took a firm line. The more violent of the soldiers were ordered to be dismissed or transferred to places where the scope for mischief was comparatively less. A more important measure was to raise fresh levies in order to have a counter force. In a few months' time about 6000 Dogra recruits were enlisted and formed into 8 battalions of infantry and 3 units of light artillery[35]. These measures, however, were not crowned with immediate success. Rather, it seemed that the mutinous soldiers were all the more offended. Sher Singh now felt so demoralised that he approached the British Agent at Ludhiana to help him restore order in the country. But when the British spelt out[36] their terms for assistance, the Maharaja had second thoughts and decided to withdraw his request[37]. The mutiny with fits and starts continued for about 6 months and then disappeared. This was a great success of the firm attitude which the government had shown all along. The fear of a British invasion also helped chasten the turbulent elements.

The end of the mutiny removed just one source, *albeit* a major one, of Sher Singh's anxiety. He was still much worried on account of the seditious activities of Rani Chand Kaur and the Sandhanwalias. The British government had granted recognition to Sher Singh's sovereignty but at the same time had granted political asylum to Ajit Singh and Attar Singh Sandhanwalias. The Sandhanwalias chiefs were openly trying to mobilise support in favour of the Rani. The Rani, meanwhile, had shifted to a *haveli* outside the fort, and had spurned all offers of marriage from Sher Singh. She was suspected of making efforts to establish intriguing contacts with some important Sardars. It was thought that she was also secretly in touch with Ajit Singh and Attar Singh Sandhanwalias residing in British territory[38]. Sher Singh's worry was also derived from the possibility of Sahib Kaur giving birth to a male child. In case this thing came to pass, he feared he might be derived of power. On the other hand, in order to minimise the degree of risk involved in it Chand Kaur had managed to procure a Kashmiri girl with pregnancy of the same duration. Sher Singh could not tolerate this and soon matured his plans to eliminate the causes of his anxiety. Sahib Kaur was administered poisonous medicines which killed the child before its birth. The lady was delivered of a still-born son[39] in July 1841. Hearing this Sher Singh felt greatly relieved. But he had still to deal with Rani Chand Kaur. For this purpose the female attendants of the Rani were bribed. They first tried to administer poison to her and when she fell ill doing to its evil effects, her head was battered with stones. There is no doubt that both Maharaja Sher Singh and Raja Dhian Singh were party[40] to this brutal act. This happened in June 1842.

The disappearing of Rani Chand Kaur permanently from the scene gave a new turn to the situation. Sher Singh now feeling fully secure began to spend more and more time in drinking and other pleasurable pursuits. In consequence the affairs of the state suffered. The minister Dhian Singh failed to persuade him to pay more attention to his official duties. After a time the Maharaja began to feel sick of him and wanted to reduce his influence. The Sandhanwalias also had rethinking after the death of Chand Kaur. Realising that they now had no candidate to support as against Sher Singh they became anxious to make up with the Maharaja and to return from their self-imposed exile. This suited the interests of Sher Singh who thought that they would be a useful counterweight to Dhian Singh[41]. The British felt equally interested in the new political alignments[42]. Like Sher Singh they also wanted to have a less powerful minister at Lahore. So they encouraged the Sandhanwalias in their desire to get back home, and the British Agent, actually took the opportunity of his visit to Lahore to advise the Maharaja to pardon them and allow them to return. The Maharaja accepted the advice promptly. Lehna Singh and Kehar Singh Sandhanwalias were released from imprisonment. Ajit Singh Sandhanwalia returned in November 1842. All of them were received with great honour and all their confiscated properties were restored. Attar Singh Sandhanwalia was still staying at Thanesar. He was more cautious and wanted before his return to see what treatment was meted out to Ajit Singh.

The restoration of the Sandhanwalias to favour led to a fresh round of party strife. Sher Singh from now onwards was more guided by their advice than by that of his minister Raja Dhian Singh who had hitherto served him so faithfully. In the words of M'Gregor[43]: "Neither by night nor day was he (Sher Singh) ever separated from them: they were his boon companions and no demand from either Lena Singh or Ajit Singh was resisted". Sher Singh now became all the more indifferent towards his duties. He failed to give audience to ministers and secretaries even when their business was urgent. When sober, the pleasures of the chase were more important to him than affairs of the state[44]. Things deteriorated to an extent that some of the older chiefs Lehna Singh Majithia and Fakir Azizuddin felt it necessary to tell him not to neglect the state business. Instead of heeding their sound advice the Maharaja started working on plans to get rid of Raja Dhian Singh. Henceforth, both of them began to suspect each other. They had to swear goodwill to each other every third day of the seek. The

Sandhanwalias now got the opportunity they had been long looking for. They decided to get rid of both. They hated Sher Singh for his murder of Rani Chand Kaur and Raja Dhian Singh for his sending them into exile. Moreover, they were ambitious and wanted to capture power, possibly the throne also[45]. They conspired with Sher Singh to kill Raja Dhian Singh and with Raja Dhian Singh to assassinate Sher Singh. They outwitted both and murdered Sher Singh, his son Prince Partap Singh and Dhian Singh all on a single day, 15 September 1843[46].

V

But the assassins did not survive for more than 24 hours after the foul deeds perpetrated by them. Raja Sochet Singh and Raja Hira Singh happened to be encamped just a few miles outside the city. As soon as the news of the murders reached them, they went to the cantonments and apprised the army of what had happened. The army immediately decided to punish the culprits and marched upon the city. Within a few hours the fort was captured and both Ajit Singh and Lehna Singh Sandhanwalia were seized and despatched. Dalip Singh[47], just a five-year old child at that time was then proclaimed Maharaja and Hira Singh was raised to the high office of *Wazir*. Pandit Jalla, tutor and mentor of Hira Singh, was appointed *mashir-i-khas* and all secretaries were instructed to submit their papers through him. Whereas the overall responsibility related with Hira Singh, in practice he left the entire administration of civil and revenue matter to his tutor, himself concentrating mainly on the management of the Khalsa army.

Two prominent leaders of Sandhanwalia party had been eliminated. A third leader, Attar Singh Sandhanwalia, had saved himself by returning to the British territory immediately on hearing about the deaths of Ajit Singh and Lehna Singh[48]. But the supporters of the Sandhanwalias still remained to be dealt with. The more important among them,

Bhai Gurmukh Singh, Misr Beli Ram and his brother Ram Kishen, and Mehr Ghasita were arrested and executed one by one. Malik Fateh Khan Tiwana who was also a supporter escaped from Lahore. He crossed over to the other side of the Indus and seizing the fort of Tank raised the standard of revolt against the Lahore Darbar. A number of other people who were suspected of pro-Sandhanwalia leanings were dismissed from service or imprisoned.

The elimination of the Sandhanwalias as a rival political group did not, however, end the internal feuds of the Darbar. Under Raja Hira Singh some new tensions arose, and where old tensions existed, they reappeared in new forms. The result was that the difficulties of administration increased all the more. In spite of his levelbest efforts, Hira Singh managed to tide over them only for a short period and ultimately had to pay with his life for his failure.

Trouble started from Hira Singh's own family which was from now onward the victim of a serious rift. His uncle Raja Sochet Singh was not happy over Hira Singh's elevation to the position of Prime Minister. He was extremely handsome, possessed a noble and commanding figure, was brave and chivalrous as a soldier and was popular with the Khalsa army. He thought that he had a far better claim to be Prime Minister than his nephew who was just a young lad of 24 years at that time. Added to this was the fact that the two, uncle and nephew, had never liked each other for a long time now[49]. In his dislike of Hira Singh, Sochet Singh was abetted by Rani Jindan and her brother Jawahar Singh. The Rani nurtured the grievance that though she was the Queen Mother she was not given the importance due to her status.[50] Her brother Jawahar Singh shared the Rani's resentment against both Hira Singh and Pandit Jalla. He was also on the look-out for an opportunity to oust Hira Singh from power and to take his place. On 24th November 1843 Jawahar Singh managed by a stratagem to remove the young Maharaja from the palace and carried him out of the city to the cantonments. He told the troops that Hira Singh had laid a plot for the destruction of the Maharaja and implored them to take him under their protection[51]. The troops declined to believe the story and separating the Maharaja from him put him under chains. The imprisonment of her brother exasperated the Rani who now redoubled her efforts to instigate Raja Sochet Singh against Hira Singh. For a time Raja Gulab Singh used his elderly restraining influence to safeguard the unity of the Dogra family. However, the rift which had been caused did not disappear and in December 1843 both Sochet Singh and Kesri Singh left Lahore and proceeded to their estates in the Jammu region and from there watched the situation closely.

About this time another cause of anxiety arose. Princes Kashmira Singh, and Peshaura Singh, two surviving sons of Maharaja Ranjit Singh, became agitated. The main cause of their trouble was their *jagirs* at Sialkot and Kurianwala. It is said that Raja Gulab Singh covered these territories and wanted to oust them from there. To achieve this sinister objective the Dogra chief accused them of being a party to the Sandhanwalia conspiracy against Raja Dhian Singh[51]. They denied the charges but the Dogras managed to get evidence in support of their charge from one of the managers of the Princes' estates. Soon after, an attack was made on them by a Dogra army sent by Gulab Singh. Failing to stand the attack the Princes took shelter with a holy man, Mahtab Singh[51a] of Kotli Loharan. Through the intercession of this saint and due to the resentment of the Khalsa army, Hira Singh was forced stay his hand. The Princes were permitted to go back to their estates after signing a pledge of loyalty to the new government and promising not to cause any harm to Kapur Singh. In spite of this undertaking Kapur Singh was beaten to death. This gave Hira Singh the handle to prepare a case against the Princes. Troops were sent from Lahore to capture them. When the Princes decided to resist the attack, the troops refused to open fire on them. Two regiments of irregular infantry even offered to help them. A number of men from irregular battalions on their way to Peshawar under orders of transfer deserted their colours and took the road to Sialkot[52]. Kashmira Singh sent a confidential messenger to the British Agent at Ludhiana. Raja Sochet Singh from Jammu extended his moral support to them. Even the Mussalman *Najib* battalions of Lahore army who were sent to Sialkot declined to fire on the sons of their late Maharaja unless the Khalsa joined in. Ultimately, it was the old Dogra battalions of Raja Dhian Singh who launched the attack and secured the surrender of the Princes.

The persistent harassment of Kashmira Singh and Peshaura Singh by Hira Singh created strong feelings against him and his government among the Khalsa army. The army *panchayats* held meetings and made a scathing criticism of Hira Singh's administration. On 24th March a deputation of the *panchayats* met the Raja and demanded[53] on behalf of the Khalsa that Jawahar Singh should be released, the campaign against Kashmira Singh and Peshaura Singh should be stopped and an undertaking should be given that they would not be ill-treated in future. They also demanded the surrender of Pundit Jalla, Raja Lal Singh and Shaikh Emamuddin. Raja Hira Singh was awed and he immediately promised compliance with the demands. Though he did not carry out the undertaking in full, he dared not to touch the Princes who were released soon after their arrest. The Princes used the opportunity to unite themselves with Baba Bir Singh of Naurangabad[54].

At this juncture Raja[55] Sochet Singh being informed that the army at Lahore was disaffected and would gladly obey his orders, came down from his *jagir*, Ramnagar, with a small force towards the capital. He arrived on the morning of 26 March at Shahdara with a small band of 40 trusted men including Rai Kesri Singh and Mian Bhim Sen. The expected support from the Khalsa army did not come and he was greatly dismayed to find that Hira Singh by dint of largess and promises had prevailed upon the army not to desert him. Raja Sochet Singh, true to his Rajput blood, refused to go back and died fighting along with his companions against the forces (20,000 Strong) of Hira Singh on 27 March 1844. Hira Singh is said to have shed tears at the fate of his gallant uncle but it was too late.

Not only the Sikhs but also the British seemed to be well disposed towards Bhai Bir Singh because they found Hira Singh not pliable enough to suit their interests. It was a very sensitive problem and for quite some time Hira Singh did not know how to deal with it. His appeals to the army to march upon the *dera* of Bhai Bir Singh went unheeded. The army was not prepared for an attack on a saint. However, the situation suddenly took a favourable turn for the Raja when the news that Attar Singh Sandhanwalia had entered the camp of the Bhai was received in Lahore on 3 May 1844. The Raja immediately addressed a meeting of the Khalsa troops and made a strong case for immediate steps to put an end to the evil. Attar Singh, he said, was sponsored by the British and had come under the instructions of the British. If he was not checked in time, he would sell the country to the British[56]. The Khalsa responded to Hira Singh's argument. On May 5 a strong force moved out of Lahore: 11 infantry battalions with 50 guns under Gulab Singh Calcuttia and 4000 cavalry including 2300 *ghorcharas*, with 300 swivels under the command of Mian Labh Singh Dogra. The efforts to settle the matter peacefully failed because in the course of negotiations Gulab Singh Calcuttia was shot dead by Attar Singh Sandhanwalia. On 7 May the two sides fought a brief action in which Bhai Bir Singh's side suffered heavy losses. The Bhai, Attar Singh Sandhanwalia and Prince Kashmira Singh[57] were counted among the slain. About 200 of their people were drowned in the Sutlej in a bid to escape to the other side of the river. In all 300 men died, 600 on the side of the Bhai and 200 on that of the Darbar.

Hira Singh was naturally pleased because he had successfully tided over a very great crisis. A royal welcome was accorded to the victorious army on their return to Lahore. But the contingent was denounced and ridiculed by other troops who taunted it with the epithet *gurumar* (murderers of the guru)[58]. Hira Singh tried to appease them by liberal rifts of money. He promised also to build a *smadh* over the ashes of Bhai Bir Singh and grant a *jagir* worth Rs. 5000 per annum for the maintenance of the Bhai's gurdwara at Sarhali[59]. The tactics of the Raja again prevailed and the anger of the army gradually subsided.

However, even after this Hira Singh did not enjoy peace for long. This time the trouble came from his own uncle, Raja Gulab Singh. Gulab Singh possessed extensive territories. Besides his own estate, he had got into his hands the estates of his brothers Raja Dhian Singh and Raja Sochet Singh. In the beginning when the mutual relations of Gulab Singh and Hira Singh were cordial, Hira Singh had granted him some additional areas, such as Hazara, Khatur, Rawalpindi and Chach. Still Gulab Singh was not satisfied and wanted more and more territories. He was anxious to get Kashmir and was prepared to pay 5 lakhs more than Diwan Sawan Mal if he was assigned Multan. He also tried hard to oust Kashmira Singh and Peshaura Singh from Sialkot and Kurianwala, but he could not succeed in his nefarious object due to the Khalsa army coming to the rescue of the Princes. All the same he got away with Kashmira Singh's property worth about one and a half lakhs of rupees. On top of this, when he was asked by the Darbar to pay up the large arrears of revenue due from him, he only procrastinated. He developed a special hatred for Pandit Jalla whome he thought was the real man at the back of the persistently made demand for the clearance of arrears. He arrested the brothers and other members of Jalla's family residing in the vicinity of Jammu, tortured them and then relieved them of a large portion of their wealth. All this was done to exert pressure upon Jalla to make him refrain from harassing him with demands for arrears. Raja Hira Singh's differences with Gulab Singh first arose after the death of Raja Sochet Singh towards the end of March 1844. Gulab Singh disapproved of Hira Singh's conduct for which Hira Singh later made amends by asking his pardon. On the other hand Hira Singh developed a grudge against his uncle for occupying the entire estate of the deceased Raja. When asked to share it with Hira Singh, he refused by saying that it was not with him but his son Mian Ranbir Singh whom Sochet Singh had adopted his heir. This did not satisfy Hira Singh. Another great grievance was that Gulab Singh was neither paying the arrears nor was he willing to accept the enhanced rates of revenue/*nazrana* imposed by the Darbar. The quarrel[60] dragged on for several months. Gulab Singh attempted all that he could to embarrass the Darbar. He tried to instigate on Queen Mother and her brother Jawahar Singh against Hira Singh and Jalla. He sent secret emissaries to the units of the Khalsa army at Lahore to excite them against the government. He prompted Chattar Singh Attariwala to raise a revolt of *zamindars* in the region of Rawalpindi. There were troubles in Hazara, Bannu and Tank. Instead of helping the Darbar in the suppression of these disturbances he extended his moral support to them. He also espoused the cause of Peshaura Singh giving out that he had a better claim to the throne than the infant Dalip Singh. He did not stop even at that. He forcibly occupied the estate of Jasrota belonging to Hira Singh and even threatened to seize the persons of his two brothers living in the hills. Hira Singh threatened to confiscate all his property in the plains and after some time even sanctioned the march of a large army upon Jammu. This brought Gulab Singh to his senses and he ultimately agreed to settle his differences with his nephew. The settlement which was reached towards the end of October 1844 was, however, more favourable to Gulab Singh than to the Darbar. The fact is that Hira Singh failed to deal with the intransigence of his uncle effectively.

Barely two months had passed when another crisis overtook the government of Hira Singh. This was the most serious of all the internal troubles which led not only to the fall of the government but also to the deaths of both Hira Singh and his mentor Pandit Jalla. The trouble began on 12 December 1844[61]. It was a *sankrant* day. Rani Jindan wanted to give away in charity some articles of gold and silver. Jalla questioned her right to take so much wealth from the treasury and even used abusive language for her. She resented it and secretly complained to the army against Jalla's misbehaviour. The army was already angry with Jalla and demanded his immediate surrender. Hira Singh refused to accept the demand. The army had still another grievance against Hira Singh. He had recently ordered the dismissal of 500 soldiers. The army demanded their reinstatement for which the Raja was not ready. The army also demanded that Jawahar Singh should be assigned a military command[62]. Hira Singh did not agree but consented to grant him a *jagir* on the condition that he should live on his *jagir*. Jawahar Singh did not obey and went to Amritsar instead and from there began to work against the government of Hira Singh. Hira Singh now, by the advice of Jalla, "determined not only to cut him (Jawahar Singh) off, but to dethrone Dhuleep Singh and place the infant son Sher Singh upon the gudi[63]". Getting a clue of their plans, the *panchayats* formally renounced their allegiance to Raja Hira Singh and pledged themselves to acknowledge no authority but that of the Rani and such minister as she should appoint. The Rani on her part declared that unless Hira Singh retired from office, she would withdraw, with her son, from Lahore. On 19th December Hira Singh ordered that Jawahar Singh should be confined in his own house and prepared a plan to seize him with the help of his Dogra troops. This was no sooner known than the army assembled and the minister was compelled to abandon his designs. Next morning the Raja summoned the officers of the army and harangued them in his usual manner. The troops required time to consider the matter. In the meantime the Rani got in touch with the *panchayats* and promised large rewards for their help in removing a wicked minister who oppressed the people and meditated the destruction of their sovereign. On 21st December Jawahar Singh took the Maharaja to an assembly of troops and placed him under their custody. He was accompanied by many other influential chiefs present at Lahore. Hira Singh and Jalla were now convinced that the game was up and they made preparations for flight to Jammu. At dawn on the 22nd of December, the Raja secretly quitted Lahore accompanied by Jalla, Mian Labh Singh, Mian Sohan Singh, a few other adherents and a body of 600 *sowars*, with some elephants laden with treasure. They were pursued by Jawahar Singh, Sham Singh Attariwala and Mewa Singh Majithia at the head of a large force and were overtaken about 13 miles away from Lahore. Finding himself helpless Hira Singh offered to surrender but was immediately killed. Jalla, Sohan Singh Dogra and Labh Singh Dogra were also killed, and the heads of all these people including that of Hira Singh were brought as trophies to the capital where they were paraded through the streets and then exhibited publicly outside the city gates.

Thus ended the stormy ministry of Raja Hira Singh. Throughout his tenure of fifteen months and a quarter (16th September 1843 to 21st December 1844) he had to grapple with a long succession of formidable problems. All these difficulties were the outcome of conflicting interests of different groups in the state polity and each one of them if not handled tactfully and firmly could have toppled the Raja's government. But if he was able to meet for a time the challenges posed to his authority one after the other, in the long run, as a result of his measures, his position was weakened rather than strengthened. His fall was the natural result of the state of complete alienation in which he found himself after a year's rule. His own uncle Raja Gulab Singh was offended with him. The widow of his other uncle Raja

Sochet Singh was constantly working against him. Most of the chiefs of the Darbar bore grudge against him. Members of the royalty were unhappy with him. The Khalsa army which had saved him from several critical situations in the past, also finally lost faith in his sincerity and turned against him. Things became so bad for him that even the escort of 600 *sowars* which was with him when he fled the capital did not remain true and deserted his cause. Indeed, Hira Singh's power rested on no solid foundation and in a little over a year fell to pieces by a slight blow. It was a political revolution, practically without any bloodshed[64].

VI

If things were bad under Raja Hira Singh, they became worse after him. The country was now faced with a situation of great political uncertainty. A number of people aspired to the exalted office of the *Wazir*. So far as the opinion of Rani Jindan was concerned, she wanted her own brother Jawahar Singh to hold the office. He had played a notable role in the overthrow of the previous government and claimed that he should be rewarded for his services. But the Khalsa did not entertain a good opinion about him and were not prepared to accept him as head of the government. Even when the Rani recommended his name for the post, the Khalsa refused to budge from their stand. Then efforts were made to get in touch with Lehna Singh Majithia for the *Wazir's* office and Prince Peshaura Singh for the post of Commander-in-Chief. Lehna Singh who was at that time residing at Banaras declined the offer. Peshaura Singh, however, agreed to come. When he actually came on 1st January, 1845 from Ferozepur, the place where for the time being he was staying, to Lahore, he was accorded a warm reception by the troops but Rani Jindan and Jawahar Singh stood in the way and granting him a *jagir* of Rs. 40,000 sent him to Sialkot. The troops too changed their stand in deference to the wishes of the Rani[65] and advised the Prince to accept the *jagir* and leave the capital. Another aspirant for the office of *wazir* was Attar Singh Kalianwala[66]. He too failed to get support from the Khalsa.

Failing to get concensus on the appointment of a *Wazir* the Rani make a stop-gap arrangement to run the affairs of the state. She set up a council under her own presidency consisting of her brother Jawahar Singh and Bhai Ram Singh. Fakir Nuruddin, Diwan Dina Nath and Bakshi Bhagat Ram were required to assist the council. This arrangement was continued until May when taking advantage of the outbreak of a terrible cholera epidemic[67] in Lahore the Rani quietly elevated Jawahar Singh to the office of the *Wazir*. The troops did not think it proper to raise any controversy about the matter and consented to the Rani's decision. Jawahar Singh was formally installed in the office on 14th May 1845[68].

Earlier in the month of February a 9000 strong contingent of the Khalsa army was ordered to march upon Jammu and seize the wealth which Raja Gulab Sing had cleverly acquired during the ascendancy of Raja Dhian Singh and Raja Hira Singh. The decision to this effect had been taken as early as 23rd December 1844 at a grand *darbar*[69] held to celebrate the victory over Hira Singh and Jalla, and the troops, the chiefs and the Regent (Rani Jindan) were all united on this question. The troops were successful in seizing a portion of the wealth of Mian Jawahar Singh, brother of Raja Hira Singh, stored in the fort of Jasrota[70] but when they came to Jammu, Raja Gulab Singh played his cards so dexterously that the commanders of the Darbar troops stood completely outmanoeuvred. Fateh Singh Mann and Wazir Bachna lost their lives in the course of the proceedings. Exasperated at this act of treachery the Lahore troops attacked Jammu and in the fight that took place Gulab Singh killed a large number of their men including several officers of distinction[71]. Still Gulab Singh was able to placate the army and get from it a guarantee of safe conduct in case he agreed to go with them to Lahore. Then Gulab Singh accompanied the army to Lahore to settle the account of his arrears with the Darbar. On his arrival in the capital on 6 April 1845, he was accorded a warm reception by the Rani. While the troops were under obligation to make sure that nobody caused any harm to him, the Rani brought about a compromise between her brother and Gulab Singh. Gulab Singh was even offered the post of *Wazir* which he politely declined. After a stay of about 3 months at Lahore the Raja returned to Jammu in early July after signing a paper to the effect that he would pay 68 lakhs of rupees by way of arrears. So long as the Dogra Raja remained at Lahore, he did not sit quietly by constantly indulged in intrigues. Through his secret emissaries like Mian Pirthi Singh he tried to work up the Khalsa troops against Jawahar Singh. He also tried to create a rift between Lal Singh and Jawahar Singh. In these activities he seems to be primarily motivated by considerations of personal safety. In case and till they remained divided they could do no harm to him, he thought; nor could they dictate terms to him in matters of payment of arrears.

While Gulab Singh was still stationed at Lahore, the Khalsa started agitating for the dismissal of Jawahar Singh. On 5 June 1845, within less than a month of his installation as *Wazir*, the *panchayats* proceeded in a body to the palace to remonstrate against Jawahar Singh's continuance in the government, reproaching the *Wazir* to his face with drunkenness incapacity. They went to the Rani and insisted that Jawahar Singh should be removed from the *wuzarat* and replaced by Diwan Dina Nath, Lal Singh or Bakhshi Bhagat Ram or the three jointly. Obviously this was the result of Gulab Singh's secret manoeuvres. But Jawahar Singh's own incapacity also had a great deal to do with it. As *Wazir* he proved himself a total misfit. The dignity of the court had never fallen so low as it did under him. Indulgence in alcoholism and debauchery was preferred to performance of state duties[72].

The critical situation developing at the capital and the growing opposition to the continuance of Jawahar Singh in the office of *Wazir* induced Prince Peshaura Singh to revolt against the Lahore Darbar and proclaim himself the Maharaja instead of Dalip Singh. This could not be tolerated by the Rani who immediately despatched General Mehtab Singh to proceed against the Prince and seize his estate in Sialkot. The Prince offered stiff resistance[73] but ultimately sought safety in flight across the Sutlej in the British territory. In fact he was deliberately permitted to escape, as the army was opposed to killing him. Leaving his family in the British territory he re-entered the Punjab and proceeded towards the Indus. By the middle of July, with the help of his Pathan sympathisers he surprised and took over the important but weakly garrisoned fort of Attock. Here he again declared himself the Maharaja and issued *parwanas* to important people to this effect. The *Wazir* Jawahar Singh commissioned Chattar Singh Attariwala to curb the evil. Chattar Singh had a personal stake in the matter because only recently his daughter had been betrothed to Maharaja Dalip Singh. He could therefore be thoroughly depended upon. Malik Fateh Khan Tiwana was ordered from Dera Ismali Khan to proceed to Attock and assist the Attariwala Sardar. Prince Peshaura was helpless against such a formidable force and had to surrender. Chattar Singh then by a trick persuaded him to accompany him to Lahore on the assurance that he would be pardoned and reinstated in his old *jagir* and other privileges. But when he was encamped at Hassan Abdal on his way to Lahore, he was caught by stratagem, put into the dungeon at Attock and secretly strangled to death[74]. This happened on 31st August 1845.

When Jawahar Singh received the news of Peshaura Singh's death, he was so elated that he actually ordered that a salute should be fired and the city illuminated[75]. This created a big storm in the army which issued orders in the name of the Khalsa summoning the Rani, the Maharaja, and

Jawahar Singh to their camp. The Rani endeavoured to negotiate with the troops but found them inexorable. Jawahar Singh vainly hoped to offer resistance with the troops in the fort but they were not ready to fight against the Khalsa. He also attempted to run away with the Maharaja but all gates were strongly guarded by the troops[76]. Then Diwan Dina Nath, Attar Singh Kalianwala and Fakir Nuruddin were sent to talk to the troops. The troops imprisoned Dina Nath and Attar Singh and sent back Nuruddin to warn the Rani of the consequences of any further delay in compliance with the orders. There was nothing that she could do now except to obey the army. On 21st September 1845 she proceeded to the camp of the army with her son and her brother Jawahar Singh. When they reached there, Jawahar Singh was immediately separated from the rest of the party and killed. The dead body was handed over to the Rani next morning and she was allowed to return along with the Maharaja.

VII

The killing of Jawahar Singh removed an idiot and a buffoon from the scene and saved the Darbar from a further decline in its dignity. The Rani wept and lamented bitterly over the murder of her brother but in fact the tragic occurrence proved a blessing in disguise for her. An important change occurred now in her personality. She grew in stature and began to conduct herself with a sense of decorum unknown to her before. As it were, she "seems to have been roused by the exigency of her circumstances to act with energy and spirit[77]". Seeing this the army changed its attitude towards her. They recognized her as the Regent and allowed her to manage the affairs of the state. They even left the selection of the new *Wazir* to her discretion though a section of the Khalsa was in favour of Gulab Singh Dogra being elevated to that post. When the Rani appointed Lal Singh the *Wazir* and Tej Singh the Commander-in-Chief of the armed forces, there was no opposition from any quarter in spite of the fact that Lal Singh was very unpopular with the troops[78].

The quarrel, however, did not end with that. It now appeared in a new form. It was no longer one faction fighting against another for power, as had been broadly the case since the reign of Maharaja Kharak Singh when internal fighting first broke out. Now the battle lines were drawn between the army on one side and the ruling elite on the other. The demonstration of military might on the occasion of Jawahar Singh's death terrorized practically all Sardars[79] and a wide-ranging sympathy was created for the Rani. Encouraged by this she with the advice of her counsellors, Lal Singh and Tej Singh, started working secretly for a direct confrontation between the Khalsa and British armies. The task presented no difficulty because the British were already getting ready for an attack on the Punjab. The Khalsa army was fully aware of this danger from outside and was prepared to make any sacrifice in defence of the independence and integrity of their state. Whatever may be said about the participation of this army in the political affairs of the state, there is no doubt that it was a highly patriotic army fully committed to the country's cause. This being the situation of the army, it was not difficult to instigate it against the British. The Rani and her agents worked up the anti-British sentiments of the army and prepared it for a march across the Sutlej[80]. On the other hand the Rani's chief advisers, Lal Singh and Tej Singh, offered their good offices to the British and entered into a secret league with them to get their own army defeated and smashed. The British for their own reasons welcomed these moves. When the war broke out, the authorities of the Lahore Darbar proved true to their plighted words and betrayed their own forces in all the battles—Mudki, Ferozshah, Aliwal and Sobraon[81]. Raja Gulab Singh who took over the *Wazir* after Lal Singh had left for the battle-field, behaved no better. He had his own axe to grind and was anxious to please the British. He had already come to terms with the British.

The taking over of the *Wazir's* office gave him a much-valued opportunity to feather his nest by serving the interests of the British. His services for bringing about the defeat of the Khalsa troops in the battle of Sobraon[82] were later acknowledged and he was rewarded with grant of a separate independent state of Jammu and Kashmir. Unlike all these people the Khalsa soldiery acquitted itself valiantly and nearly defeated the enemy at Ferozshah. Still the insincerity of their commanders led to their defeat ultimately. After the war a great majority of them were dismissed from service and sent back to their homes to turn their swords into ploughshares.

VIII

Thus we find that the Khalsa state had to pay an exceedingly heavy price for its internal feuds. The troubles broke out soon after the death of Ranjit Singh and continued with unabated ferocity until 1845. During this short span of 6 years the state was repeatedly convulsed. About half a dozen governments rose and fell. The maximum life of a government was 2 years and 9 months under Sher Singh while there were regimes which did not last more than a few months. As was to be expected, the administration suffered a grievous damage. The weakness of central authority induced laxity, inefficiency and not unoften corruption in the local authorities. The *nazims, kardars* and farmers of revenue fell into large arrears[83]. The *jagirdars* in their estates arrogated authority to themselves and began to behave as if they were independent rulers[84]. Many of the *jagirdars* extended their estates by usurping crown lands that adjoined their own. While the state revenues fell, the expenditure of the state increased enormously. In the *Fauj-i-Ain* (regular army), for instance, the total strength of the army rose from 35,242 in 1839-40 to 51,452 in 1843-44 and its salary from Rs. 42,11,292 to 87,30,108, Similar increase took place in the case of the *Fauj-i-Ghair Ain*[85] (irregular army). The accumulated wealth in the treasury of the state was practically exhausted. One thing, the treasury had been subjected to plunder on more than one occasion, as for example when Raja Gulab Singh marched out of the fort in January 1841 after the fall of Chand Kaur, or when Raja Hira Singh and Pandit Jalla fled the capital in December 1844. Then, each new incumbent of government helped himself and his supporters and favourites to large quantities of wealth in the *toshakhana*. Also, enormous wealth was given away as gifts and donatives to placate the army, or to reward its services from time to time. Thus a grave financial crisis had been created.[86] What is still worse, the situation was steadily deteriorating and there was no ray of hope of the rot being stopped in the near future.

Another major result of the internal feuds of the Darbar was the emergence of military predominance. Each party which sought power invoked the support of the army, and this gradually gave a central role to it in the politics of the state. Realising its power, the army started dictating terms and lest its demands should be ignored, set up a well-organised system of *panchayats* to speak on its behalf. After some time the army claimed to be the Khalsa and demanded a say in appointments to high offices and in important matters of state policy. The result was that a situation was created in which the authorities of the Darbar and other members of the ruling elite were arrayed in direct confrontation with the army. This factor of internal crisis later became one of the causes of the war of 1845-46, in which the Darbar authorities helped the British to inflict a defeat on their own army.

Still another tragic result of the internal quarrels of the Khalsa state was the great opportunity afforded to the British to prepare themselves for invading the Punjab. They greatly strengthened their military stations of Ludhiana, Ferozepur and Ambala, set up supply depots and collected pontoons to throw a bridge across the Sutlej to be able to cross over in time of need. They also bought over a number of leading figures of the Lahore government. But we need not dwell on this aspect here any more because this forms the subject of a separate chapter.

REFERENCES

1. Kanwar Sher Singh did no accept the accession of Kharak Singh willingly. He made a bid for the throne urging his superior merits upon the attention of the English Governor-General and seeking his intervention on his behalf. He also made an abortive attempt to seize the hill fort of Kangra. But he received no encouragement from the British. Therefore, when a deputation consisting of Mr. Clerk and Capt. Osborne (Military Secretary to the Governor-General) proceeded to Lahore in July 1839 to compliment the new Maharaja on his accession, Sher Singh hastened to make his peace with Kharak Singh, and by the intercession of Raja Dhian Singh was favourably received and honoured with a grand title.

   Thomas Henry Thornton, *History of the Punjab*, p. 207; J. D. Cunningham, *History of the Sikhs*, p. 202.
2. *The Real Ranjit Singh* (New Delhi 1976—first printed in London in 1965), p. 151.
3. J. D. Cunningham, *op. cit.*, 202; Thornton, *History of the Punjab*, p. 200—a contemporary work, first published in 1846 in London, reprinted at Patiala in 1970.
4. Ganda Singh (ed.). *Punjab in 1839-40*, p. 54 (news dated 22.6.1839). Also see Mufti Ali-ud-din, *Ibrat Nama*. Vol. I, p. 505; Ganesh Das Vadera, *Char Bagh-i-Punjab* (Amritsar, 1965), p. 327. Sohan Lal, *Umdat-ut-Twarikh*, Daftar III, Part V, p. 147.
5. Waheeduddin, *op. cit.*, p. 205.
6. Mufti Ali-ud-din speaks highly of the way he applied himself to the affairs of the state before he was replaced by Chet Singh Bajwa. The good work he did created a wholesome impression upon all except Chet Singh and a few other people who felt jealous of him. *Ibrat Nama*, Vol. I, p. 506.
7. There is ample evidence to show that Nau Nihal Singh was from the very first anxious to have an effective say in the affairs of the state. While at Peshawar he held frequent *darbars* where he repeatedly expressed his resolve to return to Lahore and look after the affairs of the government. According to *Punjab Akhbar*

dated 19 July 1839. Nau Nihal Singh at Peshawar made all the Sardars about him sign a document confirming Maharaja Kharak Singh's succession and his own *mukhtari* or ministry. He conveyed this information to the Lahore Darbar. He also sent *parwanas* to all important chiefs at Lahore to defer the *tilak* ceremony of his father till his return to Lahore.

8. He was married to a niece of Mangal Singh, brother of the Maharaja's favourite wife Ishar Kaur. At the time of his appointment Chet Singh Bajwa was a raw youth in his early twenties. Writing about him M'Gregor says that he had nothing to recommend him but arrogance and sycophancy. *History of the Sikhs,* vol. II, p. 5. (Reprint 1979, Allahabad). Also see Thornton, *op. cit.*, p. 210.

9. "The Prince (Nau Nihal Singh), a youth of eighteen, was in his heart opposed to the proclaimed minister and the Rajas of Jammu, but the ascendancy of Chet Singh over the weak mind of the Maharaja, and Kharak Singh's own desire of resting upon the influence of the British agent, induced the two parties to coalesce first for the destruction of the minion, and afterwards for the removal of Col. Wade".

   J. D. Cunningham, *op. cit.*, pp. 202-03; M'Gregor, *op. cit.*, Vol. II, pp. 4-5.

10. Ganda Singh, *The Punjab* in 1839-40, pp. 101, 117. For instance it was reported to the Maharaja on July 23, 1839 that Diwan Sawan Mal had issued orders to his people not to sell any grain to British officers. On August 19, 1839 the Maharaja ordered him not to raise any objection to such purchases.

11. *Ibid.*, pp. 107-08—news dated 26 July, 1839.

12. Fauja Singh and M. L. Ahluwalia (ed.), *Maharaja Kharak Singh* (Patiala 1977), pp. xxxvi-xxviii.

13. Thornton, *op. cit.*, p. 211; Mufti Ali-ud-din, *op. cit.*, p. 506.

14. Debi Prasad, *Gulshan-i-Punjab* (1872), p. 42; for more information on this aspect see Major G.C. Smyth, *History of the Reigning Family of Lahore* (reprint, 1970), p. 28.

15. Cunningham, *op. cit.*, p. 203.

16. There were, however, some ripples. Misr Beli Ram and his brothers were imprisoned for their support to Maharaja Kharak Singh over the appointment of Chet Singh as the *de facto* prime minister, The Maharaja constantly demanded that they should be released. In this he was supported by some important

courtiers, particularly the Bhais. The Kanwar hesitated because the Dogra Rajas were opposed to this. After some time he made up his mind and released the Misrs. Thereupon, Raja Dhian Singh and Raja Gulab Singh got angry and getting leave left for Jammu. The Kanwar soon realized that he could not ignore them and in utter disregard of the opinions of Bhai Ram Singh and Jamadar Khushal Singh sent a special messenger to Jammu to bring Raja Dhian Singh immediately. *Maharaja Kharak Singh*, pp. xxxix-xl.

17 Thornton, *op. cit.*, p. 215.

18. *Ibid.*, pp. 214, 217, 218. Thornton further writes: "He was a young man of very promising talents, brave, high-spirited, active, with great firmness of character, and many of the better qualities of his grand-father, but rash and self-willed". In his moral habits he was an example, being sober and comparatively temperate. His person and manners were agreeable and his countenance was intelligent though not handsome".

19. For details see Sita Singh Kohli, *Sunset of the Sikh Empire* (1967), pp. 21-25.

20. Sita Ram Kohli, *op. cit.*, pp. 18-19.

21. Thornton, *op. cit.*, p. 216. In the words of M'Gregor: "He was popular with the army for he had been a soldier from his boyhood, and was of a brave and indomitable spirit, united, at the same time, to great caution, discretion, and forethought. Ranjit Singh was very fond of Nonehal, and fondly anticipated that in him the Sikhs would find a successor worthy of filling the throne of Lahore and preserving his kingdom entire". *op. cit.*, p. 5.

22. *A History of the Sikhs*, p. 208.

23. Sohan Lal, *Umdat-ut-Twarikh*, Daftar IV, Part I, pp. 70-71.

24. G.C. Smyth, *op. cit.*, pp. 35-36.

Smyth bases his account on the evidence of Capt. Gardner who says that he was present on the occasion. But the story of Gardner, an unreliable man, cannot be accepted unless it is corroborated from some other sources. No such corroboration is available. On the other hand Dr. Honigberger who examined the Kanwar immediately after the accident disproves the theory of Gardner and Smyth.

25. Besides Sher Singh, there were 5 other sons of Ranjit Singh still alive: Tara Singh, twin brother of Sher Singh (born in 1807), Peshaura Singh (born in 1818), Kashmira Singh (b. 1819), Multana Singh (b. 1819) and Daleep Singh (b. 1836). Of these Sher Singh

was the eldest and the only one who had been privileged to have a seat in the Khalsa Darbar along with the heir-apparent, Kharak Singh.

26. This group included the Jamwal party, Bhai Gurmukh Singh, Sham Singh Attariwala, Dhanna Singh Malwai, Fakir Azizuddin and his two brothers, and the European officers.

27. These were all varying brands of co-regency. For instance, it was first proposed that the Rani should be the nominal ruler and Sher Singh the executive head. Then it was suggested that the Rani should be the ruler as well as the executive head while Sher Singh should only look after military affairs. Since the Rani was determined not to have any association whatsoever with Sher Singh, all attempts at compromise proved unsuccessful.

28. Sohan Lal, *op. cit.*, Daftar IV, Part II, p. 8.

29. Debi Prasad, *op. cit.*, pp. 46, 50.

29a. *Foreign Secret Consultation*, 8 February 1841, No. 88; also see Major Smyth, *op. cit.*, pp. 59-60. Gulab Singh filled "his tumbrils and waggons, sixteen in number, with silver money.....Furthermore, a bag of gold mohurs was entrusted to the care of each of five hundred of his most faithful adherents; and again a quantity of jewellery and valuable trinkets was delivered to the charge of his own orderly Gorcharas or mounted body-guard". He also took away 12 of the best horses in the stud and many valuable articles of *pashmina*.

30. M'Gregor, *op. cit.*, Vol. II, p. 8.

31. Sita Ram Kohli, *op. cit.*, p. 36; Thornton, *op. cit.*, p. 231. Kohli refers to a letter which one Harsarn Das wrote to Clerk on behalf of the Rani. This letter shows that the Rani had declared herself willing to accept a British Resident at Lahore and to be guided by him in forming her ministry. Sher Singh offered, if the British would come to his help, to transfer to them either the province of Kashmir or one-fourth of the annual revenues of the entire Punjab, and one year's revenue from Kashmir as a personal gift for Clerk.

32. "Had the city been taken by storm, it would not, probably, have suffered more". *Calcutta Review*, No. 11, p. 488.

33. Even the Maharaja and Dhian Singh were defied, hooted and disgraced. K. Sajan Lal, *News letter*, No. 36.

34. Thornton, *op. cit.*, pp. 234-36.

35. Even after this the policy of raising such levies continued. For instance, in February 1842 orders were passed to raise 10,000

hill men and Muslims. *Foreign Dept. Secret Cons.*, dated 28 Feb., 1842, No. 45.

36. Cunningham, *op. cit.*, p. 214. For a force of 12000 British soldiers, the British wanted to take the cis-Sutlej Sikh districts and 40 lakhs of rupees in coin.
37. The promptitude with which the British got ready to help him frightened him. It "made him think himself in danger of his life at the hands of his subjects and of his kingdom at the hands of his allies". Cunningham, *op. cit.*, p. 214.
38. Sita Ram Kohli, *op. cit.*, p. 43. Some correspondence between the Sandhanwalias and some regiments of the Khalsa army was intercepted by British in December 1841. See *Foreign Department Secret Cons.*, dated 17 Jan., 1842, No. 68. On 31 March 1842 Clerk in his letter to T. H. Maddock, Secretary to Government of India, wrote that Attar Singh Sandhanwalia was planning to invade the Punjab in support of Rani Chand Kaur. *Foreign Dept. Secret Cons.*, 8 April 1842, No. 36. The Maharaja complained to Clerk in April 1842 about the objectionable activities of the Sandhanwalias such as raising of troops and planning to make a nigh attack on the Punjab. *Foreign Dept. Secret Cons.*, 29 July 1842, No. 134.
39. Thornton, *op. cit.*, p. 239.
40. Sher Singh went out on the pretext of a hunting excursion. Mahan Singh, the *thanedar* of Lahore, was taken into confidence by Dhian Singh and charged with the responsibility of executing the plan. The four maid-servants who killed the Rani were later banished from the country. Their tongues were cut off to prevent them from disclosing the secret.
41. Cunningham, *op. cit.*, p. 230.
42. *Ibid.* The British interest is clear from the fact that though the Sandhanwalias were openly indulging in anti-Sher Singh activities they were never stopped, even when the correspondence between them and some sections of the Lahore army was intercepted. On this other hand the British Agent, Clerk, pleaded with Sher Singh, Raja Dhian Singh and Fakir Azizuddin for reconciliation with the Sandhanwalias. This happened in April 1842. See *For, Dept. Sec. Cons.*, 29 July 1842, No. 134. In May 1842 Clerk observed in a letter to Maddock saying; "I have now fixed my attention and the hopes of the Sandhanwal chiefs on mediation by me between them and the Maharaja". *Foreign Dept. Secret cons.*, 1 June 1842, No. 22. Rani Chand Kaur was yet alive when the British had started their efforts to persuade the Maharaja to readmit the Sandhanwalias into his favour.

43. M'Gregor, *op. cit.*, Vol. II, p. 13; Cunningham, *op. cit.*, p. 231. M'Gregor goes still further and says: "In their hours of revelry, it happened that the Maharaja and his favourites often quarrelled among themselves, and Ajit Singh frequently threatened to kill the Maharaja but the latter did not regard the threat, and hugged himself in a perfect security while he possessed to careful and wise a servant as Dhyan Singh".

44. Sita Ram Kohli, *op. cit.*, pp. 62-63. Bhai Gurmukh Singh, besides the Sandhanwalias, played a sinister role in widening the Gulf between Sher Singh and Dhian Singh.

45. According to L. Griffin (*History of the Punjab Chiefs and Families of Note*), Amir Singh Sandhanwalia in 1803 tried to kill Ranjit Singh and in 1825 when the Maharaja was seriously ill, attempted to capture the Gobingarh Fort by a clever stratagem. His intention probably was to take the place of Ranjit Singh as Maharaja. It appears that in 1843 the Sandhanwalias also cherished the ambition of first seizing power and then the throne. Kanwar Partap Singh was killed so that there should be no one left in the family of Sher Singh to claim the throne after his death. Kanwar Dalip Singh was preferred to the other surviving sons of Ranjit Singh, namely Kashmira Singh and Peshaura Singh, on the ground that Dalip Singh was just an infant whereas the latter were grown-ups. If the Sandhanwalias had survived in all probability one of them would soon have taken the place of the infant Maharaja Dalip Singh. S.R. Kohli, *op. cit.*, p. 63.

46. For details see G.C. Smyth, *op. cit.*, pp. 73-77.

47. Apart from the fact that Dalip Singh was to be preferred because he was an infant unable to take part in state administration, there was the consideration that Dalip Singh's mother being under Dogra influence would not create any problem.

48. According to Cunningham, before Attar Singh recrossed the Sutlej, he "made a hasty attempt to rouse the village population in his favour through the influence of Bhai Bir Singh", but in vain. *op. cit.*, p. 232.

49. Thornton, *op. cit.*, p. 290.

Mufti Ali-ud-din (*Ibrat Nama*, vol. I, p. 512) mentions still another cause of the quarrel. Raja Sochet Singh had rendered great help to Hira Singh in the matter of crushing the power of the Sandhanwalias, but when the victory had been gained, Hira Singh and Jalla monopolised the power and Sochet Singh was kept out completely. He felt sore and humiliated. He was later offered the governor-ship of Peshawar, which was declined by him. *Punjab Intelligence*, dated 31 December 1843 and 15 January

1844.

50. The Rani complained, for example, that her son was secluded by Hira Singh, that she was not regent during his minority and that Hira Singh had rejected a proposal of marriage made to Dalip Singh by the Sardar of Rupar on behalf of his daughter, Thornton, *op. cit.*, p. 291.

51. He even held out a threat that if the army did not help him, he along with the Maharaja would cross the Sutlej and seek shelter in British territory.

51(a). Debi Prasad, *op. cit.*, p. 66.

52. *News letter* dated 13 March 1844—H.R. Gupta, *Punjab on the Eve of First Sikh War*, p. 249.

53. Hari Ram Gupta, *op. cit.*, pp. 261-263—*Abstract of Intelligence* dated 24 March 1844.

54. Sita Ram Kohli, *op. cit.*, pp. 73-74; Mufti Ali-ud-din, *op. cit.*, Vol. I. p. 517.

55. T.H. Thornton, *op. cit.*,. 293. Mufti Ali-ud-din says that Raja Gulab Singh was keeping a close watch on Sochet Singh because he did not want that he should participate in any movement against Hira Singh. Sochet Singh therefore had to use the pretext of a hunting excursion to leave his place and march towards Lahore. *op. cit.*, Vol. I, p. 513.

56. Thornton, *op. cit.*, p. 295.

    He "told them that Uttur Singh was coming to seize the Sikh kingdom, and give it up to the British". A summary of Hira Singh's speech on this occasion is contained in the intelligence abstract of 3 May 1844. H.R. Gupta, *op. cit.*, pp. 312-13.

57. Prince Peshaura Singh had deserted the camp of Bhai Bir Singh a few days before the fight took place. He proceeded straight to Lahore and assured Raja Hira Singh of his loyalty. From there he went to his *jagir* at Kurianwala. Thornton, *op. cit.*, p. 297; *Punjab Intelligence*, Lahore, dated 5 May 1844.

58. The *News letter* for 17 May 1844 indicates the strong feelings of the soldiers who openly talked of replacing Raja Hira Singh as Prime Minister.

59. *Intelligence Abstract* dated 17 and 18 May 1849—H.R. Gupta, *op. cit.*, pp. 330-32.

60. For this dispute see *Punjab Intelligence, Lahore* under dates 28 June 1844; 25 June 1844; 4, 12, 17, 21 July 1844; 3, 4, 5, 6, 7, 8, 11, 22, 23, 26 August 1844; 3, 7, 22 September 1844; 22, 23 October 1844.

li, *op. cit.*, p. 88.

cit., p. 302.

Debi Prasad, *op. cit.*, p. 78, for an account of the n this occasion.

64. Thornton, *op. cit.*, pp. 306-07.

65. One cause of this change in the attitude of the army was that the Rani had promised to raise the monthly salary of a soldier by half a rupee. Sita Ram Kohli, *op. cit.*, p. 91.

66. He belonged to the famous *naherna* (barber) family of Kalianwala. He was not acceptable because of his low origin.

67. The epidemic first appeared on 5 May 1845. In the month of May it took a terrific toll of life carrying 500 to 700 victims each day. Before the pestilence began to abate in the following month, it is calculated that not fewer than 22000 persons had perished.

68. Before this happened, the office was offered to Raja Gulab Singh when he was in Lahore. On his appointment both the Rani and the troops were united. But Raja Gulab Singh declined the offer. He, however, supported the Rani's idea of appointing Jawahar Singh to this high office.

69. Thornton, *op. cit.*, p. 309.

70. *Ibid.*, p. 310.

71. *Ibid.*, p. 314.

72. *Ibid.*, p. 318. The vuzeer was often so drunk, having caroused all night with his favourites and women, that he could not hold a Darbar." On occasions he would not hold the daily Darbar. On one occasion he "dressed himself as a dancing girl and danced with them". There may be some exaggeration in these statements but the conclusion that he was inefficient is inescapable.

73. Both in Sialkot and later in Attock some battalions sent by the Darbar to attack him went over to his side and helped him in his resistance to the Darbar. On one occasion he even seized 6 lakhs of government treasure. Thornton, *op. cit.*, p. 319.

74. Devi Prasad, *op. cit.*, pp. 86-87. It is stated here that Raja Gulab Singh, too, had a hand in the murder of Peshaura Singh. It was on his recommendation that Chattar Singh Attariwala was appointed for this purpose.

75. Debi Prasad, *op. cit.*, pp. 88; Major G.C. Smyth, *op. cit.*, p. 146. According to Thornton (*op. cit.*, p. 319) the plot to kill the Prince was prepared at Lahore before Chattar Singh left for Attock. The murder was carried out by him in accordance with that plot.

76. Thornton, *op. cit.*, p. 322.

77. Thornton, *op. cit.*, p. 327.

78. Smyth, *op. cit.*, p. 167.

79. This fact comes out clearly from Shah Muhammad's account of the first Anglo-Sikh War (1845-46).

    Var Shah Muhammad edited by S.R. Kohli, pp. 153-54, 157; Cunningham, *op. cit.*, pp. 256-57. "As the authority of the army began to predominate and to derive force from its system of committee, a new danger threatened the territorial chiefs and the adventures in the employ of the government. They might successively fall before the cupidity of the organized body which none could control, or an able leader might arise who would absorb the power of all others and gratify his followers by the sacrifice of the rich, the selfish and the feeble. Even the Raja of Jammu, always so reasonably averse to a close connection with the English, began to despair of safety as a feudatory in the hills, or of authority as a minister at Lahore, without the aid of the British name, and Lal Singh, Tej Singh and many others all equally felt their incapacity to control the troops. These men considered that their only chance of retaining power was to have the army removed by inducing it to engage in a contest which they believed would end in its dispersion..".

80. *Var Shah Muhammad*, p. 160.

81. *Foreign Secret Proceedings*, 26 December 1846, No. 889; Cunningham, *op. cit.*, pp. 263, 265; *The Calcutta Review*, June 1849, p. 549.

82. Cunningham, *op. cit.*, pp. 278-79, 287; *Foreign Secret Proceedings*, 26 December 1846, No. 889.

83. Maharaja Sher Singh repeatedly referred to this problem of arrears. For instance, he said on 24 April 1842 that the arrears due from the chiefs and farmers amounted to 2 crores at that time. Diwan Dina Nath joined in and stated that lakhs of rupees were due from Raja Gulab Singh, Raja Hira Singh, Diwan Sawan Mal and Shaikh Emamuddin of the Doaba while other chiefs owed only thousands *(For. Dept. Sec. Cons.*, 8 June 1842, No. 43—*Punjab Intelligence, Lahore)*. In July 1842 the Maharaja issued orders to the amount of 25 lakhs in the names of the officers of Raja Dhian Singh, Raja Gulab Singh, Raja Hira Singh, Raja Sochet Singh, but Raja Dhian Singh stopped them. (*For. Dept. Sec. Cons.*, 31 August 1842, No. 62—*Punjab Intelligence, Lahore* for Ist to 10 July 1842). In January 1843, Diwan Kirpa Ram told the Maharaja that a balance of a crore of rupees would be found against the

Jamwal Rajas, Diwan Sawan Mal and Sh. Emamuddin of the Doaba, if accounts were called for. *For, Dept. Sec, Cons.*, 15 Feb., 1843, No. 36—*Punjab Intelligence, Lahore* for 13 January 1843).

84. "The Sikh chiefs in their feudal castles ruled as petty sovereigns". Thornton, *op. cit.*, p. 312.

85. Sita Ram Kholi, *op. cit.*, p. 85.

86. In all, the expenditure rose from Rs. 1,27,96,482 in 1839 to 2,46,30,767 in 1845. F.S. Bajwa, *op. cit.*, p. 97. Things became so critical that in 1845 Broadfoot anticipated a total financial breakdown and complete disintegration of the state.

Foreign Secret Consultation, 20 December 1845—Broadfoot to Governor-General, dated 15 October 1845.

For the difficult state of finances see *Punjab Intelligence Lahore* under the following dates; 18 Feb. 1844, 23 Feb. 1844, 14 March 1844, 8 April 1844, 23 May 1844, 28 May 1844.

For instance it was reported on 8 April 1844 that in the Moti Mandir Treasury there were only 30 lakhs of rupee remaining.

The position was already very difficult under Maharaja Sher Singh but Raja Hira Singh's enormous expenditure incurred on the management of the army by way of grant of increases in salaries and donatives made it all the more difficult. His retrenchment measures and reduction of confiscation of *Jagirs* failed to meet the crisis which became deeper and deeper with the passage of time.

Index

□□□